Human Capital

Thomas O. Davenport

Human Capital

What It Is and Why People Invest It

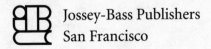

Jossey-Bass Publishers
San Francisco

Jossey-Bass books and products are available through most bookstores. To contact Jossey-Bass directly, call (888) 378–2537, fax to (800) 605–2665, or visit our
website at www.josseybass.com.

Substantial discounts on bulk quantities of Jossey-Bass books are available to corporations, professional associations, and other organizations. For details and discount information, contact the special sales department at Jossey-Bass.

 Manufactured in the United States of America on Lyons Falls Turin Book. This
paper is acid-free and 100 percent totally chlorine-free.

Library of Congress Cataloging-in-Publication Data

Davenport, Thomas O.
    Human capital : what it is and why people invest it / Thomas O.
Davenport.
        p.   cm. — (The Jossey-Bass business & management series)
    Includes bibliographical references and index.
    ISBN 0-7879-4015-1
    1. Human capital.   2. Personnel management.   I. Title.
II. Series.
    HD4904.7.D38   1999
    658.3—dc21   98-45840

FIRST EDITION
HB Printing   10 9 8 7 6 5 4 3 2 1

The Jossey-Bass

Business & Management Series

⎯⧟⎯ Contents

Preface   xi

The Author   xvii

Part One: Providing Context

1   Worker as Investor: A New Metaphor   3

2   Human Capital Investments and Returns   17

3   Human Capital and Competitive Strategy   44

Part Two: Taking Action

4   Hiring Human Capital Investors   65

5   Setting the Stage Through Workplace Environment   94

6   Paving the Way for High Investment   121

7   Building Human Capital   143

8   Holding On to Human Capital Investors   169

9   Optimizing and Measuring Human Capital Investment   202

Notes   227

Index   243

To Sue and Emily, who have invested so much in me.

⟿ Preface

Career politicians, a group roughly as popular as fire ants, can teach us something about the value of human capital. Cynics said the Washington careerists won a victory in March 1995, when the U.S. House of Representatives voted against term limits. The vote followed months of overheated oratory, with House members debating the evils of making careers from posts that our founding fathers meant to be temporary.

Embedded in the House vote, however, was another message—that wisdom gained with experience, a critical form of human capital, has value that should not be lost. Representative Henry J. Hyde, a Republican from Illinois, stated his opposition to term limits by recalling the words of American statesman Robert Livingston. In the 1788 debates over constitutional ratification, Livingston questioned the wisdom of term limits, asking, "Shall we then drive experience into obscurity?" Expanding on Livingston's point, Hyde argued, "To do your job around here you've got to know something about environmental issues, health care, banking and finance and tax policy, the farm problems, weapons systems, Bosnia-Herzegovina, North Korea, foreign policy, the administration of justice, crime and punishment, education, welfare, budgeting in the trillions of dollars, immigration. The list is endless, and we need our best people to deal with these issues. . . . Tradition, history, institutional memory—don't they count anymore?"[1]

Whatever our views on term limits, we can all agree that governing the country requires knowledge and judgment heightened by experience. And so do jobs in the modern corporation. In the early 1990s, executives seemed oblivious to this reality, as they tried to downsize their way to prosperity—or to survival, anyway. Companies viewed workers as costs, and they treated people just the way they treated other costs—by cutting. As the decade progressed, however, organizations awakened to the reality that human capital—the abilities, behaviors, and energies of workers—could not be ignored as managers looked for ways to squeeze out a competitive advantage. Somewhere in mid-decade an epiphany occurred. Employees evolved, in managerial jargon at least, to a higher form. No longer costs, employees became assets. Executives, management-wise men and women, and the business press joined the chorus extolling workers as assets. Employees took their places in the corporate pantheon right next to desks, computers, and the executive jet. To be sure, considering people as assets instead of costs elevates their status and acknowledges their value to organizational success. But does it reflect the way people behave or the way managers should expect to deal with them? I think not; here is why.

THESIS: WORKERS ARE INVESTORS

Persistent low unemployment has taught managers a lesson—when human capital owners have the upper hand in the market, they do not behave at all like assets. They behave like the owners of a valuable commodity. They contribute it carefully and demand value in exchange for their contribution. In fact, people are not costs, factors of production, or assets. They are investors in a business, paying in human capital and expecting a return on their investment. Managers who deal with human capital investors will not worry just about downsizing, delayering, and deploying. They will invest their own human capital in figuring out how to develop indispensable worker-investors—people who get so much value from the organization and give so much back that the company could not survive, let alone prosper, without them. Managers owe it to themselves (and their shareholders) to ask these questions:

- How should we go about defining the kinds of human capital we need most?
- How can my company ensure that it hires top performers who have critical knowledge, skills, and talents and who value the returns on investment my company can offer?
- What kind of work environment best paves the way for maximum effective investment of human capital?
- What kinds of initiatives, by both workers and companies, build performance capacity most quickly and effectively?

- In an increasingly risky world, how can we keep the best people (those who have the most employment options) committed to the organization and engaged in their jobs?
- How can an organization balance the interests of human capital investors and other stakeholders and measure success at using human capital to achieve a competitive advantage?

This book suggests responses to each of these challenges.

WHAT THIS BOOK IS— AND WHAT IT IS NOT

At its heart, *Human Capital* is the exploration of a metaphor. In the words of philosopher and humanist José Ortega y Gasset, "The metaphor is probably the most fertile power possessed by man."[2] I suggest that thinking of employees metaphorically as investors awakens managerial minds to the reality that workers are free agents; therefore, organizations can win their allegiance through one means only— returning value for value. I do not mean the metaphor to be depressing, however; quite the opposite. Although the worker-as-investor idea suggests that the bonds of ownership or free-floating loyalty are broken, it also points toward a different, stronger set of binding cords. These are the golden (though not always monetary) bonds of mutual benefit, not the iron chains of ownership.

I also hope the investor metaphor acts as a Trojan horse, breaching the walls of managers' minds and spreading useful ideas about people management. The asset metaphor, I observe, has become bankrupt, a noble sentiment devolved to a cliché. I hope the metaphor of people as investors opens a few eyes and a few minds and lets in both light and thought. Some ideas in the book are new; some are as old as capitalism itself. But all, I think, are sound, and all deserve more attention than they usually get, even from conscientious managers. The book is not, however, a human resource (HR) manual. Do not look for the definitive discussion of performance appraisal and management, employee communication, benefits planning, or pay package design; these and other worthy HR topics receive only passing mention. Look instead for perspectives about how both companies and individuals can prosper by changing how they define their relationship.

Clients admonish me constantly to provide practical advice. Readers will, I hope, find a good deal of that in this book. I have used examples, suggestions, models, and systems to convey useful applications of worker-as-investor ideas. I have also tried to place much of the discussion in the middle ground of principle, which lies between theory and practice. Practice without principle is aimless; theory without principle is useless. *Human Capital* contains some of each and bridges all three.

At the risk of violating my own precepts about the need for precision in the framing of a metaphor, I decline to be doctrinaire about specific terms and concepts. Change the words, reclassify the ideas, juggle the order if you want, but keep this basic notion in mind—if employees are assets, managers should worry about how to increase and measure the corporation's return on its investment in them. A better approach is for managers to view workers as human capital owners willing, under the right circumstances, to contribute to an organization's prosperity. From this perspective, we conclude that workers produce the greatest value for companies when companies generate the greatest value for workers. This thought captures, as clearly as a single phrase can, the theme of this book.

TARGET AUDIENCE AND SCOPE

Human Capital will appeal to three audiences: senior executives, middle managers and first-line supervisors, and employees. All must take responsibility for developing, preserving, and profiting from human capital.

Executives who face continued pressure from shareholders to increase company value will gain a new perspective on value and its sources. They will see why their people-related strategies must extend beyond layoffs and disinvestment on the one hand, and beyond escalating retention bonuses on the other. Managers who fight the day-to-day competitive battles must get human capital into their organizations and make the most of it. This book describes the tools they need. First-line supervisors will learn how their contribution to human capital management encompasses at least four critical roles: contract maker, investment adviser, provider of return on investment, and source of risk-management information. Workers who read the book will come away with a new framework for their workplace contribution and a heightened sense of their strategic value. They will learn how to get the most out of work by managing their jobs and careers in a value-optimizing context. In trying to engage these audiences, I have often used *we* as the subject of the sentence. Interpret this not as the editorial *we,* but rather as the collegial *we.* Although author and reader cannot converse directly, I consider this a dialogue. While writing, I imagined discourse, debate, and consensus (or not). This book is a partnership, or as close to one as I can get from my side of the computer screen.

Because the issues treated here are not limited to a single industry or type of company, the book covers the broad landscape of American business. It explores the implications of a range of current and emerging workplace issues, drawing on psychological research as well as individual and company experiences. At times I speak as consultant, at times as researcher, occasionally as manager, and now and again as reporter.

ACKNOWLEDGMENTS

A book like this represents the culmination of thoughts and ideas from a thousand sources. Some of them—an insightful boss, an enlightened teacher, a helpful colleague—exercise influence in ways an author may not even recognize. Others make a more direct, or at least more recognizable, contribution. In the case of *Human Capital,* these include Ken Alvares of Sun Microsystems, Libby Bishop of the Institute for Research on Learning, Bill Bradford of Cypress Semiconductor, Peter Cappelli of the Wharton School, Tom Cross of Pacific Bell, Robin Gower of AirTouch Communications, Devashree Gupta of the Corporate Leadership Council, Leslie Miller of Industrial Indemnity Financial Corp., Bryan Orme of Sawtooth Software, Andy Rich of Williams-Sonoma, Mike Rodriguez of Pacific Bell, Sherri Rose of Apple Computer, Susan Stucky of the Institute for Research on Learning, Joyce Sziebert of Cypress Semiconductor, Jack Unroe of Accountants, Inc., and Jack and Marilyn Whalen of the Institute for Research on Learning.

The project that comes to fruition as this book has taken many turns along the way, all of them for the better. Continuous improvement does not happen by accident, however. I thank the reviewers whose kind but firm guidance has caused me to question and improve both direction and expression. In particular, my gratitude goes to Rich Iorio and Sheryl Turping, colleagues at Towers Perrin, who read the manuscript cover to cover and offered many valuable suggestions. They have my appreciation not only for the value of their contribution but also for their tenacity in working through early, rough material. Other Towers Perrin brethren—David Lough, Chaille Maddox, Charlie Watts, and Sharon Wunderlich—read one or more chapters and provided useful comments. Monny Sklov and Samir Shah, quantitative jocks extraordinaire, did statistical analyses, crunched numbers, and built models. My hat is off to them, the salute of a word guy to two numbers guys.

More broadly, Towers Perrin provided a forum for shaping many of these ideas and a crucible for testing them. The firm was also generous in giving me time to do the research and writing. Most important, Towers Perrin let me use the services of Carol Bunce, Katie Jarcik, and Linde Virtue. The first two can wrangle word processing software with the best; without them, the manuscript might never have come to be. Linde translated my thoughts into sensible graphics. Had it not been for their investment of human capital, my ideas would never have made it onto the printed page. These pages are tribute also to the superb staff at Jossey-Bass, whose encouragement and liberal definition of deadlines made it possible for all of this to come together. All these people get a large share of credit for the useful, interesting ideas you find here. For the dubious, boring ones, however, I accept full responsibility.

My wife, Sue, and my daughter, Emily, deserve final mention. Many's the weekend and holiday they entertained themselves while I toiled away in the den. Besides relief that the project has ended, I hope they share my satisfaction with its completion. Both, in their way, contributed to the work: my wife through appraisal of ideas and text, willingness to reflect on her own work experience, and stamina in reading and rereading the manuscript as it evolved from incipience to final form; my daughter, through her example of how fast one individual (albeit a nine-year-old) can amass and deploy human capital. To both of them, I promise I will do my best to produce a return on their investment.

San Francisco, California   THOMAS O. DAVENPORT
January 1999

⟶⟋⟍⟍⟋⟍⟋⟍ The Author

Thomas O. Davenport is a principal in the San Francisco office of Towers Perrin, a worldwide consulting firm. He provides counsel on human resource strategy, organization effectiveness, and business strategy to Fortune 500 clients in the service and manufacturing industries, and in the public sector. Although his work is diverse, his practice centers on a single theme—helping companies improve business performance through their management of people. Davenport has published articles on productivity measurement and improvement, strategy implementation, and merger integration in a variety of business publications. He is a frequent speaker on human capital issues.

Davenport received his B.A. degree in English (Phi Beta Kappa) in 1975 from the University of California, Los Angeles. He also holds a Master of Journalism degree (1976) from the University of California, Berkeley, and an M.B.A. degree (1982) from the Haas School of Business at the University of California, Berkeley.

Human Capital

PART ONE

Providing Context

CHAPTER ONE

Worker as Investor
A New Metaphor

As stressful as today's workplace has become, most of us do not have to worry about being eaten alive by rats.

In Upton Sinclair's muckraking novel *The Jungle*, one young boy, assigned to carry beer for other workers, sneaks too many samples and falls asleep in the corner.[1] The next morning, his factorymates find only what the rats have left behind. Horrific as it is, this image is no more striking than many others that Sinclair created. His rendering of the danger, fear, and squalor that workers endured in turn-of-the-century meat-packing plants set the stage for widespread reform in the American food processing industry. And of all the degradation heaped on workers by the rulers of Packingtown, which weighed heaviest? It was, in Sinclair's view, that the Beef Trust treated workers as *assets,* just like the animals they butchered:

> Jurgis [the protagonist] recollected how, when he had first come to Packingtown, he had stood and watched the hog killing, and thought how cruel and savage it was, and come away congratulating himself that he was not a hog; now his new acquaintance showed him that a hog was just what he had been—one of the packers' hogs. What they

wanted from a hog was all the profits that could be got out of him; and that was what they wanted from the working man. . . . What the hog thought of it, and what he suffered, were not considered; and no more was it with labour.[2]

"Workers are assets" has become the dominant metaphor of late twentieth-century management. In some ways, it represents a worthy elevation of employees to the status they deserve. People are, after all, the chief engine of prosperity for most organizations. What other factor of production contributes so much to strategic success? In other ways, however, the asset metaphor falls short of fully expressing the value that people bring to the workplace and the control they exercise over its investment. With luck, by the end of this chapter, I will have convinced you that we have a better metaphor at our disposal.

WORKERS AS ASSETS: A GOOD START BUT . . .

Executives and management gurus alike sing the praises of worker assets with a variety of vaulting phrases. Adam Smith beat them to the punch by two hundred years, however. In his *Wealth of Nations,* published in 1776, Smith drew the analogy between people and equipment: "When any expensive machine is erected, the extraordinary work to be performed by it before it is worn out, it must be expected, will replace the capital laid out upon it, with at least the ordinary profits. A man educated at the expence of much labour and time to any of those employments which require extraordinary dexterity and skill, may be compared to one of those expensive machines."[3]

Why spend time contemplating this common managerial expression? The reason, simply put, is that language matters. Indeed, some sociologists believe that the essence of management is skillful use of language to create meaning.[4] Confucius, when asked what he would do if he ruled a country, said that his first act would be to fix the language.[5] Given the potential power of metaphors, it is easy to see why managers become enamored with their use. To leaders, they represent a tool not merely to describe reality, but also to create it. To observers, they provide a window onto the managerial landscape. The asset metaphor exemplifies the evolution of a figure of speech—and of the underlying attitude toward workers—over the better part of a decade. In the late 1980s and early 1990s, workers had not yet ascended to asset status in the minds of most senior managers. downsizing trend of that period suggests, managers viewed v as costs to be cut back whenever economic pressures forced an expense reduction. The downsizing phenomenon hit its peak in 1990–1991. Some 56 percent of the firms responding to an American Management Association survey said that they had gone through workforce reductions during that period. Overwhelmingly, the rationale for staffing cuts centered on actual or anticipated business downturns.[6] Perhaps because they saw no point in developing the skills of people who represented little more than expenses on the income statement, companies also cut their training budgets in 1991. Respondents to the annual *Training* magazine survey said that their total training budgets declined to $43.2 billion in 1991, down from $45.5 billion the prior year.[7]

Things turned around over the next several years, however, and we entered the Age of the Employee Asset. Although job cuts continued at high levels, they nevertheless decreased from the 56 percent of 1990–1991 to the mid-forties for the next several years.[8] Training budgets improved as well, topping $50 million in 1994.[9] "Employees are our most important assets" became the expression of choice for annual reports and press releases. But the phrase often had a hollow ring. In its *People Strategy Benchmark Awareness and Attitude Study*, for example, consultants from Towers Perrin noted: "An overwhelming majority of corporate executives seem to be giving lip service to the notion of people as strategic assets." The study went on to say, "Although 90 percent of the 300 executives interviewed said their employees are the most important variable in their company's success, they ranked specific people-related issues far below other business priorities." When asked to rank strategic business priorities, respondents placed investing in people behind customer satisfaction, financial performance, competitiveness, and quality of products and services.[10] If companies truly treated people as valuable strategic assets, managers would see that a competent, dedicated workforce is a prerequisite for success in any of these other areas. Investing in people would surely take on a higher priority.

A manager who likens a worker to an asset has evoked two related but distinct ideas. On the one hand, the metaphor ennobles workerhood by emphasizing the value that people contribute to the enterprises in which they toil. In this sense, the asset idea helps underscore that workers represent more than grist for industrial mills. People bring ingenuity, creativity, and initiative to their companies; they deserve more respect than the average drill press. When considered from this angle, the asset metaphor represents a clear improvement over the worker-as-cost idea that lay at the heart of widespread downsizing.

On the other hand, the asset metaphor shortchanges workers by placing them in the same class as those very drill presses. Think back to Accounting 1-A, where your professor defined an asset as an object or a legal right that meets three criteria: it can produce future service value, can be owned or controlled, and can be valued in monetary terms. Obviously people do perform services that create financial value; to that point, the metaphor holds. Apart from representing value in a general way, however, workers bear little resemblance to assets. Consider that:

- With a decline in loyalty between worker and organization, a phenomenon we'll revisit shortly, the notion that a company enjoys ownership—even abstract or emotional—of employee assets has long since become passé.

- Assets are passive—bought, sold, and replaced at the whim of their owners; workers, in contrast, take increasingly active control over their working lives.

- Despite the best efforts of accountants, methods for attaching financial value to human resources have proved elusive and flawed; moreover, the effort to denominate all value in dollar terms obscures other value sources and metrics.

And consider this question: If workers are assets, what does that make managers? Buses are assets, and they have drivers. Airplanes show up on the asset side of the balance sheet, and they have pilots. Soldiers consider tanks assets, and tanks have commanders. If people are assets, then managers are clearly in the driver's seat.

The asset metaphor perpetuates the gulf between the brawn and the brains, the doers and the thinkers, the hogs and the packers. In the words of Eric Flamholtz, a management accounting expert, "To treat people as an asset is to confuse the agent that provides services with the asset itself (the expected services)."[11]

Casual users of the employee-as-asset metaphor would protest this assessment. They would declare that they mean people have value to companies, not that the companies actually own their people. One might respond that casual users need to choose their words more carefully. As Mark Twain wrote, "The difference between the almost right word and the right word is really a large matter—'tis the difference between the lightning-bug and the lightning."[12]

"EQUALLY VALUABLE CAPITAL": WORKERS AS INVESTORS

It is time to take the asset metaphor to a new level, to think of workers not as human capital but rather as human capital owners and investors. Like the employee-as-asset idea, the image of workers as investors is not exactly new.[13] In his comparison of people to machines, Adam Smith went on to say: "The work which he learns to perform, it must be expected, over and above the usual wages of common labour, will replace to him the whole expence of his education, with at least the ordinary profits of an equally valuable capital." In other words, Smith said, the individual acts like an investor.[14] He amasses personal capital (the "extraordinary dexterity and skill" mentioned in the first part of his thought) and tries to invest it judiciously, husbanding it and deploying it to the best advantage.

Two important ideas underlie the worker-as-investor metaphor: ownership and return on investment.

Human Capital Ownership and Control

Like the asset notion, the investor metaphor emphasizes value. Investorship, however, also evokes active ideas like building human capital, contributing it to organizations, and controlling its investment. People possess innate abilities, behaviors, personal energy, and time. These elements (which we will discuss further in Chapter Two) make up human capital—the currency people bring to invest in their jobs. Workers, not organizations, own this human capital. Workers, not organizations, decide when, how, and where they will contribute it. Like financial investors, some human capital investors are more active than others. The point is that, as the owners of their capital, they can make choices. In the words of two *Wall Street Journal* reporters, "People no longer hide under their desks, cowering in fear of layoffs. With unemployment at nearly a quarter-century low, the seesaw of power is tilting from employer to employee. Many feel in control of their careers to a degree not seen during this decade."[15] Control differentiates asset owners from assets, investors from the currency they invest.

Return on Human Capital Investment

A worker who acts like a human capital investor will place his or her investable capital where it can earn the highest return. This return on investment in work (which I will also define in Chapter Two) encompasses the "ordinary profits" to which Smith refers. Thinking of workers as investors underscores a fundamental reality: investment and return make up a two-way flow. Training provides a good example. Thoughtful managers understand that increasing worker knowledge improves productivity—by as much as 16 percent, according to a study cited in a National Bureau of Economic Research working paper.[16] Training therefore looks like an excellent investment in worker assets. Increased training investment was one milepost on the road between employees as costs and employees as assets. Training also contributes to improved return on people's investment in work, however. In a knowledge-intensive workplace, people believe that learning new skills will help them in finding and keeping a satisfying job—a job that pays a high return on their human capital investment. Moreover, the gratification that comes from learning is itself a return on the human capital a worker puts into the job.

Conceiving of workers as investors rather than assets emphasizes that the link between employee and company depends not on ownership, paternalism, or blind loyalty. Instead, the cord binding people and organizations derives from the ability and willingness of each to provide benefits to the other. The relationship assumes mutual benefit, with neither party elevated at the expense of the other. If I want to energize my workforce, I will tell them what I expect them to invest and how I intend to earn their investment. I will not liken them to forklifts or other line items on my balance sheet.

THE WORLD OF WORKER-INVESTORS

If the investor metaphor has legitimacy, then it must faithfully reflect the reality it is intended to express. Let us see if worker-as-investor passes muster.

Who They Are

Investorship emphasizes the primacy of personal resources, the (chiefly) mental powers that workers bring to their jobs and their organizations. These powers carry increasing importance in today's and tomorrow's workplace.

The term *knowledge worker* flows easily off the tongues of managers these days. It borders on cliché status; still, it is too important to dismiss just because people use it loosely. Economywide employment trends illustrate the growing importance of work whose value comes from what people know, instead of what they produce with their physical powers. Let us attach the term *knowledge worker* to people in managerial, administrative, professional, technical, and sales jobs. In 1983, they represented 55 percent of the full-time workforce. Workers in service jobs, production and fabrication, forestry, and farming represented the other 45 percent.[17] By 1995, continuing a steady, century-long shift, knowledge workers accounted for 58 percent of the full-time workforce.

All knowledge work is not created equal, however. The human capital market continues to evolve, with increasing demand for certain kinds of brainpower and decreasing demand for other kinds. Table 1.1 shows how companies shifted their human capital focus by apportioning job cuts across the workforce between 1995 and 1997.

Even if downsizing has subsided, human capital market shifts have not. In the year ending mid-1997, for instance, hourly jobs represented

Table 1.1. Technical Jobs Gain, Managerial Jobs Lose.

Job Category	Percentage of Jobs Created, Year Ending:			Percentage of Jobs Eliminated, Year Ending:		
	June 1995	June 1996	June 1997	June 1995	June 1996	June 1997
Hourly worker	50.3	59.8	62.3	45.0	48.7	54.6
Supervisor	9.0	8.2	7.6	17.8	15.9	15.0
Middle manager	9.3	7.1	8.6	15.3	19.9	16.7
Professional/technical	31.5	24.9	21.6	22.0	15.5	13.8

Source: American Management Association, *Corporate Job Creation, Job Elimination, and Downsizing: Summary of Key Findings* (New York: American Management Association, 1997), p. 2. Used by permission.

the largest class of new jobs added, and the biggest focus for job elimination as well. Among professional and technical workers (the core of the knowledge worker class), things looked rosy. This category had the second highest job creation percentage each of the previous three years; companies have consistently created more technical and professional jobs than they have eliminated. The opposite is true for supervisory and middle-management jobs. These groups showed the most anemic job growth and elimination percentages far above creation percentages over the whole three years.

Moreover, changes in the substance of the managerial job give further evidence of how human capital requirements continue to evolve. Two things seem to be happening at once. On the one hand, a broad spectrum of workers has taken on what used to be considered managerial tasks. At the same time, people with manager titles do not necessarily (or solely) oversee people. They may also act as analysts, coordinators, and problem solvers; they make decisions, oversee outsourced functions, and call on clients. Looking ahead to the future state of flat organizations, management guru Charles Handy says that eventually, "Everyone will increasingly be expected not only to be good at something, to have their own professional or technical expertise, but will also very rapidly acquire responsibility for money, people, or projects, or all three, a managerial task in other words."[18] Everyone will manage something, but nobody will only manage, and we will all need to know things to succeed.

What They Have to Invest

Education builds human capital the way fertilizer grows plants. In 1960, among all Americans twenty-five years or older, 7.7 percent had completed four years of college or more. By 1990, the percentage had almost tripled, to 21.3 percent; it increased to 23.0 percent in 1995. Almost 1.2 million people received bachelor's degrees in 1993, a 19 percent gain over the 1985 total. Colleges and universities awarded 411,717 master's degrees and doctorates in 1993, 29 percent more than the 1985 total.[19]

More education means more capital to invest and potentially greater returns on investment. The increased returns show up in compensation differentials by occupational type. In 1982, for example, the employment cost index (a measure of the rate of change in employee compensation and benefits) for blue-collar workers was 78; data for

June 1989 represented 100 on the index. By comparison, white-collar occupations had an index of 74, and service occupations came in at 76. By 1995, the relative positions had shifted. The index for white-collar workers hit 128, compared with 126 for workers with blue collars and 125 for people in service occupations.[20] In a knowledge-intensive world, those with more of the right human capital command higher compensation. The rift between human capital haves and have-nots will likely continue to widen.

Analysis by the Bureau of Labor Statistics (BLS) shows that a college degree provides particularly significant leverage when combined with later job training. A BLS economist looked at the economic effects of combining a college degree with additional skills training acquired after taking a job. The analysis demonstrated that having a college degree as a foundation for additional learning was associated with a big boost in earnings. This conclusion held true even for jobs that required no college degree on day 1. Table 1.2 shows the results.

The extra time and effort required to finish college no doubt imparts some valuable knowledge that translates into earning power. Getting the degree also bespeaks initiative that doubtless contributes to greater productivity and higher compensation. Whatever the source of the effect, the BLS analysis lends credence to the investor metaphor—more human capital to invest means greater investment returns.

Having more human capital also means more job opportunities. These days, well-endowed worker-investors sit in the driver's seat when it comes to finding work. Consider that while the nationwide unemployment rate hovered a little under 5 percent, the unemployment rate in Silicon Valley fell to a microscopic 2.3 percent at the end of 1997.[21] In this cradle of high-tech civilization, technically oriented

Table 1.2. Education Plus Training Boosts Earnings.

Education	Median Weekly Earnings			
	Before Taking Additional Training	After Taking Additional Training	Gain	
1–3 years of college	$383	$474	$ 91	23.8%
College degree	381	581	200	52.5

Source: A. Eck, "Job-Related Education and Training: Their Impact on Earnings," Monthly Labor Review, Oct. 1993, p. 34.

human capital means a multitude of job opportunities. The only people unemployed are those who prefer surfing the waves in Santa Cruz to surfing the net in Santa Clara.

How Much Investment Flexibility They Have

Knowledge workers have ascended; education has built human capital. By themselves, do these facts support the investor metaphor? Yes, but not much more strongly than the asset metaphor. The tiebreaker is flexibility. Financial investors move their capital when they think they can find higher returns elsewhere. This is the essence of free-market investing—taking action (or choosing not to) in response to return-on-investment results. The keys are choice and flexibility. Do human capital investors have them? Increasingly, it seems they do.

Writing in *Time*, Lance Morrow set the stage for understanding the tenuousness of today's relationship between employees and employers: "America has entered the age of the contingent or temporary worker, of the consultant and subcontractor, of the just-in-time work force—fluid, flexible, disposable."[22] This new world sounds dangerous and daunting, but it brings some distinct advantages for human capital investors. The freer the human capital markets are, the more readily an individual can shift investment to the place that yields the best bundle of returns.

The data suggest a clear increase in human capital mobility. Recent research reinforces the conclusion that workers exhibit declining propensity to remain with one employer over the long haul. Table 1.3 shows job tenure figures for four age groups.

Tenure fell in every age category except one, with the sharpest drops occurring among men ages forty-five to fifty-four and fifty-five to

Table 1.3.   Job Tenure Decreases.

	Median Years with the Same Employer			
Age Group	1983	1987	1991	1996
25–34	3.0	2.9	2.9	2.8
35–44	5.2	5.5	5.4	5.3
45–54	9.5	8.8	8.9	8.3
55–64	12.2	11.6	11.1	10.2

Source: Bureau of Labor Statistics, "Employee Tenure in the Mid-1990s," news release, Jan. 30, 1997, p. 6.

sixty-four. In the late 1980s and early 1990s, declining job duration reflected widespread downsizing. However, the continuing trend toward shorter employment tenures must reflect something more than unilateral company cuts. More likely, the trend suggests growing worker confidence in the availability of another job. In a 1997 *Inc.* magazine survey, 42 percent of the respondents said they expected to stay with their current employers for the next ten years. Almost as many, however, said they will probably change jobs voluntarily during that period. Only 4 percent expect to be forced out by job termination.[23] In Chapter Eight, we will return to the issues of job stability and turnover.

Although labor market mobility may frustrate employers, a certain amount contributes to economic health. Human capital needs to move as freely as does any other capital form, finding the highest yields on its investment. The increasing velocity of human capital flows carries a wake-up call for employers. As a reporter for the *San Francisco Examiner* expressed it, "In the emerging new deal, the very mobility of career-independent employees provides a powerful incentive to companies to keep their promises—the most important of which . . . is to provide interesting, motivating work. Otherwise, those valuable staff members will leave."[24] Their freedom to leave, to transfer this investable currency, is what makes people investors in a world where assets wait passively to be deployed.

THE REST OF THE BOOK

The worker-as-investor metaphor has launched us on a nine-chapter voyage of exploration and application. This chapter has introduced the notion of human capital investment. In the remainder of the journey, I will expand the definition and consider how to apply human capital concepts in an evolving workplace.

This chapter and Chapter Two introduce and elaborate on the worker-investor notion. They explain the basic concepts and form the foundation for later recommendations. Chapter Two describes how the interplay among the elements of human capital creates a complex investment challenge for employees and managers alike. Psychological research and hard-won experience suggest a link between an individual's investment in a job and the perceived fulfillment of return-on-investment needs. We will consider this link in Chapter Two. Chapter Three will give the strategy context, discussing how organizations can connect the requirements for business success with human capital management. It also sets up this question: How should a company go about developing the storehouse of human capital necessary for competitive success? Chapters Four through Eight propose the answers:

- Hire the right people—that is, find workers with plenty of ability, effort, and time to invest—and make a deal with them to gain their investment.
- Elicit the maximum investment from people in the organization through sound implementation of the psychological contract between individual and company and by creating an environment that encourages human capital contribution.
- Build people's human capital through formal and informal learning, and transform highly mobile human capital into less transient forms.
- Hold on to human capital by keeping its owners committed and engaged.

Chapter Nine pulls the whole system together and deals with measurement. Every company needs a way to gauge its success at delivering returns on worker investment. Measures of elusive ideas like intangible capital will never be as concrete as standard financial measures. Ultimately it may not matter. Managers do not need a precise metric. They do need to recognize that the value of human capital is important enough to justify the measurement effort.

Several themes thread their way through the book; we have touched on two already. Expect to see more discussion of choice and flexibility and of individual control over human capital investment. These are fundamental to the argument that human capital investors, like financial asset owners, hold the reins of their own destiny. We will also periodically discuss job engagement and organizational commitment, the double pillars of effective individual investment. Learning and competence building are so important to human capital investment that they too reappear several times, in the definition of return on investment, the discussion of high-investment environments, and the consideration of ways to build personal intangible capital.

Another reappearing theme is the advisability of viewing actions taken to increase human capital as part of a coordinated system. We will see that however appealing any single action may be, the synergy that arises from many orchestrated actions multiplies the effect. Still another theme centers on the role of the first-line manager. We will observe that the people who execute strategy, manage assets, and assess performance profoundly affect an individual's return on human capital investment. This holds true even in a flat-earth world of horizontal organizations and skimpy management ranks. We will note how the managerial role has evolved beyond command and control, beyond scheduling and coordinating. Managers now must create high-return work environments.

Finally, the importance of information will receive attention at a number of points in the discussion. For example, we will note its significance in linking human capital investment with strategy and its critical role in helping people cope with change.

SUMMARY: WHAT IT MEANS TO BE AN INVESTOR

Viewing workers as investors underscores an essential fact of workplace life—work is a two-way exchange of value, not a one-way exploitation of an asset by its owner. At this point in the discussion, a thoughtful reader will ask the following questions: Does this point of view have staying power? Will some new metaphor take its place in half a decade, the way other metaphors have been displaced before it? Will the next shift in our economic fortunes mean a return to the bad old days of viewing workers as costs?

My crystal ball is no clearer than anyone else's. Unemployment may well fluctuate from lower-than-a-snail's-basement numbers to buddy-can-you-spare-a-dime levels. Buyer's markets become seller's markets, and on we go.

Although the workplace will surely continue to transmogrify, I believe that substantial time will pass before economic factors undercut the value of human capital. In good times, companies need to attract the owners of valuable human capital, make a deal with them, and provide the highest possible return on investment commensurate with sound fiscal management. In cost-conscious periods, companies still need to hold on to key people, keep them engaged in their jobs despite a risky and threatening environment, and cast an even more watchful eye on the costs associated with rewarding individual contribution. The two situations call for fundamentally the same human capital management skills, applied in different ways. Moreover, regardless of what happens in the economy at large, technological evolution will continue to support human capital creation and flow in three ways. First, technology feeds on human capital, increasing the demand for people who have the knowledge, skill, and talent to create the hard and soft components of information systems. Want a career with a future? Try computer sciences. Of the five occupations expected to grow fastest as we move toward the year 2005, two require computer know-how (computer engineers and systems analysts).[25] Second, technology-based information networks enhance the marketplace for human capital exchange; witness the rise of Internet sites that reduce the time and cost required to change jobs. Third, technology spurs the speed-of-light creation and transfer of knowledge, further fueling the growth of human capital and making it harder for companies to corral.

What does all this mean for individual worker-investors? Simply this—they must deal with a constantly evolving context for human capital investment. The workplace is its own microclimate; wait a minute and the weather will change. The predictability that once characterized the employment relationship is a fossil left behind by organizational evolution. In Chapter Two, we will take a closer look at how a worker-investor evaluates and responds to options in an unpredictable world.

Human Capital Investments and Returns

I f it hadn't been for Adam and Eve, we wouldn't worry so much about work. Genesis tells us that God gave the first two humans a pretty cushy deal. By providing them access to "every tree that is pleasing to the sight and good for food," He fixed things so the first couple did not have to work at all. They merely had to enjoy the scenery and relax streamside in the Garden of Eden. But Eve, tempted by the serpent, decided to nosh on the fruit of the knowledge of good and evil. From that time, things changed. God consigned Adam, Eve, and their descendants all the way down to you and me to earn our bread by the sweat of our brows. For his part, Adam was thereafter required "to cultivate the ground from which he was taken."[1] Thus were the first work, and the first job, created. To Adam, work equaled punishment. This is the lesson of Genesis. No wonder Monday mornings are so dreadful.

Jump ahead now about six millennia to the twentieth century. In the introduction to *Working,* his book on people and their jobs, Studs Terkel quotes an American president who put a different spin on the notion of work. In a Labor Day speech, Richard Nixon said: "The 'work ethic' holds that labor is good in itself; that a man or woman becomes a better person by virtue of the act of working. America's competitive spirit, the 'work ethic' of this people, is alive and well on Labor Day, 1971."[2] If you subscribe to the work ethic, then work is not punishment, a consequence of moral failure. Instead, work becomes a virtue, a noble endeavor that proves one's worthiness. The work ethic extols honest effort, frugality, individualism, and ability. To struggle against one's environment and win is morally right. To aspire to and reap the material rewards of victory is encouraged. Under the rules of the work ethic, it is okay to flaunt it if you've got it, baby. William H. Whyte, in *The Organization Man*, quotes banker Henry Clews as he advised Yale students in 1908:

> Anyone may choose his own trade or profession, or, if he does not like it, he may change. He is free to work hard or not; he may make his own bargains and set his price upon his labor or his products. He is free to acquire property to any extent, or to part with it. By dint of greater effort or superior skill, or by intelligence, if he can make better wages, he is free to live better, just as his neighbor is free to follow his example and to learn to excel him in turn. . . . If an individual enjoys his money, gained by energy and successful effort, his neighbors are urged to work the harder, that they and their children may have the same enjoyment.[3]

In other words, Clews said, be a winner. Don't keep up with the Joneses; leapfrog them. You don't win because you deserve it; you win because you earn it and, by earning, prove yourself deserving. The core of Clews's argument remains true today. Smart investment of the best human capital puts one ahead in the race for rewards of all kinds, from personal satisfaction to financial prosperity. In this chapter, we will develop a model depicting how and why people make human capital investments and earn a return on their investments. We will also reinforce the notion of individual and organizational reciprocity by considering how eliciting human capital investment benefits organizations. Two questions receive special focus: (1) What makes up the human capital that people invest in their work? (2) What is the general process by which organizations call forth (and people make) human capital investments?

HUMAN CAPITAL: THE COMPONENTS

The term *human capital* first appeared in a 1961 *American Economic Review* article, "Investment in Human Capital," by Nobel Prize–

winning economist Theodore W. Schultz. Economists have since loaded many terms into the human capital portmanteau. Most agree that human capital comprises skills, experience, and knowledge.[4] Some, like economist Gary Becker (another Nobel laureate), add personality, appearance, reputation, and credentials to the mix.[5] Still others, like management consultant Richard Crawford, equate the capital with its owners, suggesting that human capital consists of "skilled, educated people."[6]

For our model, let us refine the definition of human capital by breaking it into elements: ability, behavior, and effort. These three, along with a fourth element, time, appear in Figure 2.1. The figure suggests a specific relationship among the factors.

Ability

Ability means proficiency in a set of activities or forms of work. Ability comprises three subcomponents:

- Knowledge—command of a body of facts required to do a job. Knowledge is broader than skill; it represents the intellectual context within which a person performs. To succeed at brain surgery, a doctor must have not only specific skill but also a general knowledge of physiology, operating room protocol, rehabilitation methods, and insurance billing procedures.

- Skill—facility with the means and methods of accomplishing a particular task. Skills may range from physical strength and dexterity to specialized learning; the common idea is specificity. Brain surgery, for example, requires skill in making minute

Figure 2.1. Adding and Multiplying to Get Human Capital Investment.

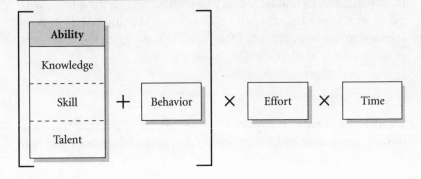

motions using delicate tools, coupled with a detailed grasp of brain physiology and function.

- Talent—inborn faculty for performing a specific task. The successful brain surgeon exhibits a talent for using her hands. She was born with it and has practiced to hone it. Talent is roughly synonymous with aptitude.

Consider the sources of each aspect of ability. Skill combines knowledge and talent (and sometimes behavior) and is often specific to a particular job or set of tasks. Knowledge of a keyboard and manual dexterity make for a good word processor. One can get many skills through use and repetition, and improve almost all through practice and additional training. Not everyone can become a brain surgeon, of course. Still, most of us can become facile enough to open a Band-Aid and put it on a cut without wrapping it into a sticky ball. Similarly, we can acquire knowledge through academic learning, specific instruction, and accumulated experience. Under our definition of human capital, experience is not synonymous with knowledge. Instead, it is a source of knowledge and a way to refine it and enhance it. Talent, in contrast to skill and knowledge, is chiefly innate. Either you can tease the sciatic nerve out of a frog or you can't. Practice can improve talent and increase the effectiveness of its application, but no amount of practice can engender a talent that was not there (in at least a latent form) at birth.

Behavior

Behavior means observable ways of acting that contribute to the accomplishment of a task. Behaviors combine inherent and acquired responses to situations and situational stimuli. The ways we behave manifest our values, ethics, beliefs, and reactions to the world we live in. When an individual displays self-confidence, forms a team with peers, or shows a bias for action, he or she has exhibited a behavior relevant to the organization. Observability is the key—for managers, what you see is what you get to deal with.

Effort

Effort is the conscious application of mental and physical resources toward a particular end. Effort goes to the heart of the work ethic. One can ask forgiveness for meager talent or modest ability, but never for middling effort. Effort activates skill, knowledge, and talent and harnesses behavior to call forth human capital investment. By applying or withholding it, we control the when, where, and how of human capital contribution. Without effort as the locomotive, boxcars full of ability sit idly on the tracks.

Time

Time refers to the chronological element of human capital investment: hours per day, years in a career, or any unit in between. Economists usually exclude time from the human capital definition because it does not reside within the human mind or body, as do the other elements. In some ways, however, time is the most fundamental resource under individual control. The most talented, skilled, knowledgeable, and dedicated worker will produce nothing without investing time in the job. In the days of Taylorist work structure, managers used time-and-motion studies to refine work processes. Frederick W. Taylor himself figured out how much time a worker should spend doing various tasks in the steel-making process. By applying his recommendations, the Bethlehem Steel Co. increased the daily total of raw materials handled from sixteen tons per man to fifty-seven tons.[7] Since Taylor's work in 1903, jobs have become more autonomous. Consequently, time allocation strategies make an increasingly important difference in how much a worker effectively invests in the job.

What better place to look for the effects of time investment than in the sales business? That is where we find perhaps the ultimate example of time under the control of the individual. Research in the stock brokerage industry shows how dramatically time allocation affects worker performance. In one study, the researchers hypothesized that experienced and inexperienced brokers would spend their time differently. They also postulated that a relationship would exist between time allocation strategies and broker performance. They discovered that less experienced brokers spend more time prospecting, seeking referrals and advice from other brokers, and making sales presentations than their more experienced counterparts. Seasoned brokers make higher average time allocations to developing corporate clients, socializing with clients in nonbusiness settings, dealing with administrative paperwork, and handling routine communications.[8] Some of this, of course, stems directly from the greater business base that more experienced brokers manage. It turns out, however, that the same basic time-spent strategies raise sales performance regardless of broker tenure. For both inexperienced and experienced brokers, sales performance correlates significantly with time allocated to dealing with corporate clients and helping other stockbrokers.

Despite the clarity of their findings, however, the researchers cautioned against assuming a straightforward time-spent-causes-performance relationship. Performance, they said, "is probably in large part a function of *how* stockbrokers carry out activities over and above *what* activities they allocate time to and emphasize."[9] This distinction takes us back to our conception of total human capital investment. In our formulation, how a worker performs a task depends on ability and behavior. The choice of one task over another at a given moment requires a time allocation decision. The combination of ability, behavior, effort, and time investment produces performance, the result (from the organization's perspective) of personal investment.

The Human Capital Equation

The elements of human capital investment come together in the additive and multiplicative relationship shown in Figure 2.1:

$$\text{TOTAL HUMAN CAPITAL INVESTMENT} = [\text{ABILITY} + \text{BEHAVIOR}] \times \text{EFFORT} \times \text{TIME}$$

Why multiplicative? Because multiplying means that increasing one element can dramatically raise the amount invested. Conversely, even a high level of one factor cannot make up for a low level of another. The key to the whole thing, as the formula suggests, is effort. I think back to one of my incarnations as a senior manager, when my organization began to suffer from disenchantment in the middle-manager ranks. We knew that turnover was rising, but we feared something worse—that even the managers who stuck with the company were disillusioned enough to cut back their effort and effectively withdraw their human capital investment, slowly but inexorably. Interviews with a selection of managers confirmed our fears. Our expectations for their investment of human capital (especially time) were high, and their perceived recompense was low. One manager expressed her concern this way: "I look at all the effort I make and how little I'm rewarded and ask, 'Should I stop trying so hard?'" We acted quickly to encourage continued effort by adjusting the relationship between the investment we expected and the return we provided.

A BRAIN SURGERY EXAMPLE

To illustrate the discussion, we can quantify an individual's investment by assigning numerical ratings to ability and behavior. We will use a scale from 1 to 10, with 1 meaning a low level of each human capital component and 10 meaning a high level. We can express time in terms of hours and effort as a percentage ranging from 0 to 100 percent.

Let us use as our hypothetical worker the brain surgeon mentioned earlier. She has excellent mechanical skills (9 on the 1–to–10 scale), strong medical knowledge (8 on the same scale), and exceptional physical dexterity and coordination (a 9 rating for talent). On the first three human capital components, she clearly comes out a winner. She exhibits moderate bedside sensitivity, so we give her a 6 on the behavioral scale. (No doubt her behavioral portfolio contains more than one element, but I am simplifying here.) She is about to operate on her favorite cousin, so her investment of effort is high, at 100 percent. The surgeon expects to undertake a six-hour operation. For the sake of illustration, then, here is her human capital investment (HCI):

$$HCI = [(9SKILL + 8KNOWLEDGE + 9TALENT) + (6SENSITIVITY)] \times (100\% \ EFFORT) \times 6HOURS = 192$$

Obviously, increasing any element raises her HCI. Let us say that her medical knowledge increased to 9 from its present level of 8 (she went back to school and took more courses in neurophysiology). Her HCI total would go up to 198, a 6-point (3 percent) gain, not insignificant if you are the one lying on the operating table. Adding a new element would also raise her HCI total. For instance, the doctor could further bolster her total by adding a behavior (say, working effectively in teams with fellow surgeons) at an 8 on the 10-point scale. This would add 8Teamwork to the total inside the brackets. Her HCI would rise from 192 to 240, a 25 percent increase.

Changes in total effort invested can also produce dramatic leverage. Suppose that instead of operating on her cousin, she is scheduled to do a procedure on her cousin's cat. She is no cat lover, so her concern about the outcome falls, as does her effort, by 20 percent. Consequently, her HCI drops from the original 192 to 154, also a 20 percent decrease. The sizable effect of effort means that the cat-owning cousin should find a way to get the surgeon more interested in feline brain function. When it comes to increasing human capital investment, it is frankly easier to conceive of a dramatic change in effort than a radical gain in ability or behavior.

THE WAY HUMAN CAPITAL INVESTMENT WORKS

We have now refined the definition of human capital, the foundation of the investment model. Next, we consider the conditions that predispose an individual to invest human capital. At the center of the discussion lie two different but related ideas: commitment to an organization and engagement in a job.

Commitment to the Organization

Commitment arises from an emotional or intellectual bond linking the individual with the organization.[10] Commitment implies acceptance of the organization's goals and direction, strong desire for membership, and tacit agreement to reject other investment tracks. It comes in several forms, each with different implications for the relationship between individual and organization. Researchers who have studied commitment divide it into three categories: attitudinal, programmatic, and loyalty-based.[11]

ATTITUDINAL COMMITMENT   Tommy Lasorda, the former manager of the Los Angeles Dodgers, had attitudinal commitment. As he told the world often, he bled Dodger blue. His dedication to the organization, and his unwillingness to manage anywhere else, bespoke profound organizational bonds. People like Lasorda have palpable connections. They identify with, are involved in, and enjoy membership in the organization. They feel motivated to work for the company's interests in large part because they value their organizational attachments.[12] As a consequence of investing their human capital, studies have shown, they work harder at their jobs than people without attitudinal commitment.[13]

PROGRAMMATIC COMMITMENT   Programmatic commitment leads people to stay with an organization because they cannot afford to leave.

Stock options that take years to vest, pension plans that are not portable, résumés that show too little experience in some areas—these are the ties that bind for the programmatically committed. Programmatic commitment without attitudinal commitment means a worker is physically on the job but does not invest his human capital fully; somebody is home, but there's no light on. Workers who feel only programmatic commitment stay with the organization not because of emotional attachment, but because the costs of doing otherwise are simply too high. Writing about commitment in 1960, sociologist Howard Becker referred to these costs as "side bets" that people make as they move through their careers. Some side bets take explicitly financial forms, whereas others stem from cultural expectations:

> People feel that a man ought not to change his job too often and that one who does is erratic and untrustworthy. Two months after taking a job a man is offered a job he regards as much superior but finds that he has, on the side, bet his reputation for trustworthiness on not moving again for a period of a year and regretfully turns the job down. His decision about the new job is constrained by his having moved two months prior and his knowledge that, however attractive the new job, the penalty in the form of a reputation for being erratic and unstable will be severe if he takes it.[14]

Becker's comments take us back to a time when employers had most of the control. In the late 1950s and 1960s, the Organization Man (and a few Organization Women) did everything possible to carve out a career in a single company. As cultural expectations have evolved, so has the significance of related side bets. Job hopping, for example, once anathema for career-minded workers, has become the norm in some job markets and industries. We have already seen how job stability has declined in an era of nearly full employment, suggesting low levels of angst attached to changing positions.

LOYALTY-BASED COMMITMENT   An individual with strong loyalty-based commitment feels tied to the organization by a sense of obligation. Perhaps the company footed the bill for a college degree, provided a job when times got tough, or put together a work group that now counts on each member for team success. Whatever the source, workers who feel loyalty-based commitment want to do what they believe is right for the organization. Consequently, commitment anchored by

loyalty will be associated with strong motivation, consistent atten-
dance, and noteworthy dedication to organizational goals.[15] In other
words, feeling an obligation to an organization produces the same
kind of dedication and involvement engendered by attitudinal commitment, although at a more modest level.

At the risk of some oversimplification, we can think of attitudinal
commitment as "I want to belong," programmatic commitment as
"It'll cost me if I don't belong," and loyalty-based commitment as "I
ought to belong."[16] The three categories are not so much different
types of commitment as different components; anybody can experience one, two, or all three. I can love my company, feel obligation to
my work group, and stick around to make sure my options vest.
Because many work experiences that predict attitudinal commitment
relate also to loyalty-based commitment, we will concentrate on attitudinal and programmatic commitment. We will treat these two categories as independent; that is, attitudinal commitment does not affect
programmatic commitment, and vice versa.[17] Indeed, the two forms
represent a kind of commitment yin and yang. Daniel Yankelovich and
John Immerwahr, in a 1983 Public Agenda study, quoted these words
to express the duality:

> Workers seem to have two separate unwritten contracts, each of which
> plays a distinct role. One contract is economic. The economic contract
> gets them to the workplace at eight or nine and keeps them there until
> five. But once they get there another contract takes over, a psychic con-
> tract. This rather different set of expectations and obligations seems
> to govern how hard people really work, and what the quality of their
> work will be.[18]

Has the psychic contract evolved since 1983? You bet it has. We will
talk more about the contract in later chapters. Meanwhile, let us move
on to the next element in the human capital investment model.

Engagement in the Job

Together, the twin concepts of organizational commitment and job
engagement are the foci of human capital investment. When
researchers study the two, they find that low levels of one (commit-

ment) tend to increase turnover, whereas a paucity of the other (engagement) links with higher absenteeism.[19]

People with high job engagement care a lot about what they do; they may or may not care about where they do it. Highly engaged people love to undertake that bundle of activities that keep them busy for eight, ten, twelve, or more hours each day. They identify with their work; they may be employees of Company X, but they are also (and perhaps foremost) programmers, accountants, salespeople, and lawyers. Nowhere is the dichotomy of commitment and engagement more apparent than in the world of information technology. There, knowledge workers thrive, and human capital commands a premium price. Info tech people work hard—all-nighters are not uncommon when it's crunch time at the end of the project—because they become enraptured by the elegance of what they do. Job engagement they've got by the bushel. But commitment to the organization is another story. In a recent survey by *Computerworld,* about one-third of information systems (IS) middle managers and professionals said that they constantly seek new job opportunities. Another 56 percent of both groups said that they are not actively looking but would consider the right offer.[20] In other words, if you are a senior IS manager, close to 90 percent of your staff are ready to take their human capital out the door at any minute. It's not just cruising the Internet that keeps IS executives up at night.

Consider also the case of Genentech, a company synonymous with the surging biotechnology business. Industry analysts estimate that some thirteen hundred biotech outfits nationwide have about 140,000 employees. That's a sizable increase over the 100,000 who were busy splicing genes in 1993.[21] The industry provides interesting, exciting, engaging work for scientists and technicians. Genentech's goal is to elicit organizational commitment from its engaged workforce. The company has succeeded, according to Judy Heyboer, the senior vice president of human resources. Genentech enjoys a lower turnover rate, she says, than its counterparts in high-tech electronics. Maybe enhanced commitment comes from the prestige of working for the granddaddy of the biotech industry. Maybe it grows out of the appreciation that comes, in turn, with the opportunity to work with the coolest technical resources. With a little more than $1 billion in 1997 revenue, the company spent $470 million on R&D.[22] The constant challenge, says Heyboer, is to get technical professionals to "love the company as much as they love their molecule."[23]

Figure 2.2 shows the placement of commitment and engagement in the chain of human capital investment.

Performance

To continue building the model, we must address the "So what?" question: "So what do commitment and engagement mean for the company?" In other words, do committed and engaged workers perform better? Do they produce higher-quality products, serve customers more diligently, save money for the organization? Excellent worker performance, after all, is what companies want. Performance, brought about by human capital investment, constitutes the company's return on its stake in human capital investment.

The link between engagement in the job and strong job performance seems obvious. It is not hard to believe that highly engaged people will be task oriented and focused on performing the parts of the job they love most. After all, they identify with their work, care about its outcome, and consider it part of their definition of themselves.[24] It makes sense that they will invest their human capital in doing job tasks well. The link between organizational commitment and performance is more tenuous, however. The hypothesis, studied and demonstrated in many research projects, is that workers who

Figure 2.2.   Commitment and Engagement Pave the Way
for Human Capital Investment.

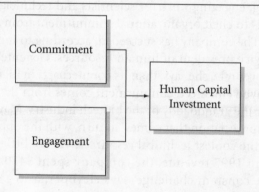

exhibit attitudinal commitment work harder at their jobs than do workers with weaker commitment. That is, they invest more human capital because of higher effort. Consequently, highly committed people should perform their work better.[25] But do they?

Some of the best research evidence I have seen of the relationship between commitment and performance comes from research by DeCotiis and Summers. In a study of the behavior of restaurant managers, they found that commitment shows a strong positive association with individual motivation. A strong correlation also exists with objective measures of performance (in this case, control of food and labor cost). Commitment also correlates negatively with desire to leave the organization and with actual turnover.[26] These findings suggest that, assuming an organization has people with the right kinds and amounts of human capital, eliciting an attitudinal commitment to invest will lead to superior performance.

We already know that commitment comes in three forms. Not surprisingly, those three forms have different implications for patterns of investment and, consequently, for performance. Attitudinal commitment finds its expression in human capital investment that produces organizationally valued forms of performance. Loyalty-based commitment has a similar but less robust relationship with performance. In contrast, research has shown, the form of commitment we have labeled as programmatic shows little discernible relationship with worker performance. Figure 2.3 shows a simple representation of these relationships.

Having added performance as the product of human capital investment, we need the component that energizes the system. We need return on human capital investment.

Return on Investment

Let us now consider what it takes to engender commitment and inspire engagement. We focus again on reciprocity, an idea central to any investment and return relationship. To quote DeCotiis and Summers, "Commitment has as its theme the notion of *exchanged expectations* [italics added] between an organization and its members, and a commitment to meet those expectations on the part of the organization and the employee. In short, when an organization commits to meeting the needs and expectations of its members, its members

Figure 2.3.   Three Forms of Commitment Yield
Different Performance Focus.

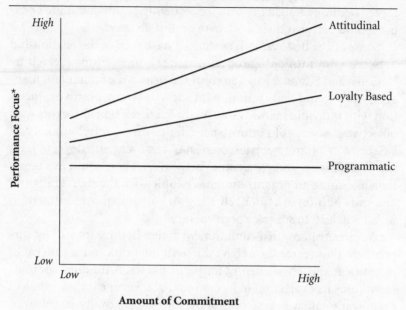

*Willingness to invest human capital to maximize organizationally valuable
performance.

commit to the service of the organization in terms of its goals and values."[27] In other words, expectancy cuts both ways. Such factors as pay, job enrichment, and influence over organizational policies influence individuals' perceptions about how much their companies appreciate and support them.[28] However, organization-generated rewards do not drop like manna from heaven, appreciated but unexpected. Workers carry their reward expectations with them from the first day on the job. Positive work attitudes, toward both the job and the organization, result from the meeting of expectations. Positive and negative experiences themselves have an effect on worker attitude.[29] That effect gets stronger—for better or worse—through comparison with expectations. The committed and engaged worker acts on behalf of the organization, receives a reward, and then continues to act in the organization's interest. We know what the worker brings to the transaction: ability, behavior, effort, and time. What does the company bring to exchange? The answer is this—return on investment. In the narrow sense, return on investment means the payback earned on human capital invested. More broadly, return on human capital investment encompasses all the rewards required to elicit incremental investment from the worker or prevent investment declines.

In searching for evidence of the link between rewards and performance, managers often focus their attention on job satisfaction. Raising job satisfaction, they reason, will surely improve performance. After all, don't satisfied people do better work, the way contented cows give more milk? As intuitively appealing as this notion may be, psychologists historically have had a devil of a time finding a causal link running from job satisfaction to performance. Ultimately, the key turns out to be rewards, and the direction of causation, reversed. Causation runs like this—strong performance brings rewards, which in turn increase satisfaction. In other words, satisfaction does not engender performance; rather, performance, through the mechanism of rewards, produces satisfaction. Some of the best support for this conclusion came from research by Edward Lawler and Lyman Porter. Writing in *Industrial Relations*, Lawler and Porter summarized their findings this way: "The data offer encouraging support . . . for the assertion of the model that satisfaction can best be thought of as depending on performance rather than causing it. . . . It is hardly necessary to note that this approach is quite different from the usual human relations one of trying to maximize satisfaction, since here we are suggesting trying to maximize the relationship between satisfaction and performance, rather than satisfaction itself."[30] Their conclusion, by the way, is no artifact of life in a postmodern, Generation X company. Lawler and Porter published their findings in 1967.

DRIVERS OF DISCRETIONARY INVESTMENT The Holy Grail for companies that employ human capital investors—just about all companies, that is—is discretionary investment. A whole gaggle of elements might make a job more pleasant or a workplace more comfortable. But what factors elicit that extra modicum of effort that ratchets up worker investment? The Public Agenda study made a point of differentiating the factors that simply make a job more agreeable from those that inspire people to work harder (that is, to invest more human capital).

Researchers found five factors most likely to be associated with inspiring harder work: good chance for advancement, good pay, pay tied to performance, recognition for work well done, and opportunity to develop abilities. Factors like relief from rush and stress, convenient location, quiet and dirt-free work environment, working with likable people, and getting along with the supervisor make the job more agreeable.[31] They do little, however, to inspire discretionary effort.

In a more recent study, researchers took a fresh look at factors that encourage discretionary effort on the job. They put a set of job-related factors into three groups: those that encourage discretionary effort, those that do not encourage it, and those that actively discourage individual initiative.[32] Factors in the first group fall into four categories:

- Having responsibility for one's work (mentioned as one of the five most important factors by 52 percent of respondents)
- Having a sense of worth in the job (mentioned by 42 percent)
- Getting the opportunity to make good use of skills (40 percent mentioned) and to develop skills and abilities (30 percent mentioned)
- Being recognized for individual contributions (mentioned by 40 percent)

Among the factors found to have the lowest value in encouraging discretionary investment were these:

- Compensation based on organizational performance (cited by 56 percent as one of the five least important factors in encouraging discretionary investment)
- Comprehensive benefits package (cited by 47 percent)
- Working on teams (38 percent cited) and collaborating with peers to get a job done (mentioned by 31 percent)
- Having trust in senior management (33 percent mentioned)

Note that the first two factors in the second list might well encourage programmatic commitment, even though they have little effect on engagement in the job. Asked in an open-ended question to name the factors that most strongly discourage voluntary investment of effort, 30 percent of the respondents named lack of recognition and appreciation; 26 percent said mistrust of management or weak upper management.

Revisiting our definition of *return on investment* (the rewards required to elicit or maintain human capital investment), we can now ratify the key elements. From research specifically focused on what it takes to get people to invest discretionary human capital, four categories of factors emerge:

1. Intrinsic job fulfillment—Factors inherent in the job itself and its composite tasks. Intrinsic elements include the challenge of the work; the degree to which the job has interest, permits creativity, and requires the use of valued abilities; and the amount of personal satisfaction afforded by the job. Enjoyable aspects of social interaction also fall into this category. At the heart of intrinsic fulfillment is the gratification that comes from doing a challenging job well.

2. Opportunity for growth—Chance to increase abilities and thereby add to the individual's store of human capital. This factor entails opportunities to learn and grow personally, and to advance within the organization.

3. Recognition for accomplishments—Acknowledgment from peers and superiors of an individual's contribution to the organization. Recognition incorporates notions like receiving respect from one's peers, experiencing esteem as an important contributor to organizational success, and being included in important business activities like strategy formulation. Recognition can also come from outside the organization: friends, community, other companies in the industry.

4. Financial rewards—Receiving various forms of compensation and benefits, especially those based on the worker's performance and productivity.

Figure 2.4 shows examples of return-on-investment elements.

Figure 2.4.   Returns on Investment Fall into Four Categories.

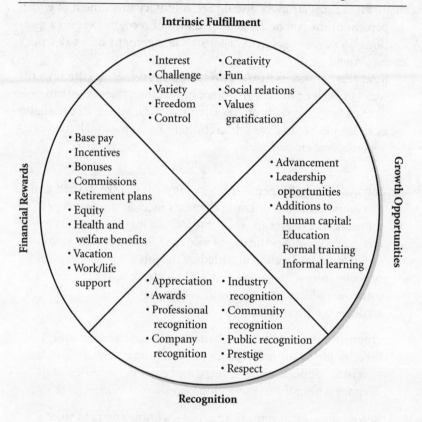

Intrinsic Fulfillment

• Interest   • Creativity
• Challenge   • Fun
• Variety   • Social relations
• Freedom   • Values
• Control   gratification

Financial Rewards

• Base pay
• Incentives
• Bonuses
• Commissions
• Retirement plans
• Equity
• Health and
   welfare benefits
• Vacation
• Work/life
   support

Growth Opportunities

• Advancement
• Leadership
   opportunities
• Additions to
   human capital:
   Education
   Formal training
   Informal learning

• Appreciation   • Industry
• Awards   recognition
• Professional   • Community
   recognition   recognition
• Company   • Public recognition
   recognition   • Prestige
                        • Respect

Recognition

THE PERCEPTION GAP

When asked what workers want most, managers often assume that people place the greatest value on high wages and job security. In reality, employees typically rank these two below such factors as having interesting work and feeling appreciated for the jobs they do. The graph on page 35 shows the contrast between what workers say they want most from their jobs and what managers think they want.

How can you explain the gap between what workers expect from their companies and what managers think they expect? After all, most managers spent at least some time in the worker ranks. Why, then, do they misapprehend worker values so badly? Here are three theories; no doubt there are others.

Managers Misunderstand What Workers Value.

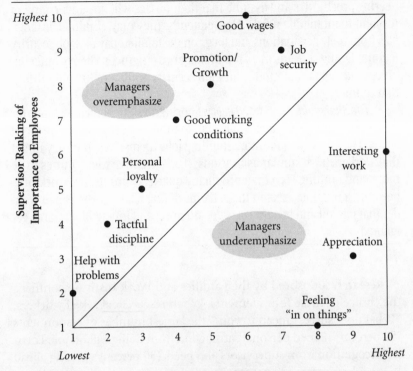

Source: Adapted from V. Niebrugge, *Declining Employee Morale: Defining the Causes and Finding the Cure* (Ann Arbor, Mich.: NOVA Group, 1992).

• *The Manager-as-Engineer Theory.* M.B.A. schools turn out management engineers—professionals who tend to look at business problems as challenges amenable to depiction on a Gantt chart. Whatever the problem, a seven-step action plan ought to do the trick. Leaders schooled in this way of thinking will naturally gravitate toward programmatic responses to the problems of acquiring and managing capital, including human capital. Turnover is up, morale is down? Engineer a solution—develop a compensation plan or a benefits strategy. These are easy levers to pull; they lend themselves to clear definition, objective analysis, and financial valuation. Fuzzier ideas like satisfying work and genuine appreciation are harder to define, tougher to value, and more difficult to deliver. Consequently, managers tend to eliminate them from the analysis.

- *The Dumbing-Down Theory.* Workers may recognize managers' engineering proclivities and assume that their bosses will not understand or respond to intangible needs. Consequently, they may eliminate intangibles from their negotiations and focus on the familiar pay and job security factors. Doing so reinforces the Manager-as-Engineer Theory and convinces managers that money and job security really are the only things that count.

- *The Shareholder Pressure Theory.* Short-term shareholder demands for returns on equity can cause managers to think of everything in financial terms. They may long for more fulfilling jobs themselves, but they forget that workers have similar aspirations. If an executive role requires little more (and nothing less) than producing quarterly profits, the workforce becomes a fungible asset in the calculus of financial returns. Small wonder that payroll and benefit costs get attention and intangible rewards get ignored.

Research sponsored by the Families and Work Institute confirms the choice of these four elements. When researchers asked workers, "What does success mean to you?" the largest number of respondents (52 percent) named personal satisfaction from doing a good job. Earning recognition from supervisors and peers (30 percent), getting ahead in the job or career (22 percent), and making a good income (21 percent) followed in order.[33]

For future reference, we will label the four factors ROI_w—return on human capital investment in work. Figure 2.5 incorporates ROI_w into the investment model.

Let us run through the workings of the model:

1. Bring a worker into a company that provides high amounts of ROI_w and you will produce commitment and engagement.

2. Human capital investment precipitated by engagement, preserved by commitment, and supported by a productive work environment and job context will yield performance.

3. Performance will produce success for the organization and return on investment to the worker.

4. Return on investment will energize the system, and the virtuous circle will continue.

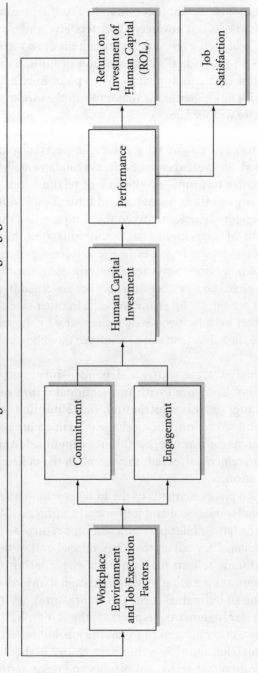

Figure 2.5. Performance Leads to Return on Human Capital Investment, Reinforcing Commitment and Eliciting Engagement.

The discussion in this chapter has focused on human capital and the return on investment it commands. Fruitful investment requires more than just ROI_w, however. Chapters Five and Six elaborate on workplace and job-level elements that help draw forth—and make effective—an individual's contribution of human capital. In Figure 2.5, these elements appear as "Workplace Environment and Job Execution Factors"; they play a major role in the investment-and-ROI_w system, as we will see later.

ANOTHER WAY TO LOOK AT ROI_w Not all aspects of return on investment in work are created equal. Some are fundamentally transactional, whereas others rely more on the web of relationships that develops within an organization. Transactional returns on investment involve an arm's-length exchange between the company and the individual.[34] Some form of agreement—stated, or unstated, but understood nonetheless—typically governs the tendering of the reward in exchange for services provided. Sometimes transactional rewards come in a global context, because they are governed by formal agreements that are similar for many workers. In other cases, they are individual, either because people earn them chiefly through individual effort or because they tend not to reinforce the subtleties of intragroup interaction.

Relational ROI_w, in contrast, depends—intuitively enough—on relationships. Compared with transactional return on investment, it is less tangible, less contractual, more implicit, and more dependent on interaction among the people in an organization. Relational returns on human capital investment seldom show up on financial statements. Instead, they come in the ephemeral currency of gratification.

Figure 2.6 places elements of the ROI_w portfolio on perpendicular transactional—relational and job—organization axes. Pay and benefits form the hard-dollar part of a worker's return on investment of human capital. They fall on the transactional part of the continuum. This positioning reflects their power at engendering programmatic commitment, at increasing total human capital investment by extending the time an individual spends in an organization. Incentive compensation arrangements, especially those emphasizing specific performance criteria, focus more on the job, but nevertheless remain transactional. Recognition is the shape shifter in the ROI_w portfolio. An organization that grinds out plaques and prizes until everyone has

Figure 2.6. Transactional and Relational ROI$_w$.

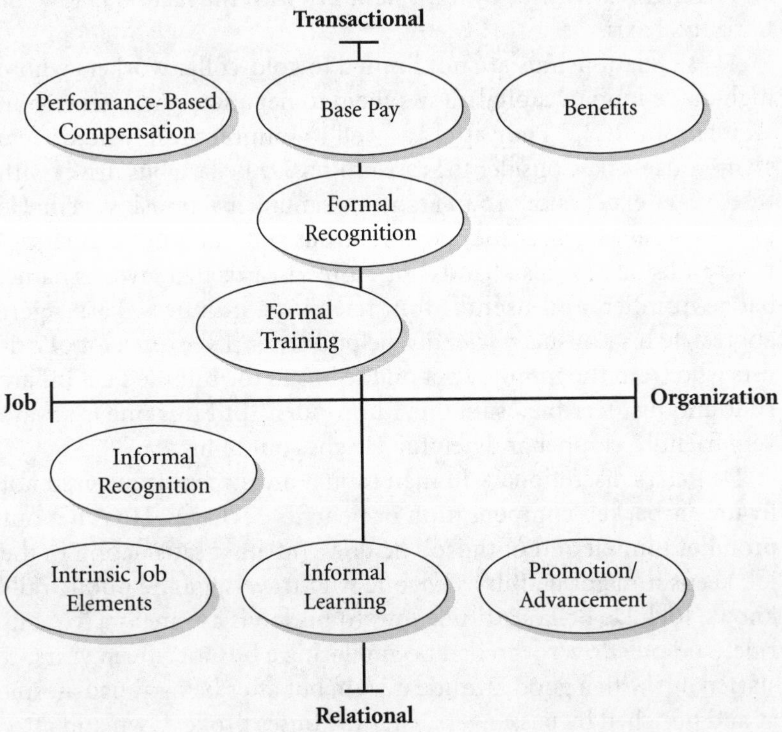

three hanging on her office wall can reduce recognition to a mechanistic transaction. Conversely, sincere recognition (with or without the plaque) given to truly great contributors can be relational.

Below the horizontal line lie other relational ROI$_w$ elements. Intrinsic job factors, many learning and growth opportunities, and some forms of recognition fall into the relational group. In the lower-right quadrant are organization-focused elements that support attitudinal commitment. Promotion up the organizational ranks and learning opportunities that build useful intraorganization knowledge fall into this category. The lower-left quadrant contains job-specific learning and intrinsically satisfying elements of work. These are the sources of job engagement. In later chapters, we will refine our thinking on what it takes to maximize human capital investment and keep well-endowed human capital investors within the organization. For now, we will simply conclude that the real power to encourage engagement and strengthen fruitful commitment lies with the factors below the horizontal axis.

These relationships are not limited to gold-collar workers whose high-value human capital allows them to negotiate packages rich in all forms of ROI_w. They apply as well to humbler folk who do less glamorous work. Consider the case of Rick De Bella, a bus driver with three years' experience in San Francisco's municipal transit system. He greets his passengers as they get on the bus and calls out the intersections and stops. He also hands out business cards that give his name, badge number, and useful Muni telephone numbers. Passengers appreciate his unusually friendly, helpful style: "I've seen a lot of drivers who from the minute I get on the bus to the minute I get off are rude and just terrible," said one Muni rider. "But this one is always very friendly, chipper and helpful. He goes out of his way."[35]

De Bella's discretionary human capital investment is inspired not by union-backed compensation or benefits packages. He is flat out proud of himself and of the job he does. Intrinsic satisfaction in the job keeps him going. But as anyone who travels via the public rails knows, Rick De Bella's attitude toward his job is as rare as a free bus ride. Said one driver who had been piloting a bus for fifteen years, "I started out with a good attitude myself, but after being yelled at, spit at and punched by passengers, after my buses broke down and after City Hall kept trying to blame Muni's problems on us, I changed some. I still take pride in my job, but I look at it differently. It's a stable paycheck." Unlike Rick De Bella, the second driver feels only programmatic commitment, engendered by a transactional element of return on investment (the pay he takes home). Feeling betrayed by the organization, he has no attitudinal commitment and only enough job engagement to get through a difficult day. If there are people like him in your organization, beware. They do not care much about the organization or its customers. Their low ROI_w means a low return on investment for shareholders.

The Returns People Want: The Same for Everyone?

Comparing the two drivers' propensities to invest discretionary human capital brings to mind lines from Milton's *Paradise Lost*:

> The mind is its own place, and in itself
> Can make a heav'n of hell, a hell of heav'n.[36]

Various points in this chapter suggest that patterns of behavior are associated with different types and combinations of returns on workplace investments. On the one hand, we can accept that certain archetypes of reward and reward-inspired action do exist. On the other, we can hardly argue that everyone wants precisely the same ROI_w components in exactly the same amounts. Workers in heavy industries like auto manufacturing, for example, take on physically challenging and monotonous work (low on intrinsic rewards) to make more money than they otherwise could. At the top end of the wage and overtime scales, some can earn more than $100,000 per year.[37] They push themselves harder than their peers by focusing heavily on one investment element (their time) and downplaying others. They care most about one element of return on investment (pay). That they are unusual underscores the point—people can exercise radical choices in how they invest their human capital and what they expect to get in return.

Some people try to increase their control over human capital investment and return by seeking alternatives to the traditional corporate environment. One indicator of this strategy is the growth in entrepreneurial businesses. By one estimate, nearly 40 percent of U.S. households include someone who has founded, tried to start, or funded a small business.[38] Entrepreneurship meets many needs, only a few of which have to do with reallocation of time and other personal resources. Nevertheless, need to get control of one's life and shift investment in ways not permitted by large corporations is one entrepreneurship motive, especially for women. In the words of Sharon Hadary, executive director of the National Foundation for Women Business Owners, "High-achieving women are leaving corporations to start their own businesses, mainly because they feel it gives them control of their lives."[39] This mobility lends further credence to the investor metaphor.

Female entrepreneurs make up one of the fastest-growing segments of the U.S. economy. Women own about 6 million of the nation's small businesses, more than one-third of such establishments.[40] Many of these operations are simple home-based businesses run on a shoestring. Others got their start because of affirmative-action programs that steer business toward firms owned by women. Many were launched, however, by sophisticated, successful businesswomen who decided that work in a large company did not offer all the ROI_w they needed. So they reallocated their human capital investment and shifted the locus of returns.

Once established within a small business, workers may hold tenaciously to the flexibility they have achieved. The story of a small company called Langlitz Leathers shows why.[41] Langlitz makes the leather jacket of choice for motorcycle enthusiasts, especially those with a rebellious streak. The customer list includes people like Bruce Springsteen and Sylvester Stallone. Langlitz refuses to make more than sixteen hundred items a year, even though demand has driven the wait for a Langlitz up to seven months. Family members who own and run the company worry that growth would endanger the relaxed environment of the fifteen-person shop. "If we grew, we'd have to work weekends," says David Hansen, general manager and son-in-law of the founder. Another family member frets, "When you get bigger, you have an executive section and a worker section, and then nobody communicates." They show a distinct willingness to give up the financial rewards of growth to control work hours and maintain an intrinsically satisfying environment. This behavior runs counter to the work ethical conduct we expect from business managers. Says one consultant, invoking the Easiest Lever Theory, "It's pretty unusual behavior. In this country, we are trained to maximize our incomes and improve our lifestyles all the time." When this kind of flexibility is both desirable and possible, the probability that an organization can craft a single, universally appealing ROI_w bundle becomes all but nil.

SUMMARY: LIVING IN THE INTANGIBLE WORLD

In Chapter Two we have continued building on the worker-as-investor metaphor. At the risk of mixing metaphors, we can say that we have added meat to the bones by defining what is fundamental to any investment—a valuable resource (human capital) and a reason to venture it (return on investment).

In defining human capital as ability, behavior, and effort, all moderated by time, we gave no single element predominance. The relative importance of any individual element depends, of course, on the requirements of the job. We noted, however, that effort acts as the catalyst that brings the other components into play. Using the human capital formulation, we developed a model that depicts why and how individuals invest their personal intangible capital in a job and an organization. The sequence that emerged ties together organizational commitment, job engagement, work environment and job-level factors, human capital investment, performance, and return on investment. We placed a special focus on the mutually supportive effects of job engagement and attitudinal commitment. At high levels, attitudinal commitment and job engagement tend to reinforce each other to produce the same performance effect—conscientious application of effort to do the job in a way that benefits the organization and the individual.

The question I phrased as, "What makes up return on human capital investment?" can be paraphrased several different ways: "What motivates people?" "What makes them care about their jobs?" "Why do they get up every morning and go to work?" We answered these questions by defining an array of ROI_w elements. We also considered the different implications for return-on-investment factors that are transactional or relational. Transactional elements have their principal effect in building programmatic commitment. Relational elements, in contrast, enhance attitudinal commitment and job engagement.

Chapter Two establishes the basis of a reciprocal exchange between worker and organization. We know what each wants and what each has to offer in trade. The exchange takes place in a strategic context within which competitive success affects both organizational prosperity and individual gains. We will consider that context, and its implications for human capital management, in Chapter Three.

CHAPTER THREE

Human Capital and Competitive Strategy

~~~

Battlefield metaphors turn up often when business leaders describe the challenges their organizations face. Companies fight for market share, outflank the competition, engage in guerrilla marketing, and take no prisoners in their quest for marketplace victory. Few other metaphors, however, have the classic military roots of the term *strategy*. The word comes from the Greek *strategus,* meaning an armed forces commander-in-chief or chief magistrate. Strategy, in turn, is the art of the commander—the art (though we too often think of it as a science) of directing the movements and operations of a military campaign. When managers use the term strategy, they usually refer to the formal effort by which an organization figures out how it will outperform its competition. Competitive advantage, in turn, becomes the means by which companies achieve their ultimate financial goal of high returns on shareholder investment.

Management professor Henry Mintzberg has developed a five-category strategy typology that elaborates on these notions.[1] He defines an organization's formal plans for achieving success as *intended* strategy. Among these intentions, some will come to fruition, and some will not. Mintzberg refers to the former as *deliberate* strategies, and to the latter as *unrealized* strategies. Occasionally companies achieve success in ways they had not planned (good things sometimes happen to good people); these fortunate events Mintzberg calls *emergent* strategy. Add up everything that succeeded, intended or not, and you have *realized* strategy.

The beauty of Mintzberg's categorization is that it incorporates both the classic view of strategy formulation and a more flexible, democratic way of looking at it. Under the traditional view, strategy formulation occurs as a result of deliberate activity that emanates from a single, usually centralized source: the strategic planning department, the executive suite, the fertile brain of the CEO's consultant. In this view, consistent with the Chapter One discussion of employees as assets, managers do the thinking, and everyone else does the carrying out. An alternative concept, Mintzberg's emergent strategy, suggests that smart ideas for business unit success need not come from a central source. The underlying assumption is that knowledge of competitors, buyers, suppliers, market substitutes, and possible new market entrants is not a rare commodity. Such knowledge rests not only with thinkers at the corporate headquarters but also with doers (who have to think as part of their jobs) in the trenches. Therefore, emergent strategy can grow almost anywhere in the organization. It sprouts from small insights, fostered by just about anyone with imagination and energy. Says Mintzberg, "All he or she needs is a good idea and the freedom and resources required to pursue it."[2]

In a later chapter, we will come back to the notions of freedom and resources as activating mechanisms not only for emergent strategy, but for human capital investment as well. In any case, the goal of Chapter Three is not to propose a detailed methodology for strategy formulation. Plenty of management gurus have wrestled with that subject; we will leave them to their labors and aim for a different objective. Instead, Chapter Three outlines a simple process for thinking about strategy in a way that leads to the identification of critical forms of human capital. We will also try to identify the ways companies might manage their human capital to make it a source of marketplace advantage.

COMPONENTS OF STRATEGY

As owners of human capital, workers have become more than moderately important in the successful implementation of business strategy. To see just how important, a Brookings Institution economist analyzed the relationship between different types of assets and market value. She did her assessment by calculating the contribution to market value of tangible assets (property, plant, and equipment) for U.S. manufacturing and mining companies. The analysis began with 1982 and covered ten years. She discovered that in 1982, hard assets accounted for 62 percent of market value in these traditionally capital-intensive industries. A decade later, tangible assets made up only 38 percent of market cap; the rest came from intangible assets, including human capital.[3] Jack Welch of General Electric (GE) has stated for the record that people-produced forms of capital have become a key source of competitive advantage: "We are trying to differentiate GE competitively by raising as much intellectual and creative capital from our work force as we possibly can. That is a lot tougher than raising financial capital, which a strong company can find in any market in the world."[4] Thus, to insightful managers, competitive advantage and shareholder value call for more than a *soupçon* of human capital. Says one senior manager quoted in *TechCapital* magazine, "In 1980 the key to success was to acquire new business. Now the key is to find the right people."[5]

Strategy: A Definition

Before exploring the specifics of how organizations identify which elements of human capital play major roles in strategic success, we need to define a few terms. Let us start by breaking down the term *strategy*. Four common threads run through the fabric of business strategy:

1. Emphasis on the business unit—Companies refer to their components as *strategic business units* for a reason. They usually focus on specific products or clusters of similar products, serve well-defined customer groups, and require internally consistent managerial skills. They frequently have their own performance measures and their own compensation plans. All of this makes the business unit the right place for strategic planning.

2. Focus on the future success of the unit—Accountants describe recent history in financial terms. Budget compilers extrapolate to the near-term future, also in a financial language. Strategy planners, in contrast, peer further into the future to define goals

and then map the organization's path down the mine-infested road of implementation.

3. Allocation of tangible and intangible resources—Strategy plans are bankrupt if they do not describe the resource augmentation, acquisition, transformation, and investment required to make the plan worth more than the diskette it is recorded on.

4. Response to the external environment—Business strategy, like military strategy, must react to competitive reality. To quote Michael Porter, the maven of competitive advantage, "The essence of formulating competitive strategy is relating a company to its environment."[6]

Strategy planning, then, calls for analysis of the marketplace, determination of what it will take to carve out an advantageous position, and assessment of the organization's internal resources. In simple terms, strategy execution boils down to an effort to match organizational strengths with requirements for competitive success.[7] In this context, a business unit (or a corporation, if it has only one such unit) will choose its course from among few product (or service) and market themes. On the product and service side, a business will decide that it must produce one of the following:

- A differentiated offering with unique (or at least superior) qualities compared with what the competition provides. Producers of a differentiated offering can charge more and thereby build their margins.

- A low-cost offering that meets reasonable quality standards but comes to market at a lower price; low-cost producers make money because their competitive prices yield high sales volumes, and their efficient production permits acceptable margins.

In the product and service context, Mercedes Benz occupies the differentiation-focused group; Volkswagen tends more toward the low-cost end of the spectrum.

Similarly, businesses have two basic market themes from which to choose. They can adopt either a niche focus, which requires them to identify and dominate a customer or geographic market, or a broader market focus, which leads them down the path to dominating the chosen market with a wide product or service array covering a broad geographic or market landscape. Think of Porsche as a niche player and Chevrolet as a would-be market dominator.

Organization Capabilities

Even these broad-brush outlines begin to suggest the array of undertakings required to carry out strategy. Strategies, after all, do not implement themselves. Companies realize their strategies by focusing their organization capabilities on achieving a marketplace advantage. *Organization capabilities* are the collective abilities of the business unit (as distinct from the individual abilities that make up human capital). Porsche, for example, strives to carve out a niche in a highly competitive automobile market, with product performance as its chosen dimension of differentiation. To win with a strategy emphasizing product differentiation and a niche focus, Porsche needs to marshal such organization capabilities as these:

- Market information management—Effective collection, analysis, and use of information on customer needs (Just how fast do they want to go? How sleek must the design be? Do they really want to listen to the stereo at 120 miles an hour?), and competitors' efforts to meet those needs (Is a Ferrari faster and sleeker? Does it have a better stereo?).

- Product differentiation and identity—Creation of a distinct image of Porsche products and of the company in the minds of customers. (Can we make Porsche seem cooler than Corvette.)

- Continuous product improvement—Ongoing enhancement of the product dimensions that customers value most and that most distinctly differentiate Porsche's cars from other cars on the market. (Can we squeeze another 10 miles per hour out of the top end, and, if so, can we still price below Ferrari?)

- Customer problem solving—Responding quickly and effectively to customer complaints, so that service and support enhance company and product image and reinforce differentiation from competitors. (How can we make sure the Porsche dealer is less snooty than the Ferrari franchise?)

It is easy to see how a low-cost producer in a broadly defined market would pay attention to a different set of organization capabilities. A competitor with that positioning would worry less about performance differentiation and more about production efficiency, distribution channel management, materials handling, and operational planning, for example.

Implementation Levers

When organizations build and strengthen their capabilities, they improve their ability to effect a winning strategy. Developing organization capabilities, in turn, calls for manipulation of a set of *implementation levers*. Here are four levers that are particularly critical:

1. Human capital—The intangible resources of abilities, effort, and time that workers bring to invest in their work

2. Organization structure—The pattern of relationships between units and individuals within the organization

3. Work processes—The series of actions and operations that yield products and services

4. Technology—The employment of mechanical means, especially scientific and computer related, to perform tasks and manage information.

To carry out strategy, an organization must decide which of these levers, manipulated in which particular ways, will build critical capabilities and thereby bring the organization a competitive advantage. By managing these four elements, companies can create and exploit other forms of tangible and intangible capital—for example, financial assets, nonfinancial components of production (machinery, raw material, and real estate, for example), and intangible assets. Intangible assets include the organizational knowledge and customer and supplier relationships that lie just out of sight but often make the difference between realized and unrealized strategies.

The flow of the strategy formulation and implementation process appears in Figure 3.1. The idea is simple—identify a source of competitive advantage, decide what organization-level abilities are needed

Figure 3.1.   Flow of Strategy Formulation and Implementation.

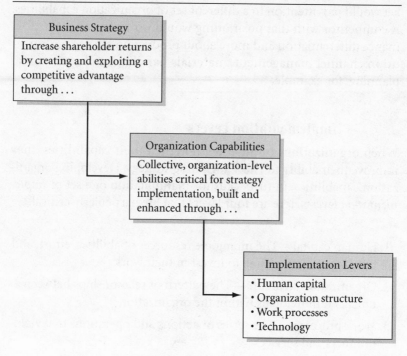

Business Strategy

Increase shareholder returns
by creating and exploiting a
competitive advantage
through . . .

Organization Capabilities

Collective, organization-level
abilities critical for strategy
implementation, built and
enhanced through . . .

Implementation Levers

• Human capital
• Organization structure
• Work processes
• Technology

to seize it, and then pull the implementation levers that create and
apply the key capabilities.

AN INDUSTRY EXAMPLE

To illustrate how organizations might link strategy execution and
human capital management, we can use the results of a Towers Perrin
analysis of the telemedia industry.[8] The telemedia group encompasses
telephone companies, cable television companies, Internet access
providers, entertainment companies, and producers of computer software. Businesses like AT&T, TCI, regional Bell operating companies,
MCI, Microsoft, America Online, and Disney fall into this industry
category—a broad and diverse group, to be sure, interesting for the
range of issues its leaders face. Deregulation, consolidation, convergence of hitherto separate industries, global and domestic competition—all keep telemedia executives awake at night. These same

factors cause insomnia for managers in other North American industries as well.

Top Ten Strategic Requirements

In the Towers Perrin survey, executives and managers in fifty-three telemedia companies evaluated a set of twenty-three strategic activities. These are the actions that managers think will make their companies the competition-crushing, shareholder-return-generating machines they aspire to be. The surveyed managers rated the importance of each activity to their organization's strategic prosperity. They also assessed their organization's success at carrying out each activity. Table 3.1 shows the ten factors rated most important by survey respondents, along with the importance and performance ratings. The column on the far right, which gives the difference between the importance and performance numbers, shows the spread between what companies say has the highest priority for them and how well they act on that priority. Think of it as the "money-where-your-mouth-is" gap. It tells how effectively telemedia managers think they have acted to make strategies become more than just flowcharts and spreadsheets.

As you would expect for an industrywide analysis, the list of important strategic activities covers vast acreage. It ranges from growth initiatives to work process reengineering, from customer retention to new-product introduction. Implementation gaps range in size as well; Table 3.1 shows five gaps of 1.0 or larger. One finding carries special significance for this discussion. Among all their challenges, telemedia managers think their companies fall shortest in trying to increase worker competency to meet emerging market demands. This strategic requirement was fourth ranked among the top ten, with an importance score of 4.4, but the respondents gave themselves only a collective 3.13 rating for performance. Evidently telemedia managers, who seek constantly to find and apply the latest virtual whizbang technology, think their biggest weakness is in managing the human capital of their workers. They also think it is one of the four most important requirements for them to compete successfully in the marketplace.

Capabilities for Executing Strategy

In the telemedia survey, respondents gave importance and performance ratings to a list of forty-seven organization capabilities. The

Table 3.1.   Top Ten Strategies for Success in the Telemedia Industry.

Strategies	Rank	Mean Importance Rating[a]	Mean Importance Rating[b]	Gap[c]
Grow market share and revenue	1	4.57	3.39	1.18
Retain customers through improved service	2	4.48	3.48	1.00
Invest strategically to gain technology advantage	3	4.43	3.55	0.88
Increase competency level of employees to meet emerging market demands	4	4.40	3.13	1.27
Understand "value" from the customer's perspective	5	4.32	3.18	1.14
Introduce new products and services	6	4.31	3.44	0.87
Expand capability to develop and deliver high-value products and services	7	4.31	3.34	0.97
Reengineer work processes to increase efficiency or improve service	8	4.30	3.14	1.16
Establish alliances or new ventures to enter markets	9	4.21	3.49	0.72
Pursue continuous improvement	10	4.16	3.24	0.92

[a]On a scale from 1 to 5, where 5 means "critical to a great extent" and 1 means "not at all critical."

[b]On a scale from 1 to 5, where 5 means "successfully executing to a great extent" and 1 means "not executing successfully at all."

[c]Importance rating minus performance rating.

Source: © 1997 Towers Perrin.

top twenty-four (all rated at 4.2 or higher on the 1-to-5 importance scale) appear in Table 3.2. The capabilities cluster into categories of management activity: people, organization, general management, customers, and products and services. Two clusters take us directly to specific implementation levers: the people management cluster (which focuses on the human capital lever) and the organization cluster (which emphasizes the importance of structural elements). The other capabilities clusters call into play, to varying degrees, several implementation levers. Let us look at one of these multilever clusters before

Table 3.2. Top Twenty-Four Organization Capabilities in the Telemedia Industry.

	Rank		Rank
People		**Customers**	
• Attract and retain people with skills to succeed	1	• Acquire new customers	2
• Engage and increase employee commitment	4	• Manage customer relationships	11
• Align human resource programs with strategy	12	• Match services to customer priorities	16
• Communicate across the organization	20	• Solve customer business problems	17
• Train and develop the work force effectively	23	**Products and Services**	
		• Provide reliable, high-quality customer service	3
Organization		• Innovate	5
• Maximize effectiveness of the sales organization	18	• Leverage technology to enhance and create products and services	6
• Optimize organizational efficiency and effectiveness	24	• Improve products and services continuously	7
General Management		• Acquire and implement leading-edge technology	9
• Measure and manage business performance	8	• Bring new products and services to market	10
• Understand and manage for profitability	14	• Develop new products and services	13
• Gain insight into competitive strategies	15	• Build brand identity	21
• Negotiate, influence, and construct profitable deals	19	• Value-price products/services	22

Source: © 1997 Towers Perrin.

returning to the capabilities that focus our attention specifically on human capital.

Implementation Levers to Strengthen Capabilities

Consider the cluster focused on how telemedia companies form and nurture relationships with their customers. The surveyed managers identified four customer management capabilities that make a critical difference in executing strategy: acquire new customers, manage customer relationships, match services to customer priorities, and solve customers' business problems. Let us suppose we attributed these findings to a single organization. The next step would be to decide how best to activate implementation levers to improve execution of the four customer-focused capabilities.

Exhibit 3.1 gives examples of how a manager might call into play each of the four implementation levers to strengthen these desired organization capabilities. The items in the exhibit represent a sample of strategy-clarification experiences across a range of telemedia businesses. Note that in this example, each lever has something to contribute. Note also that many actions resulting from manipulation of a particular lever gain support from actions associated with other levers. Take the "manage customer relationships" capability as an example. Within the organization structure lever, establishing multifunctional teams should improve this capability. Teams, in turn, should help improve the flow of information between sales and manufacturing, a work process initiative. Improved information flow will increase the effectiveness of technology applications in enhancing the customer database. And collaborative behaviors (an element of human capital) by everyone involved in teams will increase the probability that multifunctional teams can succeed.

Because our focus is human capital, we pay particular attention to the second column from the left. That column lists a sample of human capital elements that affect the four customer-focused organization capabilities. By creating a similar array for each group of critical organization capabilities, a manager can identify the bundles of human capital required for strategic success. Sometimes the investment of abilities, behavior, effort, and time will be defined in terms specific to individual jobs. Ensuring that sales representatives have the skill to prospect successfully for new customers is an example of a job-specific application of human capital. In other cases, human capital elements apply more broadly to the management of the business. Communication, teamwork, and general business acumen are examples of organization-level human capital.

WHY DON'T HUMAN CAPITAL MODELS VARY MORE?

Human capital experts notice that diverse organizations seem to search for many of the same kinds of abilities and behaviors. Even looking across different industries, the similarities are remarkable. To test this observation, we reviewed a sample of forty projects focused on defining specific human capital needs. We found that in almost every project,

Exhibit 3.1. Using Implementation Levers to Build Organization Capabilities.

Customer Management Capabilities	Implementation Levers and Actions			
	Human Capital	Organization Structure	Work Processes	Technology
Acquire new customers	• Improve sales reps' prospecting ability • Improve sales reps' knowledge of target customers' businesses	• Establish strategic marketing unit focused on key market segments • Set up national accounts function	• Shorten and simplify credit analysis process • Simplify procedure for capturing customer information	• Speed direct data entry through laptops in the field
Manage customer relationships	• Increase collaboration among sales reps • Increase collaboration between marketing and sales departments • Develop sales reps' knowledge of their company's full capabilities	• Create relationship manager position • Establish multifunction (sales, marketing, production) teams for key customers	• Improve flow of customer information across regions • Streamline flow of information between sales and manufacturing	• Enhance customer information database
Match services to customer priorities	• Increase sales reps' active listening skills	• Establish customer service functions by industry segment	• Improve market research to identify customer priorities • Shorten product design cycle time	• Put order-entry terminals on customer sites • Enhance ability to produce customized products efficiently
Solve customer business problems	• Improve sales reps' problem-solving skills • Acquire talent to enhance product design innovation	• Form alliances with complementary product providers	• Accelerate speed to market for critical products • Form joint design teams with customers	• Form data exchange links with customers

▭ Complementary initiatives

communication skill was among the most often identified forms of critical human capital. Teamwork, customer focus, and results orientation showed up on the list of desired human capital in the large majority of project companies.

Why do companies competing in different industries and employing different strategies want the same kinds of human capital? Here are some theories:

• *Similar Competitive Challenges Require Similar Responses.* This theory reminds us that when you get right down to it, companies compete along a finite range of common dimensions. It takes just two dimensions— product/service and market themes—to capture the essence of any organization's strategy. Similarly positioned companies face similar challenges of cost management, product innovation, quality, and customer service. Consider customer service as an example. Increasing expectations for high-end support inexorably drive almost all companies to focus on ways to make customers happy. This means that to some degree, every company needs people with the kinds of advanced customer-focused behaviors required to keep consumers coming back. Consequently, at some level, all companies that have customers to serve end up looking for similar service-enhancing behaviors.

• *Portable Managers Carry Their Ideas with Them.* According to a story in the *Wall Street Journal,* companies often look outside their own ranks for senior managers, including CEOs.[9] Two different university studies showed that between 17 percent and one-third of major corporations have CEOs hired from outside the company. These outsiders enter their new companies with little understanding of organization culture and politics, but with a bag of management tricks they acquired somewhere else. In place of instincts honed over years of growing up in a single organization, they substitute techniques they found successful in a prior management incarnation. As they travel from organization to organization, they are bound to seed some common practices and perspectives. To the extent that their techniques require particular forms of human capital for successful execution, these forms are likely to become more common across industries.

• *Managers Are Prone to Follow Fads.* Managers are as slavish as anyone else in their dedication to fashion. If Total Quality Management is the problem-solving flavor of the day, then ability to do root-cause analysis may become the human capital element most in demand. Looking to create cross-functional teams? Better hire people who have a propensity to work well in groups. Under this theory, widespread adoption of management fads is likely to produce commonality among the human capital elements required for execution.

There is probably some truth to each of these notions, especially the first. However, I favor two other theories to explain the frequency with which the same human capital elements show up on many companies' wish lists:

• *God Is in the Details.* Nuances make all the difference. Subtle shadings in the definitions of human capital elements are magnified when applied in a strategic context. Two companies may both look for a "bias for action" in the people they hire, but they may mean something quite different. In my pharmaceutical company, it may mean "self-motivated application of technical knowledge to develop new products." In your investment bank, you may define it as "taking steps to close a deal without waiting for unnecessary analysis or approvals from upstairs." The Details theory recognizes that industry characteristics, competitive landscape, culture, and a host of other factors color the definitions of human capital elements. Just as the DNA codes of a wolf monkey and Wolfgang Amadeus Mozart differ by only 2 percent, so may small differences in the definition of human capital elements have profound effects on strategic outcomes.[10]

• *Execution Makes the Difference.* Two companies may use similar words and phrases to define their human capital needs but take widely divergent approaches to filling those needs. Differences in hiring practices, learning strategies, work environment, reward policies, and communication can have a significant influence on the effectiveness with which organizations manage their human capital. To paraphrase Thomas Edison, the genius of human capital may reside in the perspiration of execution rather than in the inspiration of definition.

Human Capital Management Capabilities

Let us probe a little deeper into the psyches of telemedia managers to learn more about how they think about human capital. Figure 3.2 provides additional insight into the human capital management capabilities that telemedia executives think will make the greatest contribution to strategic success. For this industry at least, these five capabilities determine whether companies will succeed or fail at maximizing the strategic contribution of human capital. Requirements

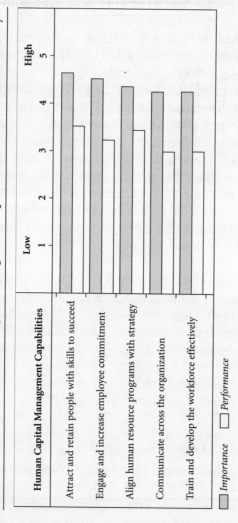

Figure 3.2. Five Key Human Capital Management Capabilities in the Telemedia Industry.

Source: © 1997 Towers Perrin.

for success range from bringing the right human capital into the organization ("Attract and retain people with skills to succeed") to providing information so people can manage their human capital investment ("Communicate across the organization"). As Figure 3.2 suggests, telemedia managers think their companies have gaps to close to become as proficient as they need to be in human capital management. The largest perceived gap exists in companies' ability to engage and increase employee commitment; the smallest gap (though still significant) is in alignment of human resource programs with strategy.

To validate the broader applicability of these five management capabilities, we ought to look at human capital from a different direction. Instead of focusing on a whole industry, let us look at a single business function.

In 1997, Towers Perrin surveyed information technology (IT) managers in some 250 companies. We had two goals: to find out what they consider important for the IT function to make the greatest possible contribution to an organization's competitive advantage, and to assess the kinds of human capital management practices in place in IT departments. The surveyed companies made up a diverse database. They came from an array of industries—more than thirty in all, ranging from aerospace to banking, metal manufacturing to retailing, insurance to pharmaceuticals. Mostly, they were sizable organizations, 71 percent having annual revenue of $1 billion or more.

The strategic concerns of IT managers reflect what is on the minds of their executive masters: understanding and increasing value from the customer's perspective, developing sound business plans, increasing employee competency, achieving better customer retention, and delivering higher-quality products and services.[11] The IT managers we surveyed put competency building in a first-place tie among these critical strategic imperatives. When we asked the IT heads which organization capabilities they believed their units would most need to support strategy execution, these five came out on top:[12]

1. Translate business needs into IT solutions.

2. Provide reliable, high-quality customer service.

3. Manage projects efficiently.

4. Efficiently use existing resources.

5. Manage change effectively.

We then took our analysis down another level and asked the IT managers what kinds of specific people-management capabilities the function would need to execute its strategic role. These emerged as the top five human capital management priorities (the percentages that follow refer to the number of respondents choosing "agree" or "strongly agree" that each factor is critical to strategy execution):[13]

1. Selecting employees, 93 percent
2. Finding employees, 93 percent
3. Rewarding high performers, 93 percent
4. Improving customer service, 92 percent
5. Developing employee skill, 92 percent

These findings line up well with the telemedia industry factors shown in Figure 3.2. The two perspectives lead us to essentially the same conclusions about what is important in human capital management. Looking for common themes, and taking some license to rearrange things into manageable groups, I would propose these as the activities that our surveyed managers think contribute most to effective human capital management:

- Bring the most strategically valuable forms of human capital into the organization.
- Create an environment that elicits high contribution of that capital.
- Increase the amount of human capital available for investment.
- Retain the people and their capital within the organization for as long as possible and give them information so they can manage their human capital investment.

SUMMARY: HUMAN CAPITAL STRATEGY

It appears we have accomplished our two goals for Chapter Three. First, we laid out a strategy-driven approach to identifying critical elements of human capital. We defined organization capabilities as the activating mechanisms of strategy—the power, prowess, and strength that make strategy manifest. We also identified four implementation levers by which organizations can build capabilities and improve their chances of realizing a winning strategy.

We accomplished our second goal when we identified another system, one comprising four management programs. This system allows an organization to marshal its human capital for maximum strategic effect. In Chapters Four through Eight, we will explore in order each of these human capital management capabilities: hiring, supporting investment, building, and retaining. We will, I hope, learn a few things about how an organization can manage its way to a competitive advantage through the handling of human capital.

The telemedia and information technology examples reinforce a central theme of the book—that people are critical to strategy *implementation*. But what about their role in strategy *formulation*? There is nothing wrong with the traditional top-down model of strategy formulation, but, as we recall from Mintzberg's typology, it is not the only way. Sometimes, Mintzberg reminds us, the best strategies emerge in the day-to-day doing of business rather than in formal planning exercises. If this is the case, then a company can place itself at a clear advantage by spreading certain key abilities widely throughout the organization.

What is it about the current business environment that places such a premium on the ability of every individual to act like a strategist? In a word, *velocity,* the pace of change. In two other words, *accelerating change,* the second derivative of velocity. Speaking about the high-technology world, a senior executive of Sun Microsystems put it this way: "The information technology industry is advancing at a whirlwind pace, with product cycles and time-to-market periods shortening and demands for continued innovation and productivity growing with each passing day. The shelf-life of a typical product in our industry is less than a year and dropping. What we will offer to the world next year has not even been invented today. In this environment, you either get the right worker and match that worker with the right position at the right time to keep you ahead of the rest of the world or you can call it a day."[14] Increasingly, the right worker is someone who can observe the environment, assess the company's position, and respond creatively. The right worker brings forth emergent strategy, guided (but unimpeded) by a formal plan.

Participating in strategy decisions has come to represent an important element of intrinsic return on human capital investment. Here again, the IT sector gives us a window into the minds of smart, well-informed workers. In the 1997 *Computerworld* survey, involvement in making and executing business (not just technical) decisions got one of the highest rankings for contribution to job-related fulfillment.[15] It seems no more than sensible for companies to make it possible for more people to develop and carry out strategically sound ideas. Doing so taps into a human capital resource that multiplies the organization's chances of beating the competition. In a competitive world, which would you rather have—one strategic planning department looking for a marketplace advantage or every employee thinking of ways to move the company to the top of the industry heap?

PART TWO

Taking Action

CHAPTER FOUR

Hiring Human Capital Investors

I n *Bartleby the Scrivener,* Herman Melville tells what happens when an employer does a slipshod job of finding the right person. The narrator of the tale (an elderly Wall Street lawyer with a thriving practice) needs to hire a person in anticipation of increased work. He is looking for a professional copyist called a scrivener. Scriveners duplicate any page requiring multiple versions, creating paper *doppelgängers* of the original. Scrivening abilities—reproducing documents quickly, accurately, and neatly—were key assets to the prephotocopy, ante–word processing law office. A lawyer would want to hire his scriveners carefully.

Despite mixed experience with scriveners in the past, the veteran lawyer hires "a motionless young man . . . pallidly neat, pitiably respectable, incurably forlorn." He makes his decision after no more investigation than "a few words touching his qualifications." In the end, the experience is disastrous for the lawyer and fatal for Bartleby. The lawyer ends up with a scrivener who refuses to do anything but copy: no proofreading, no trips to the post office, no other chores.[1] Seldom has anyone used the phrase "I would prefer not to" so often or with so chilling an effect. Had the old lawyer better probed his scrivening candidate, he might have learned about his history as a clerk in the Dead Letter office. That kind of experience would surely drain anyone's energy. He might also have better conveyed that the job required someone willing to make diverse contributions; there was no room for overspecialization. Alas, a careless selection process failed both employer and employee.

Hiring the right people, especially for skilled positions like scrivening, has, if anything, become more challenging and more important over the last 150 years. The authors of one study of differences in worker performance found that in complex jobs (attorneys, physicians, and cartographers, for example), the top 1 percent of producers generated 2.27 times the output of average producers. In moderate-complexity professions (mechanics and insurance claims evaluators, for instance), the topmost performers produced 1.85 times the average output.[2] We know from Chapter Three that attracting people with critical human capital is a requirement for strategic success. In this chapter, we adopt a human capital perspective in addressing three aspects of effective hiring in any labor market: formulating an acquisition strategy, executing a psychological contract, and managing the hiring process.

STRATEGIES FOR ACQUIRING HUMAN CAPITAL

In Chapter Three, we mapped out the road from capabilities to human capital, a road with more than a few blind corners and hairpin turns. Let us begin the discussion of human capital acquisition by visiting a business with a familiar set of challenges.

Move from Strategy to Human Capital Requirements

It's Monday morning at 9:30. You have just spent two hours with your boss, the head of your business unit, going over the strategy plan for the next year. Your unit, Perpetual Petals, faces intense competition from new market entrants. You generate about $750 million a year in revenue from your main product, silk flowers. The product competes with many substitutes: buds and blooms of plastic, paper, and metal, not to mention the genuine article. You have made it clear to the boss, and she agrees, that adding new products is critical for success. Perpetual Petals must solidify its position as a market leader in ersatz blossoms. Otherwise you will have a tough time earning the 20 percent return on equity (ROE) demanded by International Interior Novelties, your parent company.

In the terms defined in the last chapter, you have identified an important organization capability—speedy development and introduction of new products. Your next challenge (you are the head of sales and marketing) is to define the implementation lever implications for that capability and all the others highlighted in your strategic plan. On the structure side, the organization has decided to put product development in sales and marketing rather than in the research and development unit, a decision you applaud. Once you have filled out your product development staff, you will need to improve processes to accelerate speed to market. Improvements are also needed in fabric-weaving and color-mixing technology. You recognize, however, that having the right human capital will make the biggest difference in enhancing the organization's new-product capability. Using the ideas laid out in Chapter Three, you conclude new-product development will require people who have the following:

- *Knowledge* of the company's production processes and techniques for compiling market projections
- *Skill* in customer research design, defining material and manufacturing specifications, and solving problems
- *Talent* for creating appealing color and texture combinations
- *Behavior* that fosters collaboration with other units in the company

Pinpoint the Best Sources of Human Capital

You are ready for the next challenge—figuring out how to get these human capital elements into your organization and focus them on product development. Your options for constructing a suitable employment relationship are shown in Exhibit 4.1.

To choose among the options, you must answer a fundamental human capital management question: Should you develop someone within the organization or hire someone from outside? Remember that companies can develop some elements of human capital, but others lie beyond the reach of development efforts. Figure 4.1

Exhibit 4.1. Alternative Employment Relationships.

Traditional Employment	Nontraditional Employment	External Just-in-Time Alternatives	Outsourcing
Full-time employment	In-house temporaries	Agency temporaries	Outsource providers
Part-time employment	Job sharing	Consultants	Shared workforce
Overtime	Flexible time or place	Independent contractors	Service bureaus
Seasonal workers	Postretirement	Freelancers	

summarizes the available approaches to increasing human capital. Knowledge elements, for example, are trainable by definition; knowledge is information acquired through instruction and through informal, everyday contact with knowledgeable workmates and supervisors. For skills, the picture is not so clear. Skills often combine knowledge and talent; the knowledge part can be acquired, but the talent part is innate. Behaviors cover the gamut; some can be developed (like sensitive listening), whereas others resist development (such as bias for action). Organizations can nurture and reinforce knowledge, skills, and behavior through their delivery of ROI_w, as we will discuss further in Chapter Six. Nothing an organization does after hiring has

Figure 4.1. Approaches to Increasing Human Capital.

Ways to Increase Human Capital	Types of Human Capital			
	Knowledge	Skills	Talent	Behavior
Hiring				
Formal training				
Informal learning				
Reinforcement through ROI_w delivery[a]				

Impact on increasing human capital
High   Medium   Low

[a]Includes all four elements of ROI_w: intrinsic job elements, growth opportunities, recognition, and financial rewards.

much effect on values, talent, or some behaviors, however. So make sure you know the root of the human capital you need. You can probably teach a hippopotamus to catch a mouse, but it is better (and easier on the furniture) to buy a cat.

With all this in mind, let us rephrase the question: For which of the required human capital elements is development feasible? Do not think about the cost of training programs yet, or even the amount of time required to develop people. Just think about whether it is even possible to use classroom training, on-the-job instruction, or informal learning opportunities to build each human capital element. Write down the elements you can develop on a piece of paper and put it aside. Then answer two additional questions: (1) How quickly must you have this bundle of human capital? Call this *urgency.* (2) How important is it to hold on to the human capital once you have it? In other words, how important is it to your strategy over the long term? Call this *need to retain.*

These two questions both carry important strategic implications. Determining urgency and need to retain requires the kind of strategy-to-human-capital analysis laid out in Chapter Three. This is no place for guesswork. Figure 4.2 shows how ease of development, urgency, and need to retain play off each other to generate a human capital acquisition pathway. The figure illustrates a route open to the silk flower producer. Assume that the skill and knowledge parts of the role are most critical. This gives the organization the option of hiring from the outside or developing someone from within the company. Urgency

Figure 4.2. Pathways to Human Capital Acquisition.

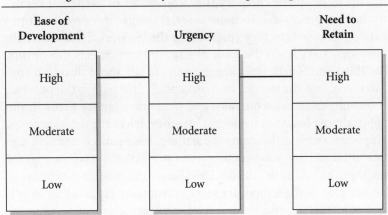

Ease of Development	Urgency	Need to Retain
High	High	High
Moderate	Moderate	Moderate
Low	Low	Low

is high; time waits for no one in the silk flower business. The company anticipates needing the product developer for the long term, because product differentiation will be a key strategic variable for some time to come. The pathway charted in Figure 4.1 reflects these factors. This pattern, in turn, suggests a two-phase strategy. Because high urgency removes the luxury of taking a long time to hire the perfect candidate, Perpetual Petals might begin by finding a consultant to start the process. Simultaneously, the organization should start a rigorous recruiting process to locate the right product manager. Once hired, she can use the consultant's analysis and product development framework to carry the effort forward.

Figure 4.2 suggests many approaches to the acquisition of human capital. Here are a few examples, with their implications:

EASE OF DEVELOPMENT	URGENCY	NEED TO RETAIN	SUGGESTED APPROACH
Low/moderate	Low/moderate	High	Hire
High	Low	High	Train/develop
Low	High	Low	Use temps or consultants
Low/moderate	Moderate/high	Low	Outsource

The first line reflects an emphasis on important talent or skills that the organization cannot easily improve, like artistic talent in our fake flower product developer. In such cases, hiring is the only option. Sometimes the more important elements of human capital fall into the developable category (like knowledge of Perpetual Petals's production processes). In those cases, the organization can adopt a learning-focused strategy (presuming the learners already have the talent necessary to do the job). The second line reflects this option. The third and fourth lines suggest ways to use short-duration contracts to obtain the needed human capital. This path is the province of consultants, service bureaus, and temporary service firms. Trainability almost becomes irrelevant; urgency drives the decision to use temporary, outside-the-company staffing. For many companies, supplemental staffing now encompasses professional and managerial functions, as well as the classic clerical and light manufacturing applications. Olsten, the temporary services company, reports that 36 percent of businesses use temporaries, contractors, or outsourcers in professional and managerial roles.[3] Accounting and information systems pros lead the pack.

Organizations sometimes find that ease of development is high, urgency of need is manageable (they have time either to train or to hire rigorously), and retention is critical. These situations pose a classic make-or-buy decision. Cost reenters the picture. A company must weigh the implicit and explicit cost of hiring against the obvious and hidden expenses associated with learning and development. Apart from the hard-dollar outlays on both sides of the ledger, return-on-investment effects also come into play. Remember that development opportunities represent a key aspect of ROI_w. Someone within Perpetual Petals probably has some of the required human capital and would blossom under the tutelage of an experienced product developer. Management must factor this into the cost and benefit analysis of hiring or developing.

Figure 4.3 summarizes the discussion so far. It tracks through Chapter Three's strategy formulation and translation processes and ties in the human capital acquisition discussion of the last few pages. We have talked about human capital acquisition in an almost modular way, as if an organization could acquire individual elements of it. In fact, human capital comes in convenient reusable packages called people. People own bundles of human capital, heavy in some areas, light

Figure 4.3. How Business Strategy Links with Approaches to Increasing Human Capital.

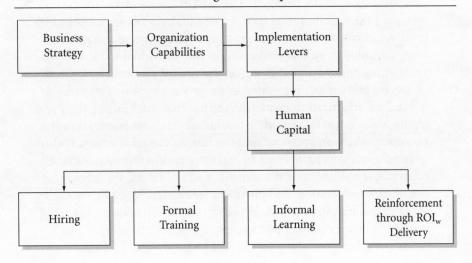

in others, but multifaceted nonetheless. If you want Bob's engineering talent, you can hire him for that, but his glibness and his impatience for detail come in the same package. You can reward the application of some elements and ignore others, but you have to take the irrelevant with the relevant.

Let us now suppose that an organization has decided to go into the labor market and hire people with the human capital required to beat the competition. The next two sections lay out some principles for hiring human capital investors. We go first to the intricacies of the psychological contract.

THE ART OF THE DEAL

An implicit contract provides the context for exchange between worker and organization, conveying what each side will provide to the other and what each will receive in return. Contracts express mutual obligations, reflecting that each party must recognize binding requirements. A formal document may capture some aspects of the relationship between worker and company, but can never encompass all the subtle interpersonal elements. Therefore, we use the term *psychological contract* to encompass the web of written, unwritten, spoken, unspoken, and ultimately ineffable aspects of the interaction between worker and company. The notion of a psychological contract is old wine, but its prominence as a term is of recent vintage. It seems that no one paid much attention to the idea of an unwritten contract until companies began to break it. Downsizing, one often reads, has destroyed the time-honored contract of a lifelong job in exchange for loyalty and reasonable performance. Nowadays, we hear, a different contract holds sway, one that requires the individual to look to the value of his human capital as the only source of job security.

We are particularly interested in the process by which an individual and an organization create such a contract. Establishing the psychological contract—making a workplace deal—is essential to the process by which an organization hires human capital investors. It also governs a worker's agreement to make the required investments. All contracts should address three distinct sets of issues. We label these duration, consideration, and provision for change. By exploring each, we can illuminate the psychological contract more precisely and examine how it defines and supports the workplace relationship.

Agree on Duration

Every contract has a stated or implied duration—the length of time covered by the contract. For a temporary worker, duration might last as little as a few hours. For a full-time worker with valued human capital and career aspirations, duration might extend for decades. The duration of a psychological contract typically reflects the period over which worker and company believe their relationship will remain mutually beneficial. Duration also has importance for the various forms of commitment. In companies that offer a rich ROI_w package, especially one hefty with intrinsic job satisfaction, attitudinal commitment may form quickly. Loyalty-based and programmatic commitment, however, takes longer to coalesce. Consider a worker who stays with a company for five years, but does so under a series of one-year contracts. Without the explicit expectation of a longer-term arrangement, that individual may never form a deep, multidimensional commitment to the organization. It is not just the length of time that is important, but also the clarity of the arrangement. To quote one observer, "It's hard to build corporate loyalty among workers who spend their days bouncing from company to company."[4] Worse than that, it is hard to build loyalty among people who do not know whether or when they *might* move to another company. In other words, uncertainty itself undercuts commitment. Reducing commitment, we know, depresses human capital investment. Also, a worker uncertain about his future with a single organization will naturally avoid acquiring skills and knowledge applicable solely to that company. We will reconsider the effects of commitment and uncertainty in later chapters, where we explore retention and risk.

It is pointless to argue that one contract length is inherently better than another for either worker or company. Companies want the freedom to reduce staffing whenever they deem necessary. Workers want to be able to move to greener pastures at a moment's (or two weeks') notice. In this context, what meaning does an agreement on duration have? To answer the question, we borrow a wrinkle from corporate finance, where duration means more than just the length of time something lasts. In technical financial terms, duration measures interest rate sensitivity, expressed in units of time. Analysts calculate duration as the weighted average of the maturities of each individual payment yielded by a fixed-income security. Securities with shorter durations (those providing more of their cash flow in the early periods of their terms) have less sensitivity to interest rate changes.

Cypress Semiconductor, a Silicon Valley chip manufacturer with $550 million in 1997 revenue, has figured out how to use this notion of duration to benefit employees and company alike.[5] Cypress has a key marketing position called product marketing engineer (PME). The PME job represents the entry point for new college graduates into the world of high-tech sales and marketing. PMEs normally have electrical engineering degrees from the best technical schools. They provide tactical support to the field sales network; PMEs help determine pricing, work with manufacturing to address quality problems, track the status of outstanding orders, and generally solve problems that impede the sales process.

In 1996, Cypress noticed that turnover among PMEs had begun to rise. When company managers investigated the problem, they found several root causes. Most prominent among these was uncertainty in the PME ranks about what the future might hold for them. They lived day to day in a high-pressure job, with demands bombarding them from all directions. They expected a challenge—that is what working at Cypress is all about—but they wanted to know where they were headed. In other words, the PMEs wanted a better sense of the rewards they could expect, given their human capital investment. They also wanted to know how rewards and investment would match up chronologically—duration, pure and simple.

To address these concerns, Cypress took a close look at the two years of a PME's life. That's about the amount of time newly hired electrical engineers spend in the position; after that, they expect to move on to another job. As Exhibit 4.2 illustrates, the company formalized PME evolution by dividing the two years into three stages: trainee, contributor, and coach. This structure makes it clear to the PME candidate what kinds of human capital investment the company expects at each stage and what the return on that investment will be. Intrinsic elements of the job come into play, as do learning and development and financial rewards. Recognition in the Cypress culture comes in the form of high-performer status, with accelerated opportunity for those who earn it. At the end of two years, successful PMEs can choose from many career paths and next-job options, including account management, strategic marketing, and product engineering. The stages are compact, with investment and return on investment synchronized. Cypress formally communicates this structure during

Exhibit 4.2.   The First Two Years for a PME.

Trainee	Contributor	Coach
Becoming socialized, getting to know the company, the job	Having maximum impact in serving customers, helping sales and marketing teammates	Preparing a replacement, beginning transition to the next job
Coach assigned to help trainee learn: The lay of the land Career options Politics Information sources	Coaching focuses on performance improvement, identification of high performers for accelerated career path	Coaching helps with transition, development of longer-term performance plan
Formal learning focused on company product line	Formal learning emphasizes specific technical knowledge (for example, end equipment architecture), development of coaching skills	Formal learning begins to focus on more advanced sales and management skills
Highly competitive base salary	Base salary increases as earned; bonus and stock options kick in	High performers eligible for additional discretionary bonus
├─────────────────────┤	├─────────────────────┤	├─────────────────────┤
About six months	*About 12 months*	*About six months*

Source: Internal company documents.

the process of recruiting a PME; everyone knows the rules from the beginning.

When investments and returns are in sync, the worker is less likely to perceive himself to be working at a deficit. This means organizations should grant promotions when earned, give recognition soon after achievements, and provide training when the need arises. Conversely, when organizations push aspects of ROI_w into the future, their value diminishes, and the uncertainty associated with them increases. Circumstances may alter their value (organization changes may devalue a hoped-for promotion, for example) and reduce their significance as returns on current human capital investment. The message—to craft an extended, mutually beneficial relationship with a worker, ensure a close matching of investment and return.

Specify Consideration

Consideration refers to the value exchanged under a contract. Managers have long viewed the hiring process as the making of a match between worker abilities and job requirements. However, there is a more basic, and perhaps more important, kind of match that takes place in the hiring process—the match between the ROI_w requirements of human capital investors and the return-on-investment elements the organization can offer.

Formulation of a recruiting approach begins with the business strategy analysis already discussed. However, following hard behind is an objective, clear-eyed assessment of what the organization has to offer the owners of needed human capital. This means going through each of the four ROI_w categories and doing an inventory of what the organization can make available, then comparing that offering with what is available from marketplace competition. Financial compensation may be the most straightforward to analyze. Most organizations have a good idea of where their financial package stands compared with the packages of their industry and labor market competition. Similarly rigorous market analysis should be done for the other three ROI_w elements: intrinsic job fulfillment, growth opportunities, and recognition. Although more difficult to describe concretely and research competitively, the key role they play in an individual's job choice makes competitive information critical.

Many organizations find that one contract size does not fit all. Even among people with similar jobs, the psychological deal may vary in subtle but important ways. Exhibit 4.3 shows a generalized example, compiled from several companies in the high-tech sector, of different deals for two similar positions. The Team Star is a gifted technical specialist who wants to polish his skills while preserving variety in his work and away-from-work life. He will take the job for a deal heavy on individual incentives and elements that build and recognize his technical artistry. The Team Leader, in contrast, wants to rise in the company. His technical human capital may not measure up to that of the Team Star, but he has something else the company values—interest in, and proclivity for, general management. He wants to work somewhere that emphasizes his group orientation, gives him exposure to current executives, and rewards him with chances to advance up the corporate ladder. An organization that wants diverse bundles of human capital must be prepared to craft different deals for different people, tailoring the contract (especially the nonfinancial elements) to particular needs and motivations.

Exhibit 4.3. Different Deals.

Return on Investment Elements	Team Star	Team Leader
Intrinsic job elements	Cool projects with smart people Frequent moves to choice of projects Access to latest technology	Exposure to senior management Involvement in big deals Opportunity to run important projects
Growth opportunities	Technical training Support for further education Assignment to key teams	Leadership training
Recognition	Eligible for annual company award based on patents granted Opportunity to present papers at professional conferences Opportunity to teach at local university Eligible for awards from project manager's discretionary fund	Eligible for recognition as head of successful project Control over discretionary funds to reward eligible employees for excellent performance
Compensation	Base salary at market average Incentive based on individual performance Options at double market average	Base salary at market average Incentive based on group performance Options at market average
Benefits	Standard health and welfare benefits 401(k) Flextime Sabbatical after six years	Standard health and welfare benefits 401(k) Standard hours

Provide for Change Through Contract Flexibility

Said the Greek philosopher Heraclitus, and many others since, "Nothing endures but change." As companies, industries, and whole economies restructure, contracts must change to reflect new realities. Not adapting is not an option. The challenge for organizations and workers alike is to construct their contracts to reflect and ensure an acceptable exchange even as the world evolves. Like circus contortionists, contracts (and contractors) must bend without breaking.

Contract flexibility affects both duration and consideration. Flexibility comes in three forms: accommodation, evolution, and replacement.

These forms vary in four ways: by the magnitude of change involved, the permanence of change, the pace of change, and the continuity with which change fits into the structure of the original contract. Exhibit 4.4 summarizes the key differences among the forms.

Accommodation occurs when one party permits a short-term, usually small change in the terms of the contract. A company that asks workers to accept a temporary wage freeze banks on their willingness to tolerate a short-lived reduction in financial return on investment. Accommodation extends this notion beyond consideration to other aspects of the contract. Take, as an example, notification by a company that it will make a onetime offer of early retirement to some employees. The company wants to shrink the workforce quickly, effectively reducing contract duration for some employees (those who choose to take the offer and leave). The effect on the workforce at large is minor, and the change initiative is temporary (presuming the organization does not expect further reductions). Also, the change occurs quickly (especially if the offer remains open for a short time only), and the preexisting contract remains largely in place.

Contract evolution involves a more dramatic change in the deal between worker and organization. Evolution takes place over a long time and moves at a measured pace. Unlike accommodation, each increment of change is permanent; the organization does not expect to return to its former contract. On the one hand, true evolution may never end; the relationship between worker and organization continues to reflect new realities as the world changes. The current (though never final) evolutionary stage may look not at all like the original. On the other hand, snapshots at different points typically reveal a con-

Exhibit 4.4.   Three Forms of Contract Change.

| | Forms of Change | | |
Change Factors	Accommodation	Evolution	Replacement
Magnitude	Minor	Major	Complete
Permanence	Temporary	Permanent	Permanent
Pace	Immediate	Slow	Fast
Continuity	Same contract	Similar for a long time, core elements often remain	Different contract

tract that resembles the version immediately preceding it and the one immediately succeeding. A central core of values remains, cherished and preserved by organization and workers. At Hewlett-Packard (HP), for example, the 1980s brought a period of acquisition and aggressive hiring. Extended contracts reflecting employment stability had been part of the HP covenant for a long time. Near the end of the decade, however, the organization found itself in a cost squeeze and needed to reduce employment. By using such approaches as an in-house service to match downsized workers with internal job openings, the organization managed to reduce its workforce without losing growth momentum. HP also avoided violating the time-honored, longstanding assumption of employment stability. The relationship between worker and company has evolved at HP, but the heart of the contract remains intact.

Contract replacement lies at the radical end of the change spectrum. Replacement constitutes major surgery—transplantation of a vital organ in the corporation.[6] A different contract comes into play, representing dramatic, permanent change brought on quickly. Waves of downsizing, announcements that workers henceforth have responsibility for their own job security, sudden creation of work teams to replace formal organization units—these are the manifestations of contract replacement.

If you worked for Ma Bell over the last decade and a half, you went through contract replacement. Here is management professor Denise Rousseau's description of the Bell System transformation:

> When divestiture was ordered by the courts in the early 1980s, the process of breaking up a highly successful, regulated business and turning it into separate competitive enterprises rewrote the deep structure of the employment contract. Employees who for generations in many cases had "bell-shaped heads" never missed a day of work, and labored loyally for a secure job and retirement began coping with the need to produce business results, and respond to market demands. A decade and a half of uncertainty, terminations, and movement of personnel from operating companies to new high-technology business units radically changed the people and their relationship to the many new organizations that the break-up created.[7]

In a perfect world, parties would define the level of expected, acceptable change at the beginning of the contract. Companies would tell people about the kinds of contract changes that had occurred in the past and, given that precedent, what the future holds. Impractical you say—predicting organizational change is like predicting the weather. Few organizations are willing to go on record about what the future might bring. Fair enough, but there are nevertheless better and worse ways to deal with changes in the workplace contract. Companies that expect a change in the psychological deal should formulate a process for working through change. My colleagues who work in change management have developed a set of steps for helping companies prepare for and make changes in the workplace contract. Their experience and research suggest that, by using a five-phase process, management can help people understand and cope with contract change.

> *Phase 1: Break with the past.* Provide legitimate, externally validated reason for change. For example, by pointing out the weaknesses of premerger performance or publicizing tougher competitive standards, management can help people grasp why the old contract must change. In effect, the organization must convey to workers why they need different human capital, or the same capital employed differently, to remain aligned with an evolving business strategy.

> *Phase 2: Mobilize for change.* Clearly signal that change is coming. The signs of change can take many forms: bringing in a new senior manager from outside, adopting a new corporate name, or changing the work locations of highly visible units. Make sure that despite change, people keep doing the jobs that need to be done. Clear short-term objectives are important when the longer-term future looks fuzzy.

> *Phase 3: Realize a new contract.* Look to line managers to forge new contracts with employees. The human resource department can help make and reinforce contracts, but the role of crafting and negotiating the new deal should fall chiefly to line managers. The role of the supervisor as keeper of the contract becomes crucial.

> *Phase 4: Embed the new contract.* Underpin the new psychological contract with change in organizational structure and people management processes (compensation and performance assessment, for instance). Expect reality testing, especially in areas that

affect employees most visibly, such as new organizational arrangements. For some, the new contract will not be real until they forge a relationship with a new superior and new peers.

Phase 5: Live the new contract. Make sure line managers from the CEO down send consistent messages about the new ways of doing business and that they reinforce words with deeds. Inconsistency breeds uncertainty, and uncertainty drains energy that should go into making change work.

If you have a change to undertake, adapt and use a process like this. Then, when you go out to hire human capital investors, tell them that you have an approach that can make any changes in their psychological deal a tolerable, and perhaps even enriching, experience. Ultimately, the ease of changing the psychological contract will depend largely on the flexibility built in at the time of hire.

THE PROCESS IS THE MESSAGE

Many recent advances in the science of selection have focused on picking the right worker out of a crowd of applicants. However, the hiring challenge extends not just to the identification of strong candidates, but also to their acquisition. Organizations should view the hiring process as a search for fit, but not just between individual and organizational values, or between human capital availability and strategic requirements. Fit also encompasses alignment between individual ROI_w needs and investment returns that the organization can offer. Consider the challenge faced by administrators at the National Aeronautics and Space Administration (NASA). NASA evolved during the early 1970s in response to President Kennedy's goal of landing a human on the moon by the end of the decade. NASA leaders had to pull together thousands of talented and dedicated people. The director of flight operations, Chris Kraft, needed to find people fanatical enough about space flight to put in sixty-hour workweeks at government salaries. NASA needed a heavy investment of technical talent, scientific knowledge, unwavering goal orientation, and boundless effort. In return, it offered enormous intrinsic satisfaction, high but indirect public recognition (the astronauts got most of the glory), and modest compensation.[8] The achievements of the U.S. space program over the past several decades stands as a tribute to NASA's success at establishing and maintaining this deal.

How must companies manage the selection process so that it marks the beginning of a beautiful relationship? Here are some tactics that might make the difference between getting and not getting workers with the right stuff. These ideas support a key theme—treat potential candidates as investors who deserve as much information out of the recruiting and selection process as they put in.

Make Sure the Selection Process Is Doubly Valid

In the words of one scholar, "Selection is not the gate through which applicants must pass before they can relate to the organization; it is itself part of that relationship."[9] The array of recruitment events that a candidate experiences represents more than just a rite of passage. The recruiting process is a message. It tells a prospective worker, "This is how we treat people who have human capital that is valuable to us." Recruiting experiences help applicants infer how potential employers deal with people once hired, how they view their social responsibilities, and even how worthy their products are.[10] The hiring process affords both parties their first opportunity to craft a deal between them.

When HR managers talk about validity, they usually refer to the legally defensible power of a selection process to identify candidates who can do the job. Individuals have their own implicit standards of validity, however, which they apply to the hiring procedure. An individual's attitude toward the hiring protocol depends on his perception of *social validity*. Social validity includes ideas like openness, fairness, respect, and rationality.[11] Social validity goes beyond face validity (the extent to which applicants believe a selection procedure reflects job content) and predictive validity (how well a procedure predicts future job performance).[12] Scholars have pondered the criteria that give some selection techniques an aura of validity and make others as appealing as an interview with Torquemada. Psychologist Heinz Schuler has suggested that four components make selection situations socially valid from the candidate's perspective:

1. Participation in, and control over, the selection process. The candidate's feeling of control over the selection process heightens the perception of validity. Several research studies support the same conclusion—interviews make people feel more a part of the process, and more in control of their own destinies, than any

other selection approach.[13] Prospective human capital investors, it appears, want their information in oral form.

2. Relevance of the selection techniques used. The perceived relevance of selection approaches depends on the candidate's ability to see how companies measure job-related traits, interpret results, and use the results to make hiring decisions. Among selection methods, work samples and focused achievement tests get the highest relevance scores.[14]

3. Provision of useful feedback to the candidate. Applicants want to know how they did in the assessment process. They don't want their results treated like the D-day invasion plans. Particularly astute organizations can gather useful information about candidates from how they react to feedback from companies. In one case described in *Forbes*, a candidate learned she had done badly on a consulting case analysis. She went out of her way to seek advice to improve her performance in other interviews. No doubt she realized that in pursuing a consulting job, she would have many more case analysis interviews. A few days after asking for the ex post evaluation, she got a job offer from the firm. The head of recruiting explained the firm's choice: "Openness to learning is very important to us."[15]

4. Information about task requirements and organizational characteristics. Selection procedures that give applicants information about the job and the organization have added validity in the minds of candidates. In particular, people want to know what tasks and demands face them, what will define success and failure, how they can take advantage of development and career opportunities, and how they can expect their earning power to grow.[16]

In human capital investment terms, they are asking about the kind of investment the organization expects and about the job-related, developmental, and financial consideration they might earn.

Forge a Full-Disclosure Deal

Following the recommendation in component 4 will ensure that individual and organization share a realistic notion of the job's basic building blocks. That is a good foundation, but it is not enough. The organization needs to go further, to pull back the seventh veil and reveal what is underneath.

Cypress Semiconductor has done just that. Cypress is the paradigm of a disciplined company. Its CEO, T. J. Rodgers, is one of the Silicon Valley's toughest-minded, most articulate leaders. His opinions on the management of human and other capital have appeared in such places as the *Harvard Business Review (HBR)* and the *Wall Street Journal*. In a 1990 *HBR* article entitled "No Excuses Management," Rodgers gave some strong clues about the culture at Cypress. This is a no-nonsense place where people make their numbers, stay within their budgets, and (as the article's title implies) make no excuses. The organization is fact driven; soft analysis carries no weight when it comes time for management decisions. Some think that the Cypress approach to management is too rigid and too data driven. Rodgers responds: "Our management systems are not designed to punish or pressure; people put enough pressure on themselves without any help from me. The systems are designed to encourage collective thinking and to force each of us to face reality every day."[17]

It takes a special sort of person to thrive in this kind of environment. However, as challenging as its culture may be, Cypress is not a place that devalues human capital. In his musings for *HBR*, Rodgers said that to succeed over the long term, his organization must do at least four things better than the competition. One is to hire outstanding people and hold on to them.[18] In 1997, the sales and marketing unit at Cypress decided that it could improve its performance at hiring and holding on to outstanding performers. HR estimated that sales and marketing experienced a 13 percent turnover in 1997—not bad in Silicon Valley terms, especially in a tight labor market, but not good enough for Cypress to remain the high-performance organization it wants to be.[19]

Teams of sales and marketing people looked at their unit from several angles, searching out performance improvement opportunities. One group analyzed the deal—the psychological contract—in place between the organization and the people in the sales and marketing unit. Naturally, they found some ways to improve the deal; many of these focused on better learning and development opportunities, improvements in manager autonomy, and more effective nurturing of high performers. The Deal Team (as it came to be called) also decided that the deal itself needed to be more formally defined and better communicated, especially during the hiring process. There is precedent at Cypress for what the Deal Team wanted to do; wide sharing of information is another tenet of the Cypress culture. This is the deal statement the team developed:

THE DEAL BETWEEN CYPRESS AND YOU

Who We Are

Cypress strives to invent, make, and sell the world's best semiconductor products.

What the Company Expects from You

Cypress hires only the best in sales and marketing: professionals who have the mental toughness, knowledge, skills, attributes, and energy to win. To be a successful Cypress sales and marketing professional, you must have a number of important abilities:

- Cypress sales and marketing professionals are smart. You possess the highest level of technical knowledge in our industry, along with a thorough understanding of Cypress products and their position in the market.

- You couple that knowledge with an understanding of our customers and their system architectural requirements to provide competitive advantage to both Cypress and the customer.

- Cypress sales and marketing professionals are customer-oriented. You empathize with our customers. You aggressively work toward customer solutions, adding value to our customers' business. You keep all commitments made to our customers and strive to exceed their expectations.

- Cypress sales and marketing professionals are goal-driven. You use analytical skills and information-driven processes to reach specific measurable objectives.

- Cypress sales and marketing professionals are solid business people. Your insight and intelligence allow you to understand the business principles that make Cypress successful. You understand your role in the company's success and maximize your value to Cypress in the ultra-competitive semiconductor market.

- Cypress sales and marketing professionals take initiative and act independently. You don't make excuses. You are used to beating the competition. You have a strong natural inclination to work hard, seize opportunity, solve problems, and *win*.

- Cypress sales and marketing professionals operate in an environment of coaching and developing. You want to grow and to help others grow as well. Cypress managers and mentors assess the development needs of others and take action to support personal and professional improvement.

- Cypress sales and marketing professionals are flexible and adapt rapidly to a dynamic environment. As marketing conditions or organizational structure shift, you are ready to modify the way you apply your knowledge, skill, and attributes to serve our customers better.

- Cypress sales and marketing professionals work in teams. Team success supersedes individual success, and team goals take precedence over individual agendas. We expect individuals to make sacrifices for the benefit of the team.

- Cypress expects its sales and marketing professionals to invest these abilities fully on behalf of the company, and to work (with help) to develop them further.

What You Can Expect from the Company

When you come to work for Cypress sales and marketing, you are a company owner. As an owner, you enter into a reciprocal arrangement with the company. Just as you have a responsibility to invest your effort and abilities with us, so we have a responsibility to recognize and reward the results you achieve through your contribution. The return on your investment in Cypress will include:

Your Job

- Challenge, with responsibility and latitude to act in ways you believe will help the company win
- Opportunity for authority and self-direction
- Opportunity to make an impact on the company's success
- Access to senior management

Development Opportunities

- Formal training programs to help develop your knowledge and skills, to help you grow and respond to our dynamic marketplace

- Rich environment for informal learning, to help you adapt to the company's changing needs
- Clear advancement path and rapid advancement for high performers
- A philosophy of mentoring and coaching for continuous learning and individual development planning

Financial Rewards

- Competitive cash compensation (base salary targeted at the 75th percentile for the industry)
- Aggressive stock option and stock purchase plans
- Special financial incentives (bonus and stock) for high performers
- Competitive, flexible health benefits
- Profit sharing
- PC purchase plan

Much about this statement of the deal is noteworthy. To begin with, it contains all the key components; it tells what human capital the company expects from its employee-investors and why. It also lets a prospective hiree know what the return on that investment will include. Indeed, it refers specifically to investment and return-on-investment ideas. And the ideas are expressed in unequivocally competitive terms. Yet it does not answer every possible question in detail. Instead, the deal statement lays out points for discussion between candidate and interviewer.

The statement gives the potential job candidate a window into the culture of the organization. Competition and winning in the market both receive three mentions. Phrases like "mental toughness," "energy to win," "goal-driven," "specific measurable objectives," and "don't make excuses" convey a sense of what it is like to work there. It is also evident from the statement that Cypress competes in a dynamic environment. In other words, "Don't come to work here unless you are prepared to adapt. Everything, including this deal statement, may change, so be prepared."

An organization can begin to bring its full-disclosure deal to life by the way it provides information in interviews. It is popular these days to ask applicants to give examples of the behaviors and abilities the organization looks for. If the company wants someone who is good at conceptual thinking, for example, an interviewer might ask, "Tell me about a time when you pulled together seemingly unrelated pieces of information to understand a problem." Suppose a company held itself to the same rigorous interviewing standard by providing specific behavioral examples of the organization's fundamental traits. Interviewees would come away a lot better informed about the organizational union they contemplate. Exhibit 4.5 contains some examples, arrayed along ROI_w lines. If the interviewee does not take the initiative and probe into the organizational psyche, provide the information anyway. Make the

Exhibit 4.5.   Examples of Company Behaviors.

If this is what you say . . .	Be prepared to back it up
Intrinsic job traits	
"This job is at the peak of the selling profession—it will really put your sales skills to work."	Give an example of the most interesting selling situation faced by someone in this position. What does the most successful seller do in that situation?
"In this company, we believe in empowering people."	Tell about the time when someone took a risk on behalf of the company to serve a customer. What did the person do, and how did the company react?
Growth opportunities	
"This is a fast-track job. You can move up quickly from here."	Describe the traits of someone the company considers "fast track." What did he do to prove his worth, and how fast did he move?
"We'll make you an expert in the latest software."	Describe how someone in the organization became an expert in this area. What did the company do to help him achieve that status: training, experience, or both?
Recognition	
"People in this position are the heart of our organization, and we recognize that."	Give an example of how an excellent performer in this position received recognition beyond his own unit.
"Everyone in the industry knows that our engineers are the best."	Describe a recent departure from the company. Why did he leave, where did he go, and what kind of job did he get?
Financial rewards	
"You have the chance to earn an annual bonus of up to 50% of your base salary."	Tell what the average percentage bonus has been over the past several years, as well as the high and the low. What exactly did the highest performer accomplish to earn the reward?

selection process as information rich for the candidate as it is for the organization. A prospective human capital investor deserves no less.

SERIOUS FUN AT SOUTHWEST

Some organizations are adept at conveying their deal not only in interviews and written statements but also in their job ads. Southwest Airlines, which shows up on everyone's list of admired companies, runs ads that reflect the company's dedication to fun. One shows a child's drawing of a dinosaur, with plenty of crayon marks outside the lines. The teacher's comment: "Bryan shows an early aptitude for working at Southwest."[21]

Working at Southwest may be an exercise in merriment, but the organization's approach to hiring produces serious benefits. Southwest gets about 150,000 job applications per year for 4,000 to 5,000 positions.[22] Most applicants are referred by friends who work at Southwest and understand the deal in place there. Word of mouth has become the chief vehicle for letting potential employees know about the Southwest culture. The organization has made itself the beneficiary of a virtuous circle:

- Under the leadership of CEO Herb Kelleher, the airline has created an attractive culture that values hard work but makes work entertaining.

- Employees who love their jobs talk about the Southwest deal with others who would fit into the culture and succeed.

- The pipeline of potentially compatible employees grows, so Southwest can choose candidates who have the human capital the company needs for competitive success (including behaviors that reinforce the lighthearted work environment).

- Well endowed with human capital, the organization beats its competition, prospers, continues to be a fun place to work, and the cycle goes on.

Southwest does not use the term *human resources* for the department that focuses on human capital issues. Libby Sartain, vice president—people, says this about her title: "It evolved out of the idea of 'human resources,' which implies that people are resources that can be used up and discarded."[22] Besides knowing how to attract the people it needs,

Southwest's human capital strategy makes a clear delineation between the elements for which they hire and those they develop through training. Says Sartain, "We hire for attitude and train for skill."

It takes courage to provide this kind of information to people who may or may not end up working for you. Your honesty will give some of them cold feet, and they will self-select out of the process. Others may take jobs with your competitors and pass what they have learned on to them. As to the first group, you probably didn't really want them anyway. As to the second, your competitors already know all of this. The veterans who quit your company and went to work for the competition told them long ago. Instead of hiding your weaknesses, tell candidates what you are doing about them and how they can contribute (and increase their return on investment in the process).

SUMMARY: CAPITAL ACQUISITION

The investment relationship between worker and organization begins to take shape not on the first day of work but at the first moment of contact. The hiring process is not a prelude to the dance, but instead the first steps in the workplace waltz.

BEWARE THE INTERVIEWER'S POWER

From the perspectives of both candidate and organization, interviewers play a central role in the hiring drama. "Interviewer" means anyone (from human resource representative to line manager) who spends time in person with candidates. Job applicants routinely give higher credibility scores to these company representatives than to written information sources.[23]

Interviewers enter the selection process with a deceptively simple goal—to find out whether the applicant can make a contribution to the organization. One study showed that recruiters come into interviews with three separate work-value definitions: the values they believe are emphasized in their organizations, their own values, and a universal set of values they view as appropriate.[24] Work values were defined as the relative importance accorded to achievement, honesty, fairness, and concern for others. In the worker-as-investor framework, these factors are salient intrinsic and recognition-oriented aspects of the job. Separate from these values constructs, recruiters also carry with them criteria by which they decide a candidate's "employability." Employability means the attractiveness of the applicant's human capital to the company and within the job market broadly.

With this programming in their mental operating systems, recruiters assess each candidate's employability and fit with organizational values. You might think that recruiters would draw their conclusions about applicant-organization fit by referring to the weight the organization places on achievement, honesty, fairness, and concern for others. Not so. Recruiters' assessments of value-based fit between candidate and organization depend mainly on congruence between the candidate and the recruiter. Surprisingly, for both value fit and employability, the perceived congruence between candidate and organization takes a back seat.[25] Recruiters personalize things, it seems. Their unique perception of the fit between the candidate's values and their own values informs their conclusions about a candidate's appeal. Yet it is candidate-organization fit, not candidate-recruiter fit, that defines actual workplace compatibility.

On top of all the other roles an interviewer plays—fact finder, interpreter, conveyer of information—there is one other worth noting. An interviewer also acts as contract maker, representing the organization in the sensitive first negotiations with the candidate. Here, too, interviewers have substantial freedom in how they express the psychological contract to the prospective employee: "Research on the unstructured interview, probably the most common selection technique, suggests that two interviewers will frequently ask very different questions and will offer distinct kinds of information to applicants. To the extent that these people convey different information, they could provide a picture of future employment that not only is not congruent, but also does not agree with any 'official' organizational position on the terms of employment."[26]

What should an organization do to channel all this interviewer power? Here are three recommendations:

- Make sure interviewers share the organization's values.
- Make sure they understand and can convey at least the broad-brush outlines of the company's psychological contract
- Supplement interviews with simulations of the jobs candidates seek. Have them analyze a customer problem, make a realistic sales pitch,

sit in with a team to brainstorm about a marketing challenge. I once had to prove I could analyze the cost structure of a vacuum cleaner manufacturer. I also had to prove my mettle as an English major by doing an impromptu recitation of Lewis Carroll's *Jabberwocky*. I landed the job.

In Chapter Four, we began by reviewing the process by which organizations translate strategic requirements into human capital needs. This is the first link in a chain of human capital management activities. I suggested that feasibility of development, urgency, and need to retain would influence an organization's choice of a strategy for getting human capital. Once the strategy takes shape, the acquisition process (the second link in the human capital management chain) begins with formulation of a psychological contract. This contract (the deal, if you will) binds workers who have the requisite human capital with the organization that needs it. This deal comprises three elements: duration, consideration, and flexibility. Each element is tricky to define and challenging to pin down. Still, the organization owes it to itself and to the individual to address the embedded issues head-on. Simply acknowledging that a psychological contract must exist and struggling with its creation are big steps in establishing a mutually beneficial worker-company relationship.

Essentially, the recruiting and selection process is the search for matches between strategy needs and human capital elements, between ROI_w needs and inducements offered, between organizational and individual values. To create the right matches, the selection process must bring about a balanced exchange of information. The process itself carries messages to the job candidate about the organization. The organization must treat candidates as human capital owners who need two kinds of information: a full disclosure of the organization's expectations for human capital investment and a comprehensive description of the return on investment it proposes to provide. For most organizations, investment and ROI_w information come chiefly through interviewing. The interview process can yield credible insights and give candidates a heightened sense of their control over the selection procedure. Courageous companies confident of their values and optimistic about their success can go as far as to present a written statement of the deal to job candidates. This step alone will set a company apart from its less perceptive, less confident competitors.

Some thirty years ago, Lyman Porter and Edward Lawler speculated that companies would eventually need to consider hiring people who valued what the organization has to offer. Although they spoke chiefly about compensation practices, their comments have relevance to recruiting and selection:

> The first step in building effective reward practices is for the company to make sure that the rewards it is providing are ones which are widely desired. This is a seemingly simple point that is often neglected. In day-to-day operations we frequently forget that, regardless of the value the giver or observer places on a reward, its motivational influence comes about only as a result of the value the *receiver* places on it. In effect, rewards that the company considers highly positive inducements may not be so regarded by many of the persons receiving them. Yet how many times do companies check this out? . . . Eventually, a company may want to consider systematically selecting the kinds of employees who will value the particular rewards that it can give most readily and feasibly.[27]

I have emphasized that hiring well is critical to acquiring strategically important human capital. But acquiring human capital is simply one link in the chain. The next link is making the most of it. What can a company do to create a high-investment environment? We will address that question in Chapters Five and Six.

Setting the Stage Through Workplace Environment

F or all his preaching on the moral primacy of individual principle and self-reliance, Ralph Waldo Emerson had an acute sense of the earthly laws of exchange. The world, he believed, enforces a constant give and take. For Emerson, this law applies as well to work as to any other enterprise:

> Human labor, through all its forms, from the sharpening of a stake to the construction of a city or an epic, is one immense illustration of the perfect compensation of the universe. Everywhere and always this law is sublime. The absolute balance of Give and Take, the doctrine that every thing has its price, and if that price is not paid, not that thing but something else is obtained, and that it is impossible to get anything without its price, is not less sublime in the columns of a ledger than in the budgets of states, in the laws of light and darkness, in all the action and reaction of nature.[1]

To Emerson, the ultimate virtue is an enlightened exchange. Our challenge in Chapters Five and Six is to define the conditions under which such an exchange can occur. We divide these conditions into two categories: elements that set the stage for investment and elements that influence investment directly. This chapter addresses the first group.

We have established that companies should define strategy in human capital terms and hire intelligently so that they can build a storehouse of human capital with which to conquer competitors. But human capital, like any other asset, lies idle if not applied. In Chapter Two we introduced the idea that effort operates as a catalyzing element to activate human capital. Yankelovich and Immerwahr, in their treatise from the early 1980s on the state of America's work ethic, quoted a trio of Marxist economists concerning effort at work: "Mainstream economists recognize that an hour of work performed by a more skilled or experienced worker is likely to be more productive than an hour of work performed by someone less skilled or experienced. But they almost always ignore something which is transparent to workers and corporations: an hour of work can be performed with widely varying degrees of intensity as well as skill."[2] A competitive advantage awaits the taking. A study by Kepner-Tregoe® showed that about two-thirds of both workers and managers said that organizations use 50 percent or less of their collective brainpower.[3] Move that number to 75 percent and you leave your competition in the dust; take it to 100 percent and you create miracles.

Here is another way to look at it—whereas forging an ROI_w-rich deal is one thing, executing it to the greatest mutual effect is another. What are the criteria for creating an environment in which the contract can come alive, for enriching the soil in which the seeds of human capital investment can grow? Research by Towers Perrin can help answer that question.[4] In 1995 and 1996, the firm conducted surveys that culminated in *The 1997 Towers Perrin Workplace Index*. Some twenty-five hundred workers at all organizational levels, from shop floor and teller line to executive suite, responded to the 1996 *Workplace Index* survey. They all came from organizations with five hundred workers or more, excluding government agencies, and represented a variety of industries. Our analysis of the data suggests that the context for maximum human capital investment consists of three principal elements:

1. Alignment with business strategy. Individual investment must be directed toward the accomplishment of business strategy. Psychological contracts that reinforce alignment with business

requirements have the best chance of producing benefits for both worker and organization.

2. Understanding. A clear understanding of job requirements and contract expectations is a prerequisite for worker willingness to invest. The contract and the job it addresses must be articulated to the degree necessary for everyone's comfort, with emphasis on the key points that anchor predictability.

3. Mutual acceptance. Both parties must trust that they will get a fair deal and that each will willingly live up to the stated and implied tenets of the deal. Enthusiastic embracing of a contract by workers will produce more investor-like behavior than grudging acceptance of the same contract terms.

Figure 5.1 shows these three criteria. They appeared as "Workplace Environment" in Figure 2.5. Figure 5.1 shows them as a frame—a visual metaphor for their contextual significance. They seem straightforward enough; as we will see, however, each has a powerful connection with individual motivation to invest human capital assets for organizational success.

ALIGNMENT WITH STRATEGY: THE POWER OF COMMON INTEREST

Workers are not stupid. They realize that unless their human capital investments align with business strategy, neither organization nor

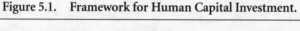

Figure 5.1.   Framework for Human Capital Investment.

individual will come out ahead. Aligning worker investment with business strategy increases the probability that the organization will succeed in the marketplace. In turn, marketplace success creates the means (financial and other) to produce the return on investment workers require. In Chapter Three, we established the high-level links between business strategy and human capital. Now we explore ways to make those links more apparent to individual human capital investors.

Let People Forge the Link

Companies that successfully hook individual investment into strategic imperatives use different means to make the link. Nevertheless, there is a critical similarity that characterizes the most effective approaches. In various ways, prosperous companies like Visa International, R. R. Donnelley & Sons (the nation's largest commercial printer), and Gateway 2000 (the South Dakota computer maker) set out to accomplish one thing—to involve individuals in defining the connection between their human capital investment and the success of the organization. Let them discover the links between customer satisfaction and organizational success. Help them define, in their own terms, what it will take for the organization to become (or remain) an industry leader. Generalizing somewhat, the approach we have found most successful is a vertical top-down/bottom-up process, shown in Figure 5.2.

Let us return to our friends at Perpetual Petals to see how they might track through their requirements for strategic success. Suppose that the chief goal of the artificial flower business unit is to generate earnings for the parent corporation, International Interior Novelties. The Perpetual Petals earnings strategy calls for it to dominate its narrowly defined market. It plans to do so by staying ahead of the competition in introducing innovative new products. In the second step of the top-down/bottom-up process, the business unit manager and his direct reports together define how creating and introducing new products help achieve the unit's earnings-contribution goal. Figure 5.3 shows the kind of contribution map they would create.

With this picture in hand, the product development department can take the analysis down a level and develop its own contribution map, as can all other Perpetual Petals departments. There is nothing magical there; translating and refining goals is a conventional man-

Figure 5.2. Connecting People with Strategy—Top Down and Bottom Up.

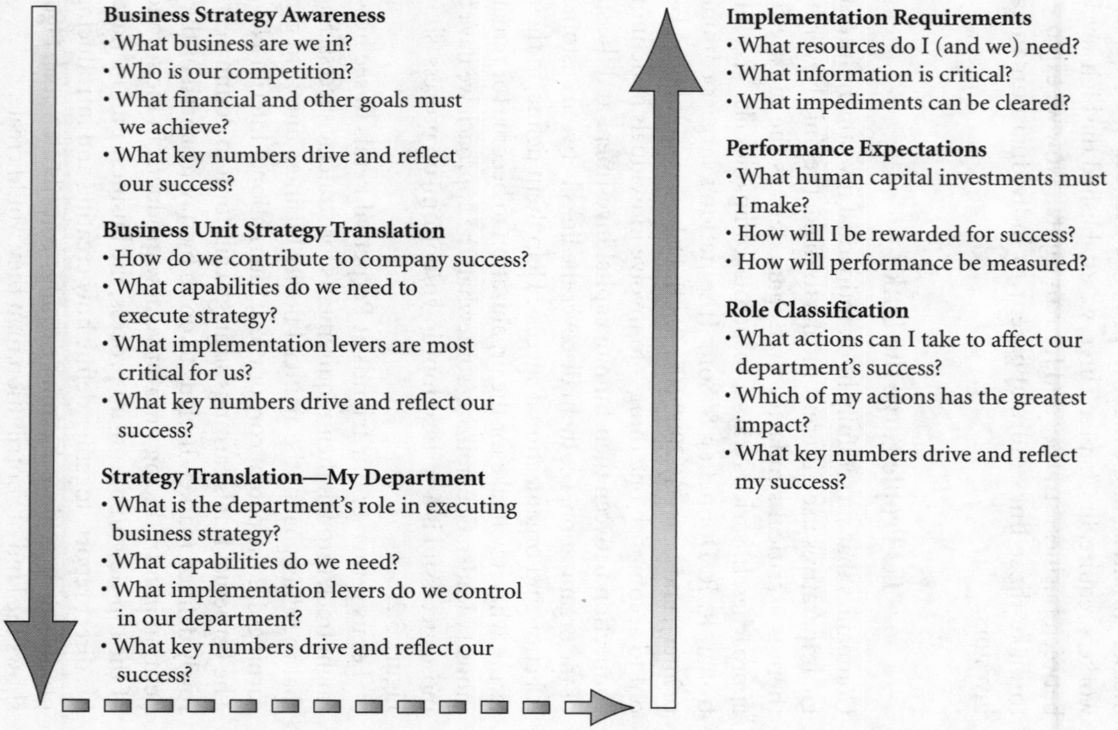

Business Strategy Awareness
• What business are we in?
• Who is our competition?
• What financial and other goals must we achieve?
• What key numbers drive and reflect our success?

Business Unit Strategy Translation
• How do we contribute to company success?
• What capabilities do we need to execute strategy?
• What implementation levers are most critical for us?
• What key numbers drive and reflect our success?

Strategy Translation—My Department
• What is the department's role in executing business strategy?
• What capabilities do we need?
• What implementation levers do we control in our department?
• What key numbers drive and reflect our success?

Implementation Requirements
• What resources do I (and we) need?
• What information is critical?
• What impediments can be cleared?

Performance Expectations
• What human capital investments must I make?
• How will I be rewarded for success?
• How will performance be measured?

Role Classification
• What actions can I take to affect our department's success?
• Which of my actions has the greatest impact?
• What key numbers drive and reflect my success?

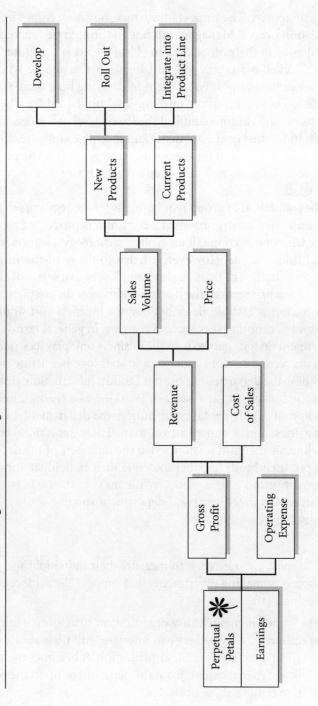

Figure 5.3. Tracing the Sources of Business Unit Contribution.

agement activity. The important nuance, however, comes in how the translation occurs. Managers will not go through this exercise alone, locked away in their offices, staring bleary-eyed at computer screens. At each level, managers will call together the people who report directly to them and involve them in defining how their areas contribute to the success of the unit one level up the ladder. The cascading process will continue until, at the lowest level of the organizational ladder, individual goal statements and incentive compensation plans tie to department and business unit strategy. This is the bottom-up part; personal goals roll up to department, business unit, and company goals.

The translation of group requirements for strategy implementation into individual contributions is a continuous process of refinement and redefinition as competition evolves, technology advances, and individual roles change. However, it helps to think of the interaction between department manager and employees as a series of three sessions. In the first session, the manager reinforces the big picture for the organization as a whole, describes how the business unit strategy contributes to corporate success, and conveys, in general terms, how the department does its part to help the business unit play its strategic role.

In the second session, manager and staff together define more precisely how the department's output (goods, information, or services) feeds the business unit's success. Working as a team, they create a depiction of departmental contribution, the departmental version of the business unit's contribution map. Their depiction serves as a guideline for the third session, when the members of the department team put their heads together to define their individual human capital contributions to the group. While making the tie between their human capital investment and department success, workers can also identify the following:

- The most accurate ways to measure their individual and group success at making investments that support the achievement of business strategy.

- The impediments (clumsy organization structure, politics, lack of resources) they believe will interfere with their ability to make the most effective possible contribution. It becomes the responsibility of management, from the department up to the business unit, to remove these obstacles.

- The low-value activities that, however deeply embedded in work processes, can be eliminated to improve the efficacy of human capital investment.
- The information they need to make intelligent decisions about how to do their jobs.

Through linking investment with strategy, people not only see their local connections better but also gain a clearer understanding of the big picture. Information is the key to reinforcing that connection and giving meaning to that picture.

Provide Information Early and Often

Making the connection between human capital investment and strategy requires that people understand just how the organization becomes successful. What does it cost to serve customers, and what factors might cause those costs to change? What goes into the making of our products and services, and how can we use those resources more efficiently? To enable people to answer those questions—not to give them the answers, but to allow them to find the answers—requires an organization to open its books. In other words, the organization would broadly release financial, operating, and strategic information. Open-book management is not a new idea. Consultants, scholars, and enlightened executives have long urged managers to teach workers how the business really functions and give them information so they can make things work better. As John Case, a well-known open-book expert, puts it, "Open-book management is a way of running a company that gets everyone to focus on helping the business make money. Nothing more, nothing less."[5]

There are enough success stories to persuade most managers to try open-book approaches. Clever companies have found imaginative ways of helping people understand how the business works and how they can control the financial and other variables that determine success. Donnelley, for example, has created a business simulation game called Celestial Cheese. Users of the simulation run a fictional company that produces different kinds of cheese on the moon. If you look below the whimsical surface, however, you find that the simulation mimics the operations of a high-volume printing enterprise. Besides having fun, users learn the nuts and bolts (or the curds and whey) of company success.[6]

With plenty of literature on open-book management available, and more than a few success stories to back it up, why haven't more organizations jumped on the bandwagon? Chalk it up to primal fear, which can take several forms.[7]

• *People will not understand how to use the information.* Good point; at first, they won't. Teaching people the basics of return on investment, gross margin, market share, or whatever else makes your business tick may be one of your best training investments. Then, too, some of your most important performance indicators do not take an M.B.A. degree to interpret. Cost overages, revenue per employee, cash in the bank—all are fairly intuitive. People can readily figure out how these numbers indicate prosperity. In fact, the contribution map they created can help workers identify and understand the critical data. For example, it would not be hard for a product developer at Perpetual Petals to zero in on a few key performance measures. Speed to market for new offerings, number of products introduced in the past year, and product profitability would all speak volumes about the department's performance.

• *People may be spooked by bad news.* People know when things are not going well. If they lack access to information, they will discount good news and exaggerate bad. Sharing information helps create an environment in which fewer bad things happen in the first place and in which people can respond effectively when they do.

• *Our competitors will get information they can use against us.* On this score, it makes sense to have some concern. You are bound to have some deep numerical secrets you don't want the competition to know. But bear in mind that employees who have left your company have already revealed some of your secrets to the competition. This information, supplemented by your financial statements, your industry press, and data your customers have shared, probably means that much of your inside information is already outside. So explain to your employees what information requires discreet handling, and then perform so well that your numbers depress your competitors because they cannot achieve your performance levels. And keep in mind that employees who benefit from business success will be loath to give away information that could be used against them.

• *Our customers could use the information to force our prices down.* Like your competitors, your customers already have access to plenty of information about your company. Besides, if you are delivering high value at a competitive price, customers presumably will want to keep being customers at that price. After all, they have a stake in keeping their vendors healthy. In the spirit of partnership, ask them to treat your performance data confidentially, and then show them how your efficiency creates value for them and life-sustaining profits for you.

• *People may figure out how much money top management makes.* If you perform well enough to earn your money, you have nothing to worry about. If you do not, the problem will not be solved by hiding the data.

At Bonded Motors, an engine remanufacturer with an improbable location in South-Central Los Angeles, management uses a daily financial report to reinforce the link between people and strategy. The reporting process carries this message—each employee has responsibility for making the company successful and needs information to do so. Says the company's founder and chief executive, "Everyone is involved in the finances of this company—the truck drivers, janitors, secretaries, everyone. If there's a problem somewhere, we've got 200 people trying to fix it." Their psychological contract says the company expects workers to care. Returns on their investment of human capital include a quarterly bonus that can equal 12 percent of base pay. Company executives say that information sharing, combined with the bonus plan, has increased company net income by 5 percent.[8]

As with any other critical initiative, sound execution of open-book management is the secret to success. Teaching people about their business can start with classroom training. You can also use simulations and games, like Donnelley's Celestial Cheese. The most powerful learning, however, comes from real-life application. Ask a unit to calculate how a change in the way they work will affect the profit line. Have a line employee explain the financials at a monthly plant meeting. Make knowledge of production costing a prerequisite for advancement. Most important of all, give people the autonomy to use information to improve the business. We will consider the importance of autonomy further in Chapter Six.

The Index of Strategy Alignment

We can use data from the *Workplace Index* to show how alignment with strategy influences investorship behavior. To achieve alignment, organizations must give individuals and work groups the means (resources, information, direction) to deliver high-quality products and services. These, in turn, allow people to meet customer needs and help push the organization to the leadership position that its strategy envisions. Six items from the *Workplace Index* reflect these requirements. These six appear in Table 5.1, along with the percentage of survey respondents agreeing with each statement. For all items except the last (linking company and customer interests), respondents gave their organizations high marks.

Now we will take these six factors and compile them into a single index, then plot the index against a survey item indicating individual willingness to invest human capital and thereby help the company succeed. In Chapter Two, we defined this kind of willingness as commitment to the organization. The results, displayed in Figure 5.4, show a clear positive relationship between strategy alignment and commitment to working on the company's behalf. In fact, the steepness of the line in Figure 5.4 suggests that a little alignment goes a long way.

UNDERSTANDING: COMMUNICATING AT TWO LEVELS

Proverbs 4:7 exhorts us: "With all thy getting, get understanding." As CEO of Apple, John Sculley promoted understanding by articulating his firm's contract in these terms: "The new corporate contract is that we'll offer you an opportunity to express yourself and grow, if you promise to leash yourself to our dream, at least for a while."[9] Sculley

Table 5.1. Index of Strategy Alignment.

Index Item	Percentage Agreeing
• My work group has clear goals for providing high-quality service.	76%
• My work group has the resources to meet customer expectations in a competent and timely manner.	69%
• My company is able to respond quickly to changing customer and market situations.	63%
• I have the resources I need to perform my job in a high-quality way.	71%
• I think my company is doing what it takes to become a leader in its industry.	74%
• What management wants me to do and what customers want me to do are usually the same.	56%

Source: © Towers Perrin, *The 1997 Towers Perrin Workplace Index* (New York: Towers Perrin, 1997).

Figure 5.4. Strategy Alignment Correlates with Motivation to
Help the Company Succeed.

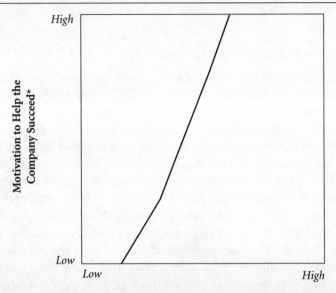

Index of Strategy Alignment

*Reflects organizational commitment, as defined in Chapter Two.

Source: © Towers Perrin, *The 1997 Towers Perrin Workplace Index*
(New York: Towers Perrin, 1997).

expressed a rough approximation of investment ("leash yourself to
our dream") and consideration ("opportunity to express yourself and
grow"). With the single phrase "for a while," he suggested a duration
but also implied open-ended flexibility. For a lean company recruiting talented, innovative, highly marketable people, he was as explicit
as he needed to be. If you talk to people who worked at Apple during
the Sculley years, you will hear that they understood and accepted this
simple compact.

In making and interpreting her psychological contract, a worker
will deal with many different organizational representatives. Corporate contract makers include recruiters, supervisors and first-line managers, senior executives, and designated representatives of the
organization (headhunters, for example). Each has the opportunity to
express an interpretation of the contract from the organization's point
of view.[10] Less formally, contract expectations may pass among
coworkers as they form teams, work on projects, or simply engage in

the conversations that take place naturally at work. For workers, cutting through the noise of multiple contract makers is critical to understanding what is expected of them.

Start with the General . . .

Companies that want to make sure people understand how they fit into the strategy for success should start by crafting a high-level statement laying out a philosophy of human capital investment and the psychological deal. At Eastman Chemical Co., for example, the chief executive laid down a formal set of guidelines called "The Eastman Way." Historically paternalistic, the company's deal called for avoiding layoffs, retraining workers to take available jobs, and providing recreation through some nineteen company-sponsored clubs. By adhering to the deal stated in its guidelines, the company eliminated time clocks and increased employee control over career management. As of 1996, the average employee had stayed with the company for 18.3 years, an impressive continuum of investment. In a chemical industry survey, employees gave Eastman an 85 percent favorable rating on providing job security; the average rating for fifteen other chemical companies was 45 percent.[11]

Fireman's Fund Insurance Company has taken a bold step in crafting a clear top-level statement of the psychological contract between individual and organization. Each employee gets what Fireman's Fund calls a *Partnership Portfolio.* The portfolio, done up to look like an investment file, starts with a letter from Fireman's Fund president and CEO, Joe Stinnette. In the first paragraph, he lays out the purpose of the portfolio: "The company has high expectations for growth as we move toward our goals for the year 2000. Meeting these goals requires a commitment from you to share your skills, your talent, and your hard work. And in return, you have a right to expect a commitment from the company. This *Partnership Portfolio* expresses our commitment to you, personally and in detail."[12]

A worker reading through the portfolio then comes to a section on work environment. These pages describe work-life balancing options like job sharing and compressed workweeks. The portfolio goes on to discuss learning opportunities, leadership development options, and community investment programs. The discussion of financial rewards comes, finally, at page 9. This part of the document contains salary and bonus information specific to the individual. The *Partnership*

Portfolio does not answer every question; still, it is one of the best efforts I have seen at giving people a philosophical framework for their psychological contracts with an organization.

. . . And Go to the Specific

As useful as high-level documents can be in stating a philosophy, the real significance for the worker comes in the way individual goals are expressed. Properly constructed, goal statements have a specific purpose—to let people know what they are expected to accomplish. Moreover, goal statements convey (sometimes subtly, sometimes straightforwardly) the kind of effort (human capital investment) required for success. They also suggest (sometimes in the same place, sometimes in another document) what the fruits of success will be (consideration). Goal statements can even give information about flexibility, to the extent that they imply possible changes in future strategic direction. When you get right down to it, statements of individual goals, when tied to the success of departments, divisions, and ultimately to business units, serve as powerful contractual documents.

Individual goal statements take various shapes, from paper forms and electronic spreadsheets to notes stuck on the edge of the desk. In our firm's San Francisco office, we are adding a new approach, one that expresses an individual's annual plan in human capital investment terms. We still have the usual multipart scorecard. It requires us to specify our objectives for the year and give each a weight. The weight reflects each objective's strategic importance and its influence on our end-of-year bonus. Thanks to the initiative and ingenuity of one of our teammates, however, we also have an easy-to-fill-out form that focuses more directly on human capital. The form calls for each of us to consider the investment we intend to make during the year and the return on investment we anticipate. My colleague named the form the IPO, short for investment plan options. Its purpose, as stated on the first page, is "maximizing your ROI_w with a personal investment plan." With some simplification, here's how the IPO works:

Section 1 of the IPO, Defining ROI_w, lays out the key concepts of human capital investment. It begins by defining ROI_w: *return* (the four elements you get out of your job), *investment* (the human capital you put in), and *work* (the role you expect to play as a member of the firm). Section 1 also explains how human capital investment helps the firm succeed so that it can pay members a return on their contribution and call forth still more success-creating investment.

Section 2, Using the Investment Plan, gives instructions for going through the IPO process:

- In January, think through and complete the document, concurrent with setting annual goals on the standard balanced scorecard.

- In March and September, review progress with mentor and manager, and make any necessary changes in the approach to investment (for example, use of time, focus of energies); also note any expected shortfalls in return on investment.

- In December, look back over the year, calculate the final return on investment (see Section 5), and review with investment adviser.

Section 3, Defining the Expected Return, takes the individual through each of the four ROI_w categories, asking him or her to specify which elements carry the greatest weight. In each category, the individual must answer such questions as:

- Intrinsic job fulfillment: What about your job do you find most exciting and challenging? What makes your job fun?

- Growth opportunities: How can the organization contribute to your competencies with skills training, education, and project opportunities?

- Recognition: When you think about the organization's awareness of your contribution, whose opinion do you most care about?

- Financial rewards: What level of base pay do you consider competitive? What kind of year-end bonus would represent a fair reward for your contribution?

That's right—the IPO asks people to state their expectations for pay. Why not? It is explicitly considered an important element of ROI_w, administered within a structure that everyone should understand. There is no reason not to put it on the table.

In a format and level of detail similar to that used for defining ROI_w, the individual specifies his or her intended investment in Section 4, Defining the Investment. This section does not call for an exhaustive inventory of a person's full human capital. Instead, the individual must consider more basic factors:

- The chief contributions he or she will make as a team member
- The major leadership contributions the team can expect
- How he or she will apply creativity and innovation to improving the firm's business
- How he or she will contribute to the development of someone else's competencies during the year

Finally, Section 5, The ROI$_w$ Calculator, asks each investor to rate on a scale from 1 (not so good) to 10 (fantastic) the quality and quantity of investment for the year. This is heavily subjective; still, most people seem able to make a clear-eyed assessment of how well they have performed as disciplined, focused human capital investors. Each also does a similar rating for the return on investment received during the year. The same rules apply; it is subjective but surprisingly legitimate. Then each person looks at the relationship between the two figures, being vigilant for obvious mismatches. Each must address any major deficits or surpluses through the next year's IPO.

Going through the IPO exercise concurrently with setting formal annual goals creates an unambiguous link between human capital investment and the business strategy that individual goals support. Review every three months ensures that investment and return never get too far out of line, consistent with the discussion of duration in Chapter Four. Perhaps most important of all, the process establishes the individual's manager or mentor as an investment adviser. In that role, the mentor-manager guides the individual in investing his or her human capital portfolio, for the maximum benefit of both the worker and the organization.

The joint challenge for manager and worker is to supplement the approaches for aligning human capital and strategy with those for understanding the psychological contract. By doing so, organization and individual can create an investment deal that:

- Reflects the terms set forth in an organization-level philosophy statement like that expressed in the Fireman's Fund *Partnership Portfolio*

• Supports strategy as articulated through a contribution map connecting business unit success with individual human capital contribution

• Specifies the individual's human capital investment and stipulates the return on investment he or she can expect

The Index of Understanding

Of the sixty items in the *Workplace Index* survey, six pertain to employee understanding of the rules of the workplace game. These six appear in Table 5.2, along with the agreement percentages for each item. Companies that follow the precepts reflected in the Index of Understanding amplify workers' insight into their connection with the company. As a result, commitment to organizational goals increases. For all but the first item on the list (understanding the reasons behind company decisions), respondents reflected high levels of agreement with the statements in this index.

Figure 5.5 shows that understanding exhibits a clear, positive relationship with commitment to help the organization succeed. As with strategy alignment, the line rises steeply, suggesting a high payoff to the company from increments of understanding.

Table 5.2.   Index of Understanding.

Index Item	Percentage Agreeing
• I understand the reasons behind company decisions that affect me.	56%
• I have a clear understanding of the overall goals, objectives, and direction of my company.	78%
• My roles and responsibilities have been clearly communicated to me.	74%
• I understand the deal I have with my company, that is, what my company expects of me and what I in return can expect of my company for my work.	75%
• I understand the factors that make my company financially successful.	81%
• I understand how I can make a difference in helping the company to achieve its business goals.	75%

Source: © Towers Perrin, *The 1997 Towers Perrin Workplace Index* (New York: Towers Perrin, 1997).

Figure 5.5.   Understanding of the Deal Also Correlates with Motivation.

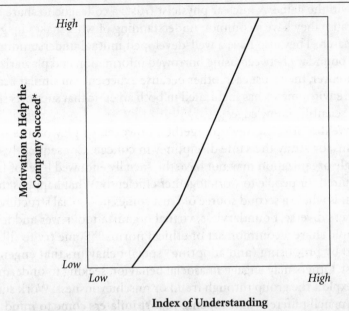

*Reflects organizational commitment, as defined in Chapter Two.

Source: © Towers Perrin, *The 1997 Towers Perrin Workplace Index*
(New York: Towers Perrin, 1997).

ACCEPTANCE: THE IMPACT OF TRUST

If each party believes a full contribution will be equitably valued, and each believes the other will live up to a desirable exchange, then each can have confidence in the predictability of the outcome. Trust is the key to confidence that the psychological contract will hold. Trust denotes the faith we have that others will treat us in ways consistent with our best interest. People who trust others are willing to make themselves vulnerable to the actions of those others, even without the ability to control (or even monitor) their actions. Like social glue, trust transforms companies, street gangs, boy scout troops, and societies from coincidental gatherings to purposeful, functioning confederations.

Trust has two sources. One source, social norms, relies on a historical base. We trust people today because we share values, beliefs, and roots embedded in prior experience. A football player trusts a teammate to throw a key block because they practiced the move a hundred times. Moreover, both understand why it is important, and both want to win the game. A nuclear physicist trusts a colleague to share data because they have a common understanding of what makes up good research. They also have a well-developed mutual understanding of the boundary between using borrowed information and plagiarizing. Moreover, they trust each other because experience in similar academic environments has inculcated in both an ethic that supports sharing scientific knowledge.

We did not all grow up together, however, or play on the same teams, or study the same disciplines in college. Consequently, any single organization may not have the socially endowed level of trust required for people to work together efficiently. What happens then? That is where a second source of trust comes in—social structure. In today's diverse, boundaryless, virtual organization, fewer and fewer people share a common set of ethical norms.[13] Some try to fill the void by proposing (and adopting) social behaviors that engender trust. Others may engage in asocial behavior, seeking to undermine or exploit the group through fraud or mischievousness. Work shirkers, pencil pilferers, and expense report inflaters come to mind. An even larger group will try to hitch a free ride, benefiting from group membership but contributing little to the common cause. Keeping the exploiters and free riders in line while furthering cooperation and sharing calls for hierarchy and rules. Francis Fukuyama, a Rand social scientist, says: "Hierarchies are necessary because all people cannot be trusted at all times to live by internalized ethical rules and do their fair share. They must ultimately be coerced by explicit rules and sanctions."[14]

Sources of trust have varying implications for the cost of transacting business. People who do not trust each other can still cooperate, but they require a heavy dose of social structure: rules, regulations, and contracts. Participants in a low-trust enterprise must negotiate, write up, enforce, and possibly litigate each agreement. This effort takes time and costs money. Widespread distrust in an organization thus imposes a kind of tax on business activity. This tax detracts from the top-line results of human capital investment.[15] Figure 5.6 illustrates the relationship between the sources of trust and the transaction costs.

When organization members follow social norms supporting trust but requiring less formal administration, cost goes down, and human capital investment produces a higher net benefit.

Figure 5.6.   Social Norms Reduce Cost.

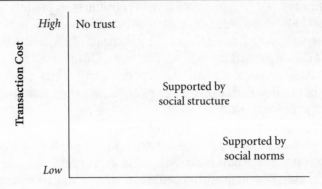

Types of Trust

Source: Adapted from F. Fukuyama, *Trust: The Social Virtues and the Creation of Prosperity* (New York: Free Press, 1995).

Build Trust Through Participation

In one study of trust, survey takers asked 103 college students to rate the impact on trust of different approaches to managing a nuclear power plant. The respondents said that only one approach produced any substantial increase in trust—establishment of a citizens advisory board with responsibility for monitoring the plant and with authority to shut it down if they believed it to be unsafe. In other words, only direct participation in, and control over, the issues that affected them increased their trust in management systems.[16] Participation accelerates the creation of behavioral norms that can substitute for more formal, rigid (and expensive) social structures. Trust that requires rules and hierarchy exacts a price from the organization. Such structures may be necessary, but they need not be permanent. Once people have created rules they can live with, and have shown a willingness to follow the rules, the rules may become superfluous. Removal of extraneous superstructure should be the first order of business once a group feels comfortable with its normative foundation.

COINCIDENCE OF VALUE

Companies are marvelous inventions. Under the corporate form, they offer limited liability and other legal advantages that entice shareholders to invest. Because they have the critical mass to buy big machines and take big risks, they benefit consumers by producing products that individuals cannot. Imagine, if you will, a sole-practitioner aircraft manufacturer. Companies can be paradigms of efficiency, as Adam Smith's classic pin-making example illustrates. He observed that ten pin makers dividing the job into discrete steps could turn out forty-eight thousand pins in a day. Each working alone, Smith estimated, would turn out fewer than twenty pins.[17]

The lesson is obvious—division of labor, made possible by the business organization, increases productivity, lowering production costs and consumer prices. Pin buyers everywhere stand to benefit. But so too does the pin maker. The company has created a market in which he can sell his human capital and multiply its value.

Companies pursue a range of programs to create and preserve the kind of success that enables them to act as human capital marketplaces. Whereas these initiatives often strengthen the organization or improve the ROI_w they offer, the results sometimes materialize in strangely imbalanced ways. In other words, some things companies do hurt workers at the expense of the organization, whereas other actions have the opposite effect. The net result of all the machinations may be positive for worker and organization, but peaks and valleys of gain and loss are evident. The table below shows how workers see the allocation of benefit from common workplace programs.

Only empowerment seems to workers to produce roughly equal benefit for both individual and company. Everything else, they believe, robs either Peter or Paul. Yet 82 percent of the respondents to the 1997 *Inc.* survey said that their employers give them the opportunity to do what they

Worker Perceptions of Who Benefits from What.

Workplace Initiatives	Benefits Worker	Benefits Company	Never Heard of It
Incentive pay	75%	18%	4%
Self-directed work teams	58	27	11
Empowerment	40	41	14
Reorganization	15	79	3
Reengineering	10	64	20
Downsizing	4	89	4

Source: Adapted from M. Hopkins and J. L. Seglin, "Americans @ Work." *Inc.*, Special Edition on the State of Small Business, 1997, 19(7), p. 82.

do best; 85 percent said their employer's mission makes them feel important.[18] When you add it all up, the workplace market for human capital works about as well as any other market. It suffers the occasional slump and subjects investors to a few unexpected turns, but it generally produces good results over the long run.

Opportunities for trust-building participation abound within most organizations. Management gurus have promoted worker participation as a cure for everything from low morale to slow inventory turn. With respect to human capital management, however, participation at a few key junctures can have a profound impact on an individual's faith in the psychological contract. Participation has the most critical effect at two points: when the psychological contract is formulated and later when review and possible modification of the contract are necessary. Consider a few examples from our discussion of the psychological contract in this and the last few chapters:

- Give job candidates a sense of participation and control by making clear links between hiring protocols and job requirements and by fully disclosing elements of the deal the company is prepared to make and abide by.
- Give people responsibility for identifying the links between business unit strategy and their personal investment of human capital; make this responsibility continuous (not a once-a-year event) because strategy is bound to change, as is the human capital required to execute it.
- Reinforce participation by educating people in the workings of the business. Give them the information they need to do all they can to influence business success.

Here is a rule of thumb for participation by human capital investors—think of them as human venture capitalists. They are not playing with OPM (other people's money); they have put their own human assets on the line. Therefore, they want the kind of control over planning and investment that the most watchful venture capitalists demand. Expect them to monitor their ROI_w closely and frequently, the way venture capital investors scrutinize quarterly results of the businesses in their portfolios. Expect to include them in any significant decision affecting the state of their portfolios. Consider the

worker a particularly active one-person board of directors with ultimate responsibility for individual investment and return results.

Once Trust Is Built, Nurture It Carefully

Even when embedded in norms and social structures, trust remains
fragile. A single broken promise can destroy it in an instant. Evidence
referred to in Chapter Two suggests that although trust does not
directly elicit discretionary human capital investment, mistrust tends
to depress investment. The implication for management is this—
promise cautiously, deliver absolutely. Compounding the fragility of
trust is its asymmetry. As expressed by risk management expert Paul
Slovic, "trust is easier to destroy than to create."[19] Slovic, who studies
trust in the public policy and government arenas, believes that:

- Trust-destroying events are more visible than positive (trust-
  building) events.
- Negative events carry more psychological weight than positive
  events.
- Sources of bad news tend to have more credibility than sources
  of good news.
- Distrust, once initiated, tends to reinforce and perpetuate
  more distrust.

When it comes to reinforcing the psychological contract, words,
written or spoken, take a back seat to actions. Writing in *Human
Resource Management,* psychiatrist David Morrison observed, "People develop their expectations by perceiving and remembering what
happens. Contracts are created from what people do, not from
what they say they will do or from what someone says they should do.
For this reason the psychological contract is more a reality than are
the formal policies. In fact, it is the reality as opposed to what someone says reality should be."[20] At the personal level, who gets hired and
fired, promoted or overlooked, well compensated or slighted speaks
to the real contract. Downsizing, reorganizations, mergers, and spin-
offs have the ring of reality, sometimes contradicting what companies
print in their employee manuals or annual reports.

Perhaps the best way to build trust through action is to stick with
an agreed-on psychological contract even when times turn from good

to bad. Think back for a moment to the late 1970s and early 1980s. If you worked in a savings and loan then (as I did), you were in for a wild ride. Deregulation began to transform both sides of the balance sheet. Variable-rate mortgages and the breaking down of barriers prohibiting savings and loans from offering checking accounts changed asset and liability management forever. Interest rates hit record highs; the prime rate peaked at 20.5 percent in August 1981. A new product called the money market account threatened to bleed banks and thrifts dry. All of this compounded the age-old borrow short–lend long dilemma faced by thrift institutions. The smarter S&Ls stopped making thirty-year mortgages. Instead, they put their money in investments that would move with interest rate fluctuations.

It was a bad time to be a residential mortgage lender, unless you worked for Golden West Financial Corp. in California. This thrift, operated by the husband and wife team of Herb and Marion Sandler, knew the value of a good loan officer. They were not about to let economic troubles, however devastating, force them into laying off the producers who had fueled the institution's asset growth. In other words, they refused to let go of all the human capital represented by loan officers' judgment and selling skill. Instead, management found positions for loan officers throughout the organization. They delivered mail, distributed office supplies, and did whatever else needed to be done. True, it wasn't as interesting as making mortgage loans. However, it was a good deal better than losing their jobs altogether, as so many of their counterparts in other organizations had. The Sandlers kept them on the payroll, preserving the core of the psychological contract and building trust. Their action also set the company up for a fast start when interest rates fell and lending became part of the strategy again. To this day, Golden West (which operates as World Savings) remains one of the best-managed consumer financial institutions in the United States.

The Index of Acceptance

Four items from the 1997 *Workplace Index* indicate the degree to which workers believe organizations accept and adhere to their psychological contracts. Together, they reflect the perception of fairness in the equity of the deal (see Table 5.3). Respondents gave lower scores to acceptance-driving items than to other items in the *Workplace Index*. Perhaps skepticism born of early 1990s downsizing remains.

Table 5.3.   Index of Acceptance.

Index Item	Percentage Agreeing
• In general, workforce policies at my company are administered fairly and consistently.	56%
• In general, promotions at my company are administered fairly and consistently.	45%
• Employees who are top performers receive more pay and recognition than average/poor performers.	44%
• If my company is financially successful I will share in that success.	56%

Source: © Towers Perrin, *The 1997 Towers Perrin Workplace Index* (New York: Towers Perrin, 1997).

Or maybe princely compensation packages paid to CEOs make people wonder whether the wealth is really being shared.

Figure 5.7 shows that the line representing the relationship between acceptance and motivation to invest starts a little to the right of the

Figure 5.7.   The Third Framework Factor: Acceptance of the Deal.

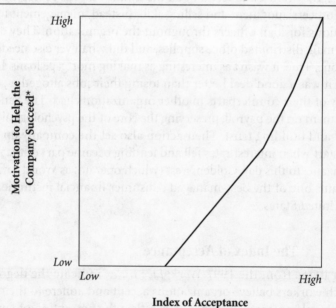

*Reflects organizational commitment, as defined in Chapter Two.

Source: © Towers Perrin, *The 1997 Towers Perrin Workplace Index*
(New York: Towers Perrin, 1997).

lines associated with strategic alignment and understanding. We might conclude that it takes relatively more units of acceptance than units of either alignment or understanding to gain the first bit of commitment. The comparison is intriguing, for it suggests that acceptance provides less initial leverage than alignment of understanding when it comes to increasing individual propensity to invest human capital.

SUMMARY: THE INVESTMENT FRAMEWORK

In establishing the framework for maximum human capital investment, this chapter focused on three factors associated with the psychological contract: strategic alignment, understanding, and acceptance. Each shows a strong positive association with individual commitment to invest human capital on behalf of an organization.

The three factors strengthen one another by their association. Organizations that effectively align strategy with human capital investment improve their chances of generating the financial and other rewards that reinforce acceptance of the psychological deal. Individual involvement in defining the links between investment and strategy not only improves alignment but also increases understanding and reinforces the trust that underpins acceptance. The actions that organizations take to establish trust increase individual understanding. And on it goes.

Two repeating themes run through the chapter: participation and information. We saw how participation at a few key points in the contract establishment and execution continuum reinforces trust. In addition, when workers take part in defining the links between investment and strategy, those links become both clearer and stronger. Consequently, so does the organization's chance of executing strategy successfully. Information supports alignment between human capital and strategy, contributes to understanding, and reinforces the trust required for acceptance of the workplace deal.

This chapter introduced one other important point—the notion of manager as investment adviser, the first of several important roles. In this capacity, managers and mentors (not the same role, but sometimes the same person) can greatly affect an individual's ability to manage the human capital investment process. We will see as we progress that the first-line manager has other important parts to play in the unfolding story of human capital investment.

As a group, the three factors explored in Chapter Five take us back to the notion of organizational commitment. Each factor functions as a tie between the individual and the company. In the discussion, I have treated the three as independent and roughly coequal. In my book, however, acceptance underscored by trust is first among equals. On the one hand, increments of trust may affect commitment less dramatically than gains in strategic alignment or understanding of the deal. On the other hand, we should think of trust as the keystone of an arch—the part on which the other stones depend for support. Without trust, strategy alignment is meaningless and understanding, bankrupt.

Chapter Five has established a set of three background criteria for the maximum investment of human capital. We move on now to three additional criteria that directly influence the way people view the jobs through which they make their human capital investments.

CHAPTER SIX

Paving the Way for High Investment

—⁓— **M**ark Twain, who did plenty of both, knew the difference between work and play: "Work consists of whatever a body is *obliged* to do. . . . Play consists of whatever a body is not obliged to do."[1] An episode in Tom Sawyer, perhaps the most famous scene in American literature, illustrates how indistinct is the line separating the two. Tom's Aunt Polly has ordered him to spend Saturday whitewashing the front fence. Tom reacts the way any other red-blooded American boy would—he tries to get out of it. At a hopeless moment, with the prospect of a ruined day looming before him, he has an inspiration. Perhaps he can work a trade with some of his friends—a fulfilling whitewashing experience in exchange for their investment of effort. He, in turn, can have the leisure he wants along with plenty of company. As it turns out, he gets more than that. He makes fence painting so attractive that his friends pay him to do the work. He acquires such treasures as a dead rat on a string (suitable for swinging), twelve marbles, six firecrackers, a one-eyed kitten, and a dog collar (without the dog).

As often happens with Twain's vignettes, this one offers insights into the state of humanity. Most relevant for us is the notion that in a well-conceived exchange, all parties are happy with the value they gain. Chapter Five established the organizational context for such an exchange. In this chapter, we move inside that framework to study the execution-focused elements that pave the way for high investment and high returns. We will consider three factors:

1. Competence. Competence comprises the whole range of skills, knowledge, talent, and behaviors necessary to do a demanding job. Organizations that emphasize worker competence not only increase potential workplace investment but also help release that potential.

2. Autonomy. Workers with the freedom that autonomy implies can formulate principles for personal behavior and then act accordingly. Autonomous workers invest more human capital than their less autonomous counterparts because they work free of restrictive rules and regulations.

3. Reinforcement. We have spent ample time on the concept of return on workplace investment, the broadly defined recompense that goes to workers in exchange for their human capital investment. What we have not spent much time on is the means by which organizations deliver ROI_w. Organizations that follow a few simple principles can ensure that the return on human capital investment has the maximum impact in eliciting the next round of investment.

Figure 6.1 places these three elements inside the frame constructed in Chapter Five. Strategy alignment, understanding the psychological contract, and acceptance of the contract form the organizational context. Competence, autonomy, and reinforcement engage individual investment in the execution of the job. Together, these six factors appeared as "Workplace Environment and Job Execution Factors" in Figure 2.5.

COMPETENCE: CAPACITY FOR ACTION

The quest for competence is the mechanism by which people understand and control their environments. "We demand a knowledge of effects" said Jean Piaget, the famous child psychologist, "and to be ourselves the producers of effects."[2] Psychologist Robert W. White, in a

Figure 6.1. Competence, Autonomy, and Reinforcement
Fit into the Investment Framework.

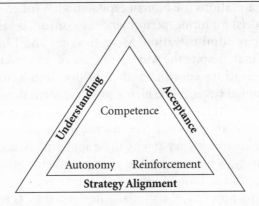

seminal article written in 1959, argued that competence works as a motivational concept. He said that people have a natural propensity to seek a feeling of efficacy by exploring novel situations and mastering new ways to control them. He referred to the motivational aspect of competence as *effectance* and described it this way: "Satisfaction of effectance contributes significantly to those feelings of interest which often sustain us so well in day-to-day actions, particularly when the things we are doing have continuing elements of novelty."[3]

Competence affects human capital investment in two ways. First, and obviously, workers with growing competence have more human capital available to invest. Both individual and organization stand to gain when investible, return-generating assets increase. Second, opportunities to increase competence act as powerful catalysts of effective human capital investment. In its *Partnership Portfolio*, Fireman's Fund expresses it this way: "When you improve your professional skills and experience, you can make better decisions than the competition, contribute more to your teams and provide better service to your customers. This helps us improve and sustain profitable growth in pursuit of our organizational goals. On your side, you build a diverse portfolio of skills, knowledge and experience which can improve performance in your current job and help you succeed in your career."[4]

Chapter Seven focuses specifically on competence-enhancing learning approaches consistent with the human capital ideas we have established. In this chapter, we will look more generally at how an organization can create an environment that fosters competence building.

Link Human Capital Models to Support Strategy

Many organizations use human capital models (often called competency models) for hiring, performance assessment, development planning, or pay administration. My colleagues and I have observed, however, that, despite the widespread use of competency modeling, few organizations coordinate their efforts into a single, coherent human capital system. The hiring protocol often does not link with the development model, and the performance assessment approach may bear only an incidental resemblance to the skill-based pay structure. Creating consistency among these applications, and linking them all to strategy, is fundamental to giving momentum to an organization's competence-building efforts.

Williams-Sonoma, the specialty home products retailer, has set about to create this link among its human capital applications.[5] Williams-Sonoma operates three retail groups that sell through both stores and catalogs; the company also has two catalog-only divisions. The organization has generated impressive growth over the past several years. Net sales increased from $440 million in 1993 to $933 million in 1997. The company operates close to three hundred stores in thirty-six states and mails some 135 million catalogs each year. Even while managing this growth spurt, Williams-Sonoma has improved quality and customer service. Management knows it cannot stand still, however. Continuously improving human capital management will play a critical role in sustaining the organization's success. Williams-Sonoma has begun an effort to coordinate hiring, performance appraisal, individual development planning, and succession planning within a straightforward ten-part human capital construct. The company's human capital model calls for managers to hire, develop, and do career planning using this one basic design; the model emphasizes such organization-level human capital elements as communication skills, customer focus, business knowledge, and thinking skills. Andy Rich, formerly the company's senior vice president of human resources, says that the secret to success is not in the specific elements of the model: "We had a hard time getting people to agree that these were precisely the right ten factors. We got everyone involved and eventually reached agreement. However, the magic is in the process of definition, not in the definitions themselves. Beyond that, the key thing is to make sure that you connect hiring, assessment, and development."

Rich agrees that despite the frequency with which companies use multifactor human capital models, the interconnections are often absent: "I believe that less than one percent of U.S. companies have linked the full continuum." Research data from Aon Consulting bears this out. Among the respondents to Aon's 1997 survey of human resource trends, 70 percent said that their companies' performance management systems need to provide greater career development support. Almost 40 percent said better linkages to development and training would improve their present performance management processes.[6]

To create these missing interprogram links, an organization must begin by defining the human capital required to carry out strategy. Chapter Three provided a strategy-formulation framework. Beyond that, linking the recruiting, selection, development, performance assessment, and compensation systems is a painstaking process of building application-specific sets of procedures on a common human capital foundation. Here are some applicable principles:

- Make sure human capital definitions are suitable for all applications; there is no point in creating a definition that guides training and development, for example, but is too complex to use as a hiring criterion.

- Assess carefully (using the kind of framework shown in Figure 4.1) whether each element can be developed by the organization or requires special attention in the hiring process.

- Do the analysis depicted in Figure 4.2 to differentiate hiring from developmental needs, and to determine how much latitude the organization has in choosing make-or-buy options.

- Involve employees and managers extensively in the design process for each of the different applications; make sure the design teams share membership to ensure cross-fertilization.

- Communicate the programs (along with the human capital foundation that underlies them) widely throughout the organization.

- Train managers and employees at all levels on the use of human capital programs; emphasize how they reinforce each other to build the company's human capital base.

- Call back teams of managers and employees for quarterly design review and modification meetings on each application; continue to meet for the first two years after program rollout.

- Set up calibration meetings periodically to check consistency among the programs and ensure they support the building of critical human capital.

Fill the Organization with Teachers and Learners

Competence, as a form of human capital, comprises two main components: teaching and learning abilities. These two aspects comprise behaviors and intellectual capacity, with some skill thrown in for good measure. Smart organizations (and organizations that want to become smart) know they must hire people who have these two traits in abundance, and then nurture their development. From their study of what they call "the teaching firm," researchers at the Education Development Center (EDC) in Newton, Massachusetts, reached this conclusion:

> Most of the factors that an organization can influence involve external reinforcement, such as financial incentives, recognition, career advancement, increased authority and responsibility, etc. As such, it would seem that the organization cannot do much to increase the tendency for people to be personally and internally motivated to learn. It would seem that the best an organization can do is select employees who seem to be internally motivated to learn. . . . The interviews we conducted clearly demonstrated that people have varying inclinations and attitudes towards learning. High achievers and self-starters were more likely to seek out opportunities to develop and grow within the organization. Traits which tended to facilitate informal learning include: ambition, curiosity, competitiveness, sociability, imagination, ability to reflect, critical thinking, and self confidence.[7]

Assessment of learning (and teaching) abilities and behaviors should become a focus of prehire assessment. In keeping with the Chapter Four argument favoring a full-disclosure deal, interviewers should describe how the organization fosters a climate supportive of learning and growth, a climate that enables people to capitalize on their competence-building propensities.

Make Competence an Organizational Value

In its research, the EDC identified several factors an organization can influence to increase individual learning: "Research has observed that organizations in which learning is integral to the culture, an organizational value, tend to create a context where individuals learn to appreciate the value of learning. In a context where learning is reinforced, valued, appreciated, and discussed openly, individuals internalize the value of learning, and incorporate it into their behaviors."[8]

As with so many other aspects of corporate life, the staying power of a value comes down to senior management action. If executives act as though competence has importance, then it will. If valuable training investments escape the knife when cost pressures rise, their significance will be underscored. If executives themselves live up to a standard of continued competence improvement, they can conscionably hold workers to the same standard. If executives have personal human capital development plans that guide them in building well-defined abilities and behaviors, then workers are more likely to embrace such plans for themselves.

For competence to become an organizational value, companies must resist headlong replacement of clever people with unclever machines. Granted, automation of routine tasks represents a tremendous boon to workers and organizations alike, but it can have a hidden price. Sacrificing human capital for its hardware and software counterparts not only strips away critical abilities but also undermines competence as a value. Analysts seldom note these losses when they formulate the business case for automation. Here are two examples that suggest why they should.

Consider first the accounts payable process. What other procedure could be more routine, paper intensive, and computer amenable? Many big companies have slashed their accounts payable staffs, some by as much as 50 percent.[9] The payroll cost savings are obvious and enticing. The problem is that a competent accounts payable clerk can do things a computer cannot: spot duplicate invoices and billing errors and detect defective merchandise. Savings in overbillings can pay the clerk's salary (and the boss's bonus) several times over. While all those staff cutbacks took place, accounts payable losses have risen 30 percent a year over the past couple of years and may run as much as $10 billion a year. Computers simply can't catch those errors. And they don't always notice when prompt payment can yield a discount. Fast and cheap as they are, computers cannot bring to bear all of the judgment, intuition, experience, and suspicion that a competent accounts payable clerk carries around in his head.

Now consider the evolving art of sales. With electronic customer databases, telemarketing, and selling via the Internet, has the day of Willy Loman faded into history? Not according to one observer. He tells of cases where personal contact enabled sales reps to renegotiate complex deals, tease out evidence of critical needs, and gather otherwise unavailable market intelligence. Writing in a *Wall Street Journal* column, guest author Jack Falvey concludes: "High-tech data collection will never substitute for the human touch: a good salesman's ability to establish trust with customers, respond to subtle and unexpected cues, and deal flexibly with customers' needs while protecting his company's interests."[10] In other words, organizations cannot easily replace the kind of competence that a good sales rep (or accounts payable clerk) exhibits. Organizations dedicated to competence relinquish such assets with fingernail-ripping reluctance. Those smart organizations understand that competence supports job engagement—and human capital investment—through its connection with performance. Higher competence produces better performance; better performance, in turn, improves the individual's satisfaction with and involvement in the bundle of tasks that make up the job. Moreover, as an element of return on investment, competence building has a positive effect on human capital contribution.

AUTONOMY: EMPOWERMENT AND BEYOND

To emphasize the importance of autonomy, let us differentiate between autonomy and its second cousin, empowerment. *Empowerment* means to give up power, to transfer control from manager to worker. To a large extent, the empowerment movement is an effort to break the enduring shackles of Frederick Taylor's scientific management. Taylor believed that giving job discretion to unmotivated workers merely allowed them to hold back effort and hamper productivity. He argued for turning control over to managers, who would plan the work flow down to the gold screws in the gnat's eyeglasses. In Taylor's own words, "The work of every workman is fully planned out by the management at least one day in advance, and each man receives in most cases complete written instructions, describing in detail the task which he is to accomplish, as well as the means to be used in doing the work."[11]

Paradoxically, empowerment can sometimes reinforce the hierarchical relationship between the one-up manager and the one-down worker. As workers often discover, organizations may empower them to do things right, but not to make mistakes. At an Easton Corp. small forge plant, for instance, management enthusiastically embraced a form of empowerment that included public group discipline for mistakes. But this kind of empowerment sometimes backfired. "They say there are no bosses here," said one long-term worker, "but if you screw up, you find one pretty fast."[12]

Autonomy means something different, a step beyond empowerment. It comes from the Greek words for self-governance. To quote psychologist Edward Deci, "Autonomy . . . is about acting volitionally, with a sense of choice, flexibility, and personal freedom. It is about feeling a true willingness to behave responsibly, in accord with your interests and values. The converse of being autonomous is being controlled, which means that you are pressured to behave, think, or feel some particular way."[13] Contrary to the fears of some managers, the true control that comes with autonomy does not require them to give up the authority they exercise. Control, in other words, need not be a zero-sum game; it expands as more people have it. Managers who understand this concept are likely to encourage subordinates to take charge of their jobs.[14] This increases worker control. Workers who make their own decisions are more likely to cooperate with management's policies. Thus, managerial influence also increases.

Nothing Pollyannaish here—just more choice and flexibility with less control. A 1994 *Business Week* article described how autonomy can work not just in high-tech, new age businesses, but also in a less elegant milieu. At Wayne Stevenson's body shop in Cambridge, Massachusetts, bodymen take ownership of a car while it is in the shop, sticking with the job the whole way. "There are a set of parameters," says Stevenson; "then they have to be responsible." Workers receive cross-training to give them new skills and go back to school annually to keep their skills up to date. The shop's traffic has doubled every year for five years.[15]

Autonomy should improve human capital investment and job performance in three ways. The first way is direct—autonomous people, provided with information and freed up to do their work, are likely to perform better than their more tightly controlled, less-informed counterparts. The second way comes through the effects of heightened ROI_w. Freedom and work control that come with autonomy constitute an intrinsic return on human capital investment, more of which produces incremental effort. Thus, both worker and company should come out ahead when autonomy increases. In its research, the Families and Work Institute confirmed the salubrious effects of worker autonomy: "Workers with more job autonomy and control of their work schedules are less burned out by their work, are more satisfied with their jobs, and take more initiative at work. In addition, workers with greater job autonomy are more committed to doing their jobs well, are more loyal to their employers, and plan to remain with their current employers longer than other workers."[16]

The third benefit of autonomy comes as reduction in the cost associated with management. More about that in a moment, as we explore a few ideas for how managers can increase autonomy.

Release the Brakes on Work Processes

In these days of knowledge work, managers have little hope of exercising anything close to a Taylorist kind of control over work processes. We live in a post-downsizing world; companies have concluded that a force of middle managers with narrow spans of control is an indefensible cost. The remaining managers have jobs too complex and strenuous to permit detailed work planning of any kind, let alone the written, day-in-advance variety Taylor advocated. As a writer for the *Wall Street Journal* said, "Managers now must supervise many people who are spread over different locations, even over different continents. They must manage across functions with, say, design, finance, marketing and technical people reporting to them. If their employers set up workplace teams, managers must play an even murkier leadership role. And they must be agents of change, champions of the latest re-engineering or reorganization, even if they have had nothing to do with creation of the plan or disagree with it."[17] On top of all this, they should plan employees' work?

The secret to creating an autonomy-supporting work environment is no secret at all; good companies have been doing it for many decades. In *Built to Last,* James Collins and Jerry Porras laud Hewlett-Packard (HP) for embedding autonomy in the corporate culture. They note that, to support autonomy at both the individual and business unit levels, "HP early on adopted a management method of 'provide a well-defined objective, give the person as much freedom as possible in working toward that objective, and finally, provide motivation by seeing that the contribution of the individual is recognized throughout the organization.' Later, as the company rapidly expanded in the 1950s, it extended this management method into a decentralized structure of highly autonomous divisions set up as little businesses."[18]

Autonomy pulls together many of the principles we have discussed elsewhere. Drawing from some prior points, and extending from the HP experience, we could conclude that companies foster individual autonomy when they do the following:

- Make sure people know what needs to get done, a state of mind fostered by individual ties to business strategy.
- Field a workforce that acts with what consultant T. J. McCoy calls "informed self-determination."[19] The critical element is information—about how the business works, how it makes money, how it measures its success, how and why individual contribution makes a difference. We touched on these points in the consideration of open-book management and top-down/bottom-up strategy linkage.
- Build the capacity to do work effectively. This takes us back to competence, which we can define as the ability to be autonomous *effectively*.

Indeed, Robert White's notion of a motivation to achieve competence ties closely with this idea of autonomy. Achievement of competence requires autonomy; too much external control over an individual's environment reduces the inherent novelty that sparks the urge to learn. An individual expands at the expense of his or her surroundings. Rigid boundaries confine the expansion of knowledge and self-governance, and so inhibit the quest for competence.

Conversely, competence supports autonomy by providing the mechanism for an individual to exercise self-determination. The way Deci sees it, "The strivings for competence and autonomy together—propelled by curiosity and interest—are thus complementary growth forces that lead people to become increasingly accomplished and to go on learning throughout their lifetimes."[20] As the matrix in Figure 6.2 suggests, only when both exist can individual and organization mutually benefit.

Figure 6.2.   Autonomy Plus Competence Improves Investment.

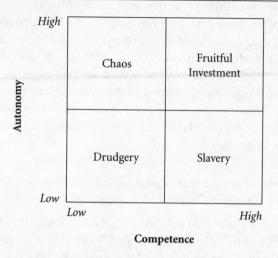

Source: Adapted from E. L. Deci with R. Flaste, *Why We Do What We Do: Understanding Self-Motivation* (New York: Penguin Books, 1995).

The goal is to create an environment that both supports autonomy and builds competence. Low autonomy with high competence means exploitation of employees. High autonomy with low competence means very little valuable work gets done.

Use Rewards for Support, Not Control

Companies set up their reward systems to try to produce (or at least enhance) motivation among workers. Managers think they know instinctively how to motivate people—reward a desired behavior, and the behavior will continue. For adherents to this behaviorist point of view, the equation is simple. Beginning with the premise that people take action only to obtain rewards or avoid punishments, they construct compensation plans that can do both. Produce more widgets, get more money. Fall below quota, and you don't get the money. With some pay-at-risk plans, your below-quota performance may even pay you less than you used to get in the days before incentive compensation.

The problem, some psychologists say, is that rewards doled out in a behaviorist system undermine autonomy and therefore reduce motivation, rather than increasing it. Those who do not subscribe to the behaviorist approach build their argument on three points. First, they say, the proffered rewards are always extrinsic. Second, extrinsic factors do not produce the self-generated discretionary effort that intrinsic rewards elicit; we know that from the discussion of transactional and relational ROI_w in Chapter Two. Third, and most subtle, monetary rewards usually emerge from a system of control, a system that undermines autonomy.

Psychologist Teresa Amabile has analyzed the relationships among monetary rewards, control, and creativity. In one study, she and her team compared the results produced by artists working under commission arrangements with those of artists doing noncommissioned projects. They discovered that artists working under the pressure of a commission delivered work judged to be less creative than the products of their noncommissioned counterparts: "What mattered was not the obvious fact of contracting for reward, but the degree to which the artist felt constrained by the terms of the commission."[21]

Amabile notes, however, that intrinsic and extrinsic rewards can coexist. Some artists, for example, considered their commission enabling, giving them the means to be creative. It is too simple to say money is either good or bad for motivation. The means of delivering money determines whether it is freeing or constraining, consistent with intrinsic sources of motivation or conflicting with them. As Amabile said in a 1997 interview on National Public Radio:

> I think it's clearly a mistake to say that creativity can be easily enhanced by the use of rewards. That's a vast oversimplification. It's also an oversimplification to say that reward will always kill creativity. And the middle ground is that people have to feel that they're doing what they're doing not in order to get a reward, but because they're interested in what they're doing and they care about what they're doing. If that's firmly in place, rewards that support competence, rewards that enable people to do something that they're excited about doing, can in fact add to higher levels of creativity.[22]

If you accept the notions expressed by Amabile, the right place for the cart of compensation is well behind the horse of job design and the nonfinancial elements of ROI_w. Instead of setting up a "do-this-because-you'll-get-paid" system, aim for "do this because . . ."

". . . you helped design how it would get done."

". . . you understand how it contributes to the organization's success."

"... it is intrinsically interesting and engages your creativity."

"... it helps you develop your skills and knowledge."

"... the organization will recognize and appreciate how it contributes to the group's success."

REINFORCEMENT: DELIVERING ROI$_w$

The idea of ensuring that rewards do not become autonomy draining opens a wider discussion of how companies should deliver ROI$_w$ to their worker-investors. The watchword is *justice*, the impartial distribution of life's goodies. Justice does not, by itself, elicit human capital investment. However, deficits in justice decrease human capital investment by putting speed bumps on the road to workplace contribution. Lost productivity may be tough to measure, but it's real nonetheless. Consider, for example, the annual compensation dance that takes place in Wall Street money houses:

> You don't know the meaning of anarchy until you've seen Wall Street at bonus time. As Labor Day recedes in the rearview mirror and Thanksgiving comes in sight, each firm creates a committee to decide the bonus for each employee while each employee tries in various ways to convince the committee that he is underpaid. The trick here has always been to point out the terrible injustice of the $685,000 you were paid last year without seeming either ridiculous or ungrateful. . . . The person who rises above the bonus fray is as Godforsaken as the man who stands back from the luggage conveyor belt at the Calcutta airport. He'll spend the rest of his life waiting for his bags to arrive.[23]

Visualize all that talent burning ergs of energy recalculating and renegotiating bonuses instead of crafting deals for clients. Also, note how the perception of justice has a relative (not an absolute) foundation. If you think you deserved a kingly $700,000 bonus, then a princely $685,000 simply will not do. Never mind that either sum will feed a Guatemalan town for a year.

By exhibiting justice, an organization's ways of operating can remove these progress-inhibiting barriers. Justice comes from two sources: the fairness of the inherent procedure and the equity of the result.[24] The first form, procedural justice, depends on the process. It requires that organizations make decisions (and allocate rewards) in a way that seems equitable to everyone's satisfaction. The second form, distributive justice, depends on the outcome. Distributive justice predicts satisfaction with individual results, like receipt of a bonus.

Ensure Procedural Fairness . . .

Procedural fairness plays a powerful role in worker satisfaction with the more conspicuous ROI_w elements. Remember the position of rewards as the factor that mediates between performance and satisfaction. Research into the effects of compensation systems shows that perceptions about the fairness of pay procedures more strongly influence job satisfaction than do actual pay levels.[25]

The experience of a small Louisville company called Lantech shows how people manipulate or circumvent systems they do not trust.[26] At one point, Lantech management defined bonuses according to the profit generated by each of five individual divisions. A worker in a high-performing division could receive an incentive of as much as 10 percent of regular base pay. However, interdependence among the divisions made sorting out the profits a nightmare. Groups jockeyed with each other, trying to shift cost to others and claim revenues for themselves. "That led to so much secrecy, politicking, and sucking noise that you wouldn't believe it," said the company's CEO. Employees even argued over who should pay for the toilet paper in the common rest rooms. Someone suggested that the accounting department allocate toilet paper costs according to the gender makeup of each division. Their rationale centered on the theory that one gender uses more toilet paper than the other.

Managers face a daunting challenge in constructing an equitable distribution system for return on workplace investment. On the one hand, the commandments for administering compensation systems are well known among human resource practitioners: make it simple, tie pay to performance, communicate the pay structure to everyone. Pay is, after all, a transactional element of ROI_w. Some sort of formal agreement or policy governs most compensation arrangements. On the other hand, when intangible, relational elements of return on investment come into play, the rules become much less clear. What guidelines apply to the allocation of recognition, for example? The compensation commandments make a good starting list, but they do not go far enough. One scholar of social equity proposes six criteria for evaluating the fairness of decision-making procedures. His criteria provide useful guidelines for managers who control the distribution of relational ROI_w.[27]

1. Consistency across time and people. Make sure today's decisions can be justified in the cold light of precedent.

2. Absence of self-interest. Don't let personal biases or favoritism influence reward decisions.

3. Use of accurate information. Rely only on information that is objective and that, upon review by all involved parties, reflects an agreed-on reality.

4. Opportunity for correction of errors. Make available an appeals process for those who believe they have received unfair treatment.

5. Concern for the interests of all involved. Don't provide benefits to one at the expense of someone else.

6. Application of ethical and moral standards. Use rewards to encourage behavior that reflects positively on the organization and reinforces organizational values.

Congratulations if you read this list and said to yourself, "These would support the establishment of trust between manager and worker and between worker and organization." Give yourself extra credit for finding another connective filament in the web of factors that elicit human capital investment.

. . . But Don't Forget Individual Equity

Psychological research supports the conclusion that people construct a personal reward-to-effort ratio. When it comes to concrete rewards like pay, the bigger the individual's ratio of reward to effort, the greater the satisfaction with both the reward procedure and the outcome.[28] Conversely, the greater the discrepancy between what I think I deserve and what I get, the less satisfied I am.[29]

Again, the annual Wall Street morality play can teach us a lesson about how people personalize their views of what they deserve. In the mid-1990s, Warren Buffet tried to change the way compensation worked at Salomon Brothers. Under his structure, all but a few of the firm's two hundred managing directors would receive a guaranteed salary of $400,000. Each would be eligible for a subsequent bonus that kicked in only after Salomon's profits had reached a certain level. As 1994 drew to a close, the firm readied itself to announce a pretax loss of nearly $1 billion. Under the Buffet plan, bonuses would be slim indeed. The resulting uproar was predictable; almost everyone who did not quit threatened to do so. Standard & Poor's cited the mass uprising and exodus as a reason for lowering Salomon's credit rating.[30] Ultimately, Salomon abandoned the Buffet rules. With them died the first attempt to introduce into a Wall Street firm the idea that the individual must sacrifice for the good of the whole.

To address this phenomenon of personalization, managers must be mindful of the myriad ways workers get information about how organizational phenomena affect them. Under the theory that actions speak louder than words, organizations must pay special attention to the critical incidents that convey organizational realities. Management professors Lisa Gundry and Denise Rousseau have used the idea of epiphanies to describe the interactional moments that leave marks on people's lives.[31] In a study of newly hired engineers in an electronics manufacturing firm, the researchers elicited a set of critical incident descriptions. The descriptions covered a variety of positive and negative experiences within a range of workplace situations. Some kinds of incidents made people feel that the organization would provide such relational ROI_w elements as achievement, self-actualization, and supportive interpersonal relations. Incidents that tended to build an individual's confidence in positive personal treatment fell into such categories as these:

- Supportiveness of the supervisor: demonstrated backing by the first-line manager
- Initiative taken by subordinates: evidence that peers had succeeded by acting autonomously
- Acquisition of greater responsibility: reinforcement of autonomy through the widening of boundaries for action
- Work on a challenging project: opportunity to experience increased intrinsic job fulfillment.

Conversely, critical incidents that undermined an individual's personal view of organizational support were associated with the following:[32]

- Violation of policies and rules
- Menial work assignments
- Interdepartmental conflict
- Alienation from the group or the manager
- Inequity in promotion or rewards
- Conflict between supervisor and subordinate

From this list of dos and don'ts come two conclusions. First, each positive experience increases an individual's confidence that just personal outcomes will result from continuing investment of human capital. In the terms defined in Chapter Five, trust increases as the individual becomes more confident that the organization will uphold its end of the deal. But beware the power of bad news; negative critical incidents have a magnified and destructive effect on trust. Second, the line supervisor has dramatic control over many critical incidents that support or undermine individual confidence in personal justice from the organization. To a large extent, the supervisor holds the scales of justice when it comes to relational ROI_w.

Give People Maximum Choice, but Be Wary of Trade-Offs

The organization will need to make individual deals with individual workers, each of whom brings different kinds of human capital to invest. This kind of customization implies the need to offer workers a choice of elements in their ROI_w array—a scary prospect, to be sure, introducing the possibility of endless negotiation and administrative hassle. But remember two points. First, people's need for a particular balance of ROI_w elements is bound to change over time. This factor alone requires managers to forget the idea of a single, long-lasting deal. Deals change not just as an organization changes people, but also as the people within the organization change. An early-career worker may want challenging work, rewards based on performance, balance between work and the rest of life, and intensive skill development. A more senior person has more interest in job security and hankers for rewards based on tenure, assistance with the transition to retirement, and opportunities for wealth accumulation. Under these scenarios, individual differences inevitably will drive an organization toward segmentation of the employee population and creation of many different deal packages.

Second, the greatest need for flexibility falls in the relational ROI_w categories, where flexibility is easiest to manage. Compensation and benefits plans come under legal, tax, and moral constraints that restrict companies from giving substantially different packages to similarly situated individuals. In contrast, companies can offer much freer choice in such areas as work group structure, choice of work type, choice of location, advancement track, and development opportunities.

The recommendation that organizations offer choice in the creation of return-on-investment portfolios does not give them license, however, to make unilateral shifts among ROI_w elements. Only workers can make such shifts. The problem is that the elements of return on workplace investment cannot be expressed in consistent units. Figure 6.3 plots the four categories of investment returns in a three-dimensional space. The axis labeled individuality shows how much the worth of a return element depends on an individual's unique measurement system for that element.[33] Highly individual returns on investment have no universally acceptable units of measure. Like beauty in the eye of the beholder, graduations in value depend largely

Figure 6.3. Return-on-Investment Components Have Widely Varying Value Metrics.

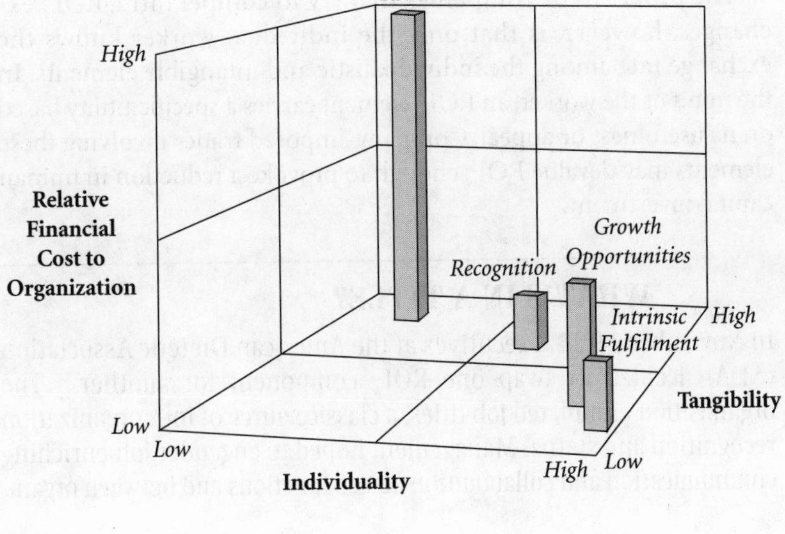

on the perception of the individual. Intrinsic job fulfillment, growth opportunities, and recognition all rate high on individuality. The valuation of money, in contrast, is much less individual. Although its importance varies among people, we nevertheless have an established and widely accepted system for denominating our money. We can therefore exchange it freely and at arm's length. The axis labeled tangibility refers to the concreteness of an ROI_w component. Financial ROI_w is clearly the most tangible of the four return-on-investment elements. Intrinsic fulfillment is the least tangible.

The third dimension is relative financial cost to the organization. Obviously, monetary rewards have the greatest financial significance. Growth opportunities, to the extent that they require a company to make an investment in training and development, carry a more moderate financial impact. For intrinsic fulfillment and recognition, the financial implications usually are (or can be) modest by comparison.

Visualizing ROI_w elements this way tells us something about the opportunities and challenges organizations face in providing attractive consideration in return for investment. We know that people do sometimes make trade-offs among ROI_w elements. They may trade among intangibles, for example, by sticking with a fulfilling job rather than accepting a promotion to a loftier but less intrinsically appealing position. They may also substitute an individualistic and intangible element with low financial impact for a greater financial reward. Teachers who leave the classroom and take up insurance sales make such a trade-off.

The problem for companies that try to compel intra-ROI_w exchanges, however, is that only the individual worker knows the exchange rate among the individualistic and intangible elements. In the mind of the worker, an ROI_w element carries a specific utility based on its usefulness or appeal. Company-imposed trades involving these elements may devalue ROI_w enough to provoke a reduction in human capital investment.

WHAT'S IN A TITLE?

In November 1994, executives at the American Dietetic Association (ADA) decided to swap one ROI_w component for another.[34] The organization eliminated job titles, a classic source of intraorganization recognition and status. Management hoped to engender job-enriching communication and collaboration across functions and between organization levels. By its action, the ADA unleashed "primal forces," said the columnist who wrote the story on the ADA move: "An egalitarian structure may appeal to you if you're completely secure about your value to your employer and couldn't care less about status, competition and career advancement. But how many of you are that well adjusted?" For their part, staff members wondered why they should invest their human capital when one form of return on their investment had effectively disappeared. "If you're not going to have something to show for it, why put in extra time?" one said. Moreover, the organization had to wrestle with how to hand out financial rewards without titles as a guideline. One executive said the organization has to heap more praise on workers to make up for lack of ego-boosting titles. "I think people feel a bit anonymous, devalued," said one senior staff member.

Managers also have a fiduciary responsibility to spend wisely the money they put into providing investment returns to workers. This means getting the maximum human capital investment for the ROI_w they provide—return on investment from the company's point of view. It is not as easy as cutting the training budget and sliding a little money over into the employee-of-the-month program. To do justice to both workers and shareholders, managers must:

- Understand the choices workers want to make to create appealing ROI_w arrays.
- Know the strategic value of the human capital investment those arrays will produce.
- Figure out the cost of delivering the desired ROI_w and compare it, at least in general terms, to the strategic value of human capital.
- Offer a selection of ROI_w choices that, to the maximum extent, elicits the investment of critical human capital while husbanding organizational resources.

Doing the optimization problem implied in the final point on the list is far from easy, of course. We will wrestle with this mixed-media measurement challenge in Chapter Nine. For now, let us simply say that organizations cannot overengineer the ROI_w packages they offer workers. Only by giving choices, defined in the context of fiscal reality, can a company hope to create individual deals that reflect the best interests of both workers and the organization.

SUMMARY: COMPLETING THE PICTURE

We now have a picture to fit in the frame established in Chapter Five. In the main, the factors discussed in Chapter Six tend to work through increased job engagement. This is especially true of competence and autonomy; the former gives a worker the resources to invest in a job, whereas the latter ensures the freedom to make that investment unstifled by job-specific constraints. Competence and autonomy form a powerful investment-eliciting combination. They are critical, for instance, in turning emergent strategy into reality.

Reinforcement has both job and organizational implications. Day-to-day relationships with coworkers and supervisors profoundly affect an individual's beliefs about whether rewards represent a fair return on investment. At the same time, organizations play a major role in reward distribution; they must fight the temptation to make unilateral shifts among ROI_w elements. Bundles of transactional and relational rewards carry denominations that vary too much and are too subject to individual definition to make company-engineered trade-offs feasible. We can categorize reinforcement as a boundary spanner; it has effects on all sides of the lines dividing job from organization, commitment from engagement. Thinking back to Chapter Five, we could put strategy alignment in the same boundary-spanning category. We saw how strategy alignment connected individual human capital investment to both job and organization.

We have advanced several other points in Chapter Six, some introduced earlier and some to come up again later. One we have seen before has to do with the importance of the supervisor. Supervisors act not just in an advisory role but also as key players in delivering workplace return on investment. We can expect to add more richness to the first-line manager role as we go on. Looking ahead, we have posed a challenge for Chapter Nine—determining return on investment from both worker and organization perspectives. Finally, this chapter introduced the notion of worker competence. We will pick up that idea in the next chapter, which deals with building human capital.

Building Human Capital

*Q*uestion: Which adds more to productivity: a 10 percent increase in worker education or a 10 percent increase in capital stock?

Answer: Put your money on education.

That appealing conclusion came from the 1994 National Employer Survey (NES) conducted by the National Center on the Educational Quality of the Workforce (EQW). The EQW-NES was administered as a telephone survey of managers and owners of approximately three thousand establishments employing twenty or more workers. Survey results suggested that increases in years of worker schooling contribute proportionally more to productivity than increases in either capital stock or work hours. Among all companies, a 10 percent increase in education is associated with an 8.6 percent gain in productivity. Increase capital stock by 10 percent, and you get only a 3.4 percent bump in productivity. In the nonmanufacturing sector, the results are even more dramatic. Increases of 10 percent in education, work hours, and capital stock correspond to productivity gains of 11.0 percent, 6.3 percent, and 3.9 percent, respectively.[1]

In Chapter Four, we introduced the notion that an organization can choose from among several different approaches to building human capital. The formal education that new employees bring to the organization is just one source. We considered the hiring option in some depth; now it is time to look at learning strategies executed within the organizational environment. Particularly for knowledge and skill elements, learning opportunities can make a significant contribution to individual—and total—human capital.

In this chapter, we assess the merits of formal training and informal learning approaches. We identify ways for organizations to use both—and to make connections between them—to create powerful momentum behind human capital growth. Chapter Seven builds on what we already know about formulating human capital strategy, hiring workers with the needed elements, and eliciting the investment of those elements.

EXAMINING THE TRAINING BIAS

Employers in general exhibit a clear (and growing) dedication to building human capital through organization-sponsored training. Among establishments of all sizes, more than 80 percent give structured or formal training either on the job or at schools or technical institutes.[2] Among large companies (those with one thousand employees or more), nearly all provide both formal and informal training. Training commands a sizable chunk of corporate change. *Training* magazine's annual survey showed that in 1998, U.S. organizations with one hundred or more employees budgeted $60.7 billion for training.[3] As a group, they increased their budgets from $58.6 billion in 1997 and from $43.2 billion in recession-plagued 1991.[4] The figures included trainers' salaries, outside expenditures, facilities, and overhead.

But here is a paradox—although most companies say they provide training, less than 20 percent of workers say they receive any formal training from their employers. Part of the problem may be a definition of terms. A manager who spends time watching an employee and helping him learn a new task may define that time as training. The worker, conversely, may view the manager's activity merely as over-the-shoulder kibitzing. This cannot fully explain the discrepancy, however. A more likely explanation is that, although most companies offer training, only a few of their workers actually receive it. When researchers Lisa Lynch and Sandra Black reviewed the data on training programs, they found a skewed distribution—better-educated workers, managers, professionals, and employees of large companies are more likely than others to receive company-financed training.[5] A Field Institute analysis of job skills training in California showed that about two-thirds of college graduates participated in job training. In contrast, only 43 percent of workers with high school degrees got similar opportunities.[6]

Data on training expenditures bear this out. Of the $60.7 billion allocated to training in 1998, companies slated $33.1 billion (54 percent) for managers and professionals. Training of salespeople claimed another $8.6 billion. All others received a training budget of $19.0 billion, a little less than one-third of the total. Whereas about 70 percent of the organizations surveyed train their middle managers, executives, and first-line supervisors, the folks who make the products and serve the customers get short shrift. Only 37 percent of the surveyed firms train production workers; customer service providers get training from 49 percent.[7] So in a world that calls for ever-increasing skills and knowledge to produce goods and serve customers, who gets the biggest piece of the training pie? Not goods producers and customer servers, but managers and professionals. A former Secretary of Labor and his coauthor put it bluntly: "The vast majority of American frontline workers get no further formal education and training at all after landing their first job."[8]

Besides its constrained availability in many organizations, formal training has another limitation—it is often not the best way for people to learn. In 1996, the Education Development Center (EDC) began an analysis of learning in the workplace. They started with a simple but powerful premise—the long-term employability and flexibility of American workers depend on their ability to learn on the job.[9] They based their study of what they came to call "the teaching firm" on a 1996 U.S. Department of Labor Statistics report that said that as much as 70 percent of all workplace learning may be informal. The EDC defined *informal learning* as the individual's gaining of knowledge in ways not determined by the organization. Informal learning takes place when an employee asks a peer how to use the graphics software, how to find a document in the electronic library, or how to file a dental claims form. The pervasiveness of continuous, casual learning should come as no surprise at this stage in our discussion. We know that people share a common drive to increase their competence through an autonomous approach to doing their jobs. Support for competence building is a key organizational value; when it is present, people do not wait until they enter a classroom to start acquiring skills and knowledge.

There are few pure types of either formal or informal learning; each typically incorporates some elements of the other. Nevertheless, the two approaches generally differ in important ways. Exhibit 7.1 summarizes the differences.

Informal learning has some advantages worth noting:

- Because people can choose what they need and want to learn, their learning efforts are relevant and focused on their immediate requirements. With formal training, the relevance of material is bound to vary among the people in the class.

- Informal learning usually involves picking up the next piece of information or taking an incremental step in understanding. Material delivered in formal training may be old hat to some and too advanced for others.

- Informal learners define how they will gain the knowledge they need and must take initiative to piece the parts together. Formal training is more packaged and more homogenized.

Exhibit 7.1.   Characteristics of Informal and Formal Learning.

Informal Learning	Formal Learning
Highly relevant to individual needs	Relevant to some, not so relevant to others
Learning varies across learners— learners learn different things, depending on need	Learning expected to be constant across learners—learners all exposed to the same thing
Small gap between current and target knowledge	Variable gaps between current and target knowledge
Learner decides how learning will occur	Trainer decides how learning will occur
Immediate applicability ("just-in-time learning")	Variable time to applicability—could be close to learning, well before, or well after
Occurs in work setting	Occurs in nonwork setting (often)

Source: Adapted from Center for Workforce Development, Education Development Center, Inc., *The Teaching Firm: Where Productive Work and Learning Converge* (Newton, Mass.: Center for Workforce Development, Education Development Center, Jan. 1998), p. 177.

- People learn informally on the job and can apply what they learn at once. Formal training often occurs in nonwork locations and at times scheduled for group, rather than individual, convenience.

Perhaps the prevailing asset-centric view of workers pushes management toward conventional but only marginally effective training investment. If workers are assets, then the more knowledge you pour into them, the greater is their worth to the organization. Like passive vessels, they have more value full than empty, so companies set about to fill them up with the elixir of learning. The rub is that no matter how you measure it, the traditional pour-the-knowledge-into-their-heads approach to training falls short in two ways: it neither takes full advantage of an individual's capacity for learning nor capitalizes on an organization's ability to provide learning opportunities. Workers are not jars to be filled; they are active participants in the quest to fill themselves with learning. Workers are human capital owners who need control over learning processes and participation in the creation and communication of wisdom.

IN PRAISE OF GUT FEEL

We have seen a few reasons for the pedagogical advantages informal learning has, in some situations, over formal learning. Some observers of conventional training methods believe, however, that its flaws lie deeper. They see the inadequacies as rooted in an incomplete understanding of the neuroprocessing systems of the human brain and body.

In Western society, we have come to accept the dualism represented by the ideas of René Descartes, the seventeenth-century French philosopher and mathematician. Descartes advocated a clean, clear split between mind and body. Not only are the two distinct, he argued, but the mind is also the more important in defining the essential self. *Cogito ergo sum,* he said; I think, therefore I am. He relegated the body to a secondary position, bestowing on it the distinctly less noble status of biological vessel. In Descartes' view, the body exists chiefly to house the mind and carry it from place to place.[10]

The separation of mind and body has influenced the modes of knowledge delivery chosen by both schools and businesses. Fully 88 percent of the organizations surveyed by *Training* magazine in 1998 said that at least some of their training courses require people to sit in chairs, away from their work, and listen to someone talk.[11] The subliminal message—train the mind and don't worry about the body. Another view, more common in Eastern philosophy, says that the body also has a role to play in the absorption of knowledge. As an alternative to Cartesian dualism, Antonio Damasio, doctor and professor of neurology at the University of Iowa College of Medicine, proposes what he calls the "somatic-marker hypothesis."[12] He observes that in many situations involving complex decisions, people do not have the time (or the capability) to analyze an array of variables and come to a rational choice. At some point, most of us go with a feeling. Damasio is talking about (and giving legitimacy to) good old-fashioned gut feel: "Because the feeling is about the body, I gave the phenomenon the technical term *somatic* state ('soma' is Greek for body); and because it 'marks' an image, I called it a *marker*. . . . In short, *somatic markers are a special instance of feelings generated from secondary emotions.* Those emotions and feelings *have been connected, by learning, to predicted future outcomes of certain scenarios.* When a negative somatic marker is juxtaposed to a particular future outcome the combination functions as an alarm bell. When a positive somatic marker is juxtaposed instead, it becomes a beacon of incentive."

How does a person gain a set of functioning somatic markers? Not by sitting in class, mind engaged and body detached, while an instructor dumps knowledge in through a funnel. Here again, the Eastern point of view is instructive. Ikujiro Nonaka, a professor specializing in knowledge management at the University of California at Berkeley Haas School of Business, describes the Japanese point of view on product development and market analysis: "In developing the products and identifying the markets, Japanese firms encourage the use of judgment and knowledge formed through interaction with customers—and by personal bodily experience rather than by 'objective,' scientific conceptualization. Social interaction between individuals, groups and organizations is fundamental to organizational knowledge creation in Japan."[13]

Individual autonomy to cope with the chaos of a new situation promotes learning by both mind and body. Indeed, it is chiefly by discovering personal meaning and making individual choices in uncertain situations that we learn how to gain control of such situations; uncertainty and the exercise of personal control are therefore inseparable.[14] In Nonaka's words, "Chaos or discontinuity can generate new patterns of interaction between individuals and their environment. Individuals recreate their own systems of knowledge to take account of ambiguity, redundancy, noise, or randomness generated from the organization and its environment."[15]

So get those people out of the classroom and into the field to deal with a customer problem, or manage an unfamiliar project, or fix a quality glitch. They may make a few mistakes, but they will learn faster than they would by staring at a white board. They will also develop a gut feel about what works and what does not—something that no amount of classroom time will ever give them.

Does all this mean that organizations should chuck their formal training programs? Not just yet; as we will see, formal training has a place in the human capital–building strategy.

SHARING TACIT KNOWLEDGE

Scholars like Ikujiro Nonaka identify two basic forms of knowledge: tacit and explicit.[16] *Tacit knowledge* encompasses what people know but cannot readily express. They pass it along through actions, symbols, analogies, metaphors, and other representations of cognizance. *Explicit* or *codified knowledge* refers to knowledge that people create and transmit through formal, systematic language. Table 7.1 gives examples of both types and suggests how each form may exist within, and pass between, individuals and groups.

This model suggests that much of the insight an individual (or a group) needs to do work is subliminal, submerged, and out of the

Table 7.1. Where to Find Tacit and Explicit Knowledge.

Types of Knowledge	Individual	Group
Explicit	• Job skills • Design rules • Procedures	• Best practices • Stories • Work processes
Tacit	• Intuition • Know-how • Common sense • Judgment	• Rules of thumb • Traditions • Sources of information • Requirements for survival

Source: Adapted from P. A. Galagan, "The Search for the Poetry of Work," *Training and Development,* Oct. 1993, p. 36.

reach of formal training. Knowledge and skill go beyond what is in the procedure manual (the explicit stuff) to encompass the sub rosa tricks that let people use the manual more efficiently. At one large copier company, for example, repair technicians circumnavigated the elaborate, sophisticated expert system intended to guide them through a repair procedure. They avoided laboriously working their way down the sequence of yes-no questions intended to diagnose problems (and do much of their thinking for them). Instead, they would skip ahead to check the answers and then apply judgment to choose the most plausible next step.[17] Rather than follow the diagnostic map, they improvised with it, using their own judgment and experience to plot a course.

Real work practice consists largely of this kind of pragmatic, impromptu exploration. Susan Stucky, associate director of the Institute for Research on Learning (IRL), a not-for-profit organization that studies how people learn, calls this "the messy, swampy stuff" that defines how people work and learn to work.[18] There is simply no way a teacher (or videotaper or CD creator) can translate it into training media. Consequently, the best way to transfer tacit knowledge among people is to create and capitalize on opportunities to put those who have knowledge together with those who need it.

Create an Environment That Supports Informal Learning

EDC researchers pinpointed thirteen work activities where most informal learning occurs.[19] Team participation emerged as the number one venue for informal learning. EDC researchers then identified a set of general factors that add to the power of teams to foster informal learning:

- Authority to decide outcomes
- Clear and achievable team goals, with sufficient time and resources to reach the goals
- Diverse perspectives among team members, supported by a climate of tolerance for risk taking
- Cooperative problem solving and collective decision making
- Effective leadership

- Reward structure tied to the meeting of goals
- Job security, so people know they will be around to apply what they make the effort to learn

After analyzing the research findings, EDC staff divided informal learning into four categories: *pragmatic* (specific knowledge and skills required for the job), *intrapersonal* (individual skills for navigating the workplace, solving problems, and coping with change), *interpersonal* (interacting, cooperating, and working with groups and other individuals), and *cultural* (understanding organizational norms and behavioral expectations).[20] EDC researchers used field analysis at companies like Boeing, Ford, Siemens, and Motorola to test and refine their understanding of informal learning.

At Motorola, the EDC studied the impact of informal learning, particularly team structures, on production performance. Researchers discovered several kinds of teams already in place at the Motorola facility they visited. Most were total customer satisfaction (TCS) teams—voluntary, short-term, project-focused teams that had their roots in a corporate initiative formed in 1989. In other cases, Motorola had established teams to address specific strategic problems that managers at the division level had identified. As one manager told the EDC researchers, "The real work of TCS teams offers a better applied learning environment than *any* classroom simulation."[21] Motorola's teams exhibited their own variations of the characteristics that support informal learning.[22]

- *Autonomy.* Team membership was voluntary. Teams were left to their own initiative to work out solutions to the problems they identified. They could choose to work on any aspect of a subject related to a business objective. Each team had an engineer or supervisor serving as an adviser, but team leaders generally came from direct labor staff.
- *Strategic focus.* Management expected the teams to select a project related to current business objectives. They were urged to identify customer requirements, set aggressive goals, benchmark best practices, use sophisticated analytical techniques, and institutionalize improvements by sharing their solutions with other Motorola teams. Teams had limited life spans; the average Motorola team lasted nine months.

- *Training support.* Team members received formal course training touching on such subjects as team building, statistical process control, use of analytical techniques, and other aspects of quality.

Of course, these are useful criteria for constructing teams even when informal learning is not an explicit team goal. Still, it is interesting to contemplate the possibility that teams constructed to be fertile learning mechanisms may not only generate more learning but also produce better direct business results.

To establish a relationship between team-generated learning and business outcomes, the EDC looked at the performance of Motorola's teams over twenty-one months, from January 1994 through September 1995. They correlated an informal learning proxy (the number of voluntary teams joined by employees) with three results measures: cost, quality, and cycle time. In three of the four departments they studied, the EDC researchers found statistically significant relationships between informal learning and lower cost. Informal learning also correlated with reduced cycle time in three departments.[23]

For one of the four departments observed, the EDC had enough information to calculate the return on Motorola's investment in informal learning. Investment consisted of the worker time spent in team meetings and activities, the cost of formal training given to team members, and the administrative expenses associated with the TCS process. They estimated that savings in production costs attributable to team activities were three to five times higher than the associated costs.[24] The EDC research team noted that their analysis of informal learning did not count the benefits of production cost savings in future years. This opens the door for another intriguing speculation—suppose a major benefit of workplace teams comes not in the near-term improvements they generate but in the learning they encourage—learning that produces benefits in future periods with little or no additional cost.

Encourage Communities of Practice

Etienne Wenger, a senior research scientist at the IRL, uses the term *communities of practice* to describe the informal, emergent work groups that form in the workplace. We can think of communities of practice as a special kind of team—one that coalesces organically, without official designation (or even recognition) by management.

Communities of practice form because people develop associations with each other while they work.[25] Salespeople and technicians who cooperate to solve a class of client problems, neighbors who band together to organize a cleanup campaign, secretaries and document producers who find a better way to control paper flow—each is a community of practice. Community members confer, collaborate, share information, and teach one another. They do all this not because the boss says they have to or the organization chart puts them in the same box. They do it because they need each other to get the job done. Organizational position and level have little to do with communities of practice. They embrace people regardless of title, education, or number of company training courses taken. Organizational boxology specifies what management thinks takes place in a company; communities of practice say more about what really happens.[26]

The IRL's Stucky tells the story of a group of Hewlett-Packard engineers who had been working toward master's degrees in electrical engineering at Stanford University.[27] When the group was moved two hours north of Palo Alto to Santa Rosa, commuting to campus became impossible. So that these students could continue their course work, lectures were videotaped and sent to them for showing in a classroom setting. A paraprofessional tutor (a practicing engineer without prior teaching experience) went along to stimulate class discussion. The tutor stopped the videotape every five to ten minutes to encourage questions and challenges. Students received handouts and homework identical to that given to the on-campus group, and their performance was evaluated in essentially the same way. At the end of the course, they earned higher grades than groups that had received direct classroom transmission or untutored video instruction. Moreover, to everyone's surprise, they also scored higher than students who took the class live.

Social learning theory may explain why. It turns out that the students in the Santa Rosa group were not simply a random gaggle of engineers. They had known each other before the class and had formed a community of practice. Consequently, they spoke a common language and shared a set of experiences. These provided the context for discussing and applying what they gleaned from the videotape. The moral of the story: "It pays to look at the social conditions. . . . Once one does, one finds that social processes in teams and their collaborative work practices have a lot to do with a group's performance in terms of learning and work."[28] In other words, learning is social (not individual) and acquired from peer interaction (not merely from instructors).

THE VALUE OF FRIENDSHIP

Everyone, it seems, loves telecommuting. Workers appreciate it because it cuts down on commuting time, frees them from the interruptions of the office environment, and lets them work in their pajamas. Bosses think it improves morale, reduces space cost, and increases productivity.[29] What it does not do very well, however, is promote the networks that make work a socially engaging, productive activity.

Advocates of work-away-from-work arrangements say that the individual and social aspects of work are completely separable—another form of dualism. People can do individual work perfectly well, they argue, from home or from any other place that accommodates a PC and a reading lamp. There lies the fallacy, according to the researchers at the IRL: "Individual work and social work are not naturally disjoint: one flows into the other; the need to collaborate with someone grows out of individual work; the result of a collaboration or communication, in turn, refocuses individual work."[30]

Friendships are one casualty of work-at-home arrangements. Conventional wisdom posits that friendships among the members of working groups may harm the group's performance. Social interaction, some observers believe, promotes frivolity rather than fruitfulness.[31] But in fact, results of one recent research study suggest that workplace friendship improves working efficiency. Researchers at the Universities of Pennsylvania and Minnesota found that work groups composed of friends outperformed groups whose members were merely acquaintances. Their conclusions pertained to both physical tasks requiring motor skills (a group model-building exercise) and decision-making jobs calling for cooperative judgment (evaluating applications for graduate school). The research pinpointed four specific reasons for the superior performance of friendship groups:[32]

1. Commitment to the group. Identifying with their friends encouraged members to work harder to protect both group and individual identity; harder work led to better performance.

2. Cooperation. Members in the group of friends helped each other on tasks and thereby increased both effort and rate of production.

3. Monitoring. Groups comprising friends tended to assess progress against deadlines and calculate the amount of work remaining to reach the team goal; this improved their collective chance of completing the task on time.

4. Information sharing. Increased exchange of information among friends made valuable insights critical to the task available to all group members.

If we do our best work in groups of friends, then what does the organization gain from sending people home to work? In pushing people out of the organizational mother ship, management may have reduced flashy office space as an expense and a symbol of corporate excess. But have we gone too far? We draw ever closer to the company without place, existing only symbolically in electronic addresses. Let us not forget that we humans are, after all, a gregarious species. We need critical mass to ignite our energies and fuel our creative fires.[33] John Donne had a message for modern managers when he wrote, "No man is an island."[34]

How can managers encourage communities of practice to form and function? They can start by realizing that communities of practice are already engaged in learning throughout any large organization. Wherever people need to learn and adapt to get the job done, practice communities have likely emerged informally, of their own accord. However, managers can do (and avoid doing) a few things to help both mature and incipient communities.[35] First, the dos:

- Recognize them when you see them, if for no other reason than to avoid disrupting their progress.

- Give them a few resources: use of a conference room, a company-funded get-together, a billboard on the Intranet.

- If they come up with something great, challenge them to find ways of promulgating their insights.

- Legitimize their work, and value the learning they create.

- Let them extend their communities outside the boundaries of the organization; they may give away some valuable information, but they will bring some back as well.

And here are the don'ts:

- Don't think you can create a community of practice by management fiat; they evolve naturally or not at all.
- Don't fund them too much, force them to develop a charter, or compel them to produce something management defines unilaterally.
- Avoid the temptation to declare them an organizational unit and give them a box on the chart.

Fine, you say—communities of practice sound just great. You pledge to let them evolve and learn and not to inhibit their growth. But what if you identify strategically important aspects of knowledge that no existing community owns? What direct action can an organization take to develop the knowledge it needs to win in the marketplace?

One answer focuses on the boundary-spanning role of a broker who can carry information or bring about cooperation.[36] A broker knows enough about the substance of several practices to have credibility with members in more than one group. Such a person can bring new information to a practice or focus several practices on a common problem. A sales representative who is conversant with the technical side, a hospital administrator who used to be a nurse, a human resource generalist who once worked in the field—each may function as a broker who can pass through practice boundaries to forge truly cross-functional teams. Recognize them, encourage them, reward them, and give them time to play the broker role, for they can energize communities to concentrate on problems critical to the larger organization.

Ultimately, communities of practice are too evanescent to be engineered. It is possible, however, to combine formal training with social learning to ensure that critical knowledge emerging from practice communities spreads beyond the communities themselves. In the next section, we will define the steps organizations must take to distribute the knowledge developed in practice communities. By doing so, they turn local wisdom into an asset accessible to the organization at large.

TRANSMITTING EXPLICIT KNOWLEDGE

The discussion to this point has emphasized the value of informal learning and its principal result—the transfer of tacit knowledge from those who have it to those who need it. However, not all knowledge is tacit. There is also an explicit form, which has some valuable characteristics. Chief among these is durability. Explicit knowledge, once captured in a tangible manifestation, can remain with an organization long after the people who created and documented it have left. No matter how hard you try to retain the owners of your most valuable human capital, you are bound to lose a few you would rather have kept. (Chapter Eight considers the issues surrounding the retention of human capital investors.) Still, the reality of an active and efficient labor market means that organizations owe it to their other stakeholders to transform some human capital into a more permanent form.

Create Synergies Between Formal and Informal Learning

At this point in the discussion, one might conclude that formal training is the red-headed stepchild of human capital–building strategy. However, formal training has advantages over informal learning for some kinds of learning needs. Investment in formal training can be particularly valuable, for example, when:

- Information is especially complex or best conveyed in concentrated bursts that require full attention for comprehension.

- Subject matter requires the use of abstract concepts or models that do not have immediate application on the job.

- Topics pertain to the organization as a whole rather than to the specific job.

- Many workers need the same knowledge and skills at the same time.

- Facilitated sharing of experiences and perspectives enriches learning significantly.

Classroom training can be effective, for example, in teaching workers the financial and general business concepts that underlie openbook management. Imagine how workers in a classroom setting could debate and refine the business unit contribution map created by our friends at Perpetual Petals. Organizations seldom stick with pure forms of either formal or informal learning. Peer feedback meetings, mentoring programs, various forms of on-the-job training, learning centers stocked with books and videotapes—all represent points on a continuum that has informal learning on one end and training on the other.

Results of the EDC's work at Motorola suggested that strong ties can and should exist between what people learn while they work and what they learn in classrooms. Each form draws strength and momentum from the other. Monika Aring, codirector of the teaching-firm project, says, "The key message we're trying to get across is that corporate management can realize huge gains on the money it spends on formal training by improving the relationship between training and informal learning."[37]

When you talk with professional trainers about linking formal and informal learning, however, the discussion often heads in the direction of explicit design steps: needs analysis, curriculum development, delivery mechanisms. "What about just going to the workers and asking, 'How can we help?'" Etienne Wenger suggests. "I believe the best way to link formal training and informal learning is to go into the practice, look for formal training events to extract, and then try to figure out how to integrate those back into the practice."[38]

Wenger's suggestion about how to link formal and informal learning carries some provocative implications for the training departments of large corporations. They can set for themselves two separate but related goals. The first is to seek out teams and communities of practice and provide the targeted instruction that would help the members do their jobs better. The second is to become the means for extracting tacit knowledge from teams and communities, formalizing it, and spreading it across the organization.

What does all this mean for professional trainers? How should they spend their time? Certainly not secreted behind cubicle walls compiling next year's training catalog. Trainers should (indeed, must) consider ways to reinvent themselves.

TRAINERS SHOULD BECOME CONSULTANTS   They should search out teams and communities of practice and approach them with two questions. First, what do you need to know that would make your jobs easier and your performance better? Motorola answered this question with training focused on team dynamics and analytical processes. Second, of the knowledge produced, what aspects address strategic needs in other parts of the organization? Perhaps the company wants to improve customer service or product quality or speed of new-product introduction. Trainer-consultants can find the units that do it best now and look for the communities that may already exist in the organizational vicinity. They can seek out the bands of sales reps, technicians, or customer servers who have developed know-how that, with a little tweaking, could help the rest of the company. Trainers should confer with the members of practices and with the brokers between practices to decide how formal training can accelerate and spread learning.

TRAINERS SHOULD PRACTICE ETHNOGRAPHY   Libby Bishop of the IRL suggests that trainers adopt the live-in observational approach that the IRL itself uses with clients.[39] An ethnographer studies a population by moving in and cohabitating with it. Trainers should do the same: find people doing excellent work, sit next to them, and watch them do it, noting the elegance with which they accomplish their tasks. Through close observation of one group, trainers can identify knowledge and skills that could help other workers do things even better.

TRAINERS SHOULD BECOME TRAINERS OF TRAINERS   Let those who can, teach. Having searched out the places where good things happen, trainers should identify who in those places can best pass on the wisdom developed. The doers may need to learn how to teach others; this is an ideal role for the professionals in the training department.

TRAINING BUDGETERS SHOULD SEE THE BIG PICTURE   Regardless of the approach they take to training, companies must still set budgets and manage their investment of training dollars. Like lunch, training isn't free. Whether the bill comes as salary to an instructor, fees to a consultant, or tuition for outside classes, someone ultimately has to write a check. Classic human capital theory says that firms should pay only for the development of skills and knowledge that directly benefit the organization. Here is how Eric Flamholtz and John Lacey address the issue in their monograph on human capital theory:

> Possibly the most important implications of human capital for personnel decision making flow from the concept that expenditures on training may be investments in the sense that someone will earn a return on them. In the case of general training the returns will be earned by the employee; consequently it is an investment for the

trainee. Returns from specific training may accrue mainly to the employer; consequently it is an investment of the employer. . . . Any general training provided free may be viewed as a direct transfer payment to the employee. Such expenditures will provide little or no future benefit to the employer and should not be viewed as an investment which will yield direct returns.[40]

It seems clear enough—if training helps the company, pay for it. If it only helps the worker develop general skills and knowledge (which she could cash in at another company), let the worker pay with her own time and money. Fortunately for prospective paying organizations, much of the learning that goes on in the workplace requires little or no direct investment. Thoughtful structuring of teams or a bit of grease-the-skids funding for an emerging community of practice drains very little from the corporate coin bank.

The complexity increases, however, when we contemplate more costly investments in worker learning. How should companies decide whether and when to put hard dollars into training? The expected return on that investment is one factor, of course. A company's direct ROI from training is difficult to calculate, but the literature does contain some useful guidelines. Still, pure financial ROI does not answer all the necessary questions. An equally important concern has to do with the ROI_w value of company-provided training. If training bolsters ROI_w enough to increase worker commitment to the organization, then it may be a smart investment simply for its power to improve employee retention.

In any event, competitive advantage comes from having more knowledge (and other forms of human capital) than the next company and putting it to better use. No organization should withhold a training investment simply because the learning could conceivably benefit another organization. To do so would be like not drilling your basketball players because some might become free agents next year. A better idea is to develop them well so they win the championship and decide to stick with a successful team.

Set Up a Knowledge Marketplace

Transformation is another response to increasing worker mobility; if you cannot hang on to the people, at least hang on to the artifacts of their human capital investment.

Companies often refer to knowledge as a resource to be managed. Suppose we take that notion and elaborate on it to create a richer metaphor—by considering an internal marketplace that accelerates knowledge transformation and distribution. To function effectively, a knowledge marketplace requires the same components you would find in any other efficient market: a product, a willing producer and seller, a needful customer, and a medium of exchange.

The product is tacit knowledge changed into an explicit, enduring form: a document, a computer disk, a CD. The buyer's need for the product arises because for some reason (distance, perhaps) he cannot join a community of practice or otherwise get access to what the knower knows. This creates an opportunity for an in-the-know producer-seller to create a knowledge product and get it to the customer, to the benefit of both. Something of value must pass between customer and provider to complete the transaction.

When we talk about parties to the exchange, a third entity—neither producer-seller nor customer—enters the picture. The organization has its own knowledge transformation and transmission interests. These may include, but extend beyond, the interests of individual producers and buyers. Professional service firms, for example, want desperately for the London office to share its databases and client service approaches with the folks in New York, Los Angeles, and Singapore. People in those locations may look no farther than their neighbors down the hall when they need a new idea or a bit of information. Solutions that lie outside their literal or figurative neighborhoods may be too hard to find. Conversely, people who have full-time jobs may not want to make the effort to build knowledge products out of what they know, however valuable their insights might be to others in the organization.

Sometimes addressing these issues may be as easy as getting teams, communities, and individuals to share the insights they generate spontaneously as part of their work. In other cases, the organization may see potential for pulling together and enhancing knowledge that lies fragmented across the company. In the quest to encourage the transformation and distribution of this more explicit form of knowledge, the organization can play several different roles:

- Uncovering knowledge worthy of transformation and transmission
- Funding the transformation and distribution process

• Providing incentives to producer-sellers and customers, thereby injecting energy into the knowledge marketplace

UNCOVER WORTHY KNOWLEDGE   Assume that the management of an organization has learned of some insight, information, or skill that has emerged somewhere and could have value elsewhere in organization. The next step is to sleuth out the hidden knowledge and bring it to light. One problem with knowledge is that it is, after all, intangible. Tasteless, odorless, colorless, it is like a gas that permeates the organizational atmosphere, unnoticed but present nonetheless. Typically you will know it by the results you see, but you may have to go hunting to find out how locally developed knowledge helped boost the numbers. At Europe's Rank Xerox, a team with representatives from sales, service, and administration set out to find the best revenue-producing practices within the organization.[41] After a few weeks of analyzing sales data, the team found eight cases of dramatically strong performance. They then undertook active information extraction, sending members to each country identified as having a successful revenue-building approach. Some organizations find that chartering a SWAT team to find and document models, processes, and information can be a useful way to get at hidden nuggets of value.

FUND TRANSFORMATION   The precious metal of tacit knowledge sometimes lies deeply embedded in organizational ore. Transformation turns the raw material of tacit knowledge into the explicit form that can be used by the uninitiated. At Rank Xerox, the search team compiled their best-practices information into a book describing what the top performers did and the results they achieved.[42] That kind of effort usually requires a group of dedicated people to do information collection and product development. Because the result has broad application, the organization can expedite the process by paying for the time, travel costs, materials, and analytical support necessary to develop the knowledge product.

PROVIDE INCENTIVES TO PRODUCERS AND USERS   As with any other market system, currency exchange lubricates the machinery of transaction. For knowledge that springs in usable form directly from group and individual work, informally denominated payment may suffice to keep the product flowing. Tom Davenport and Larry Prusak identify three forms of interpersonal payment that can pass between the providers and buyers of information: reciprocity (help me later if I help you now), repute (recognize me publicly as an information source), and altruism (don't give me anything—I'll help because I know it benefits you and the company).[43]

For more elaborate transformation efforts, companies should use formal incentives to reward the team that successfully creates a knowledge product. The terms should be familiar by now—ROI_w commensurate with the human capital contributed by team members. Organizations should convey, through promotions, formal and informal recognition, and financial rewards, a single, critical point—that creators of valuable, broadly applicable manifestations of knowledge are as important to the company as those who make and sell the company's products.

Design the Knowledge Product for Maximum Appeal

In any market system, product features play a crucial role. Sometimes ideas and information require only modest transformation; people can readily apply successful sales and service techniques, for instance, much as conceived by the originators. At other times, refining and upgrading original knowledge may call for more complex transformation efforts.

To this point, we have used terms like *data, knowledge,* and *information* more or less interchangeably. Let us separate them now to emphasize the stages of transformation. Take as an example the compilation and promulgation of competitor data in the credit card business. If you are Visa, MasterCard, or American Express, you have keen interest in your competitors' card issuance numbers for recent past periods. Chances are your domestic and international regions have the figures, but the regions (and the figures) are spread out literally around the globe. By themselves, these *data* (bits of factual knowledge that form the raw material for transformation) may have little value. Add some context, however (for instance, several years' worth of figures) and format the numbers so that they reveal patterns, and you transform data into *information.* Some organizations stop there, even though information does not capture the full potential of embedded utility; more latent value remains. By delving into information, analyzing patterns, and identifying root causes and driving forces, an organization can turn information into *intelligence.* For example, if you know that a

competitor's streamlined development process speeds product introduction and increases sales volume, you have invaluable intelligence
for formulating your own new-product response. The final step in
transformation is to turn intelligence into *information capital.* This transformation comes about when organizations do the following:

- Identify which forms of intelligence have the greatest strategic
  value and institutionalize the processes for their acquisition and
  analysis.
- Share the intelligence among key users through suitably
  designed information channels.
- Create formal processes for incorporating the intelligence into
  the planning and execution of competitive strategy.

Figure 7.1 illustrates the process.

A useful information capital product should incorporate these
features:

- Context: introductory, framework-setting material that tells the
  user how the knowledge works, how it solves problems, and
  what skills and resources are required for its application.
- Comprehensiveness: answers, or sources for answers, to all concerns addressed by the product. The product may not (indeed,
  usually should not) contain every iota of intelligence on a subject, but it should have enough depth to tell the user whether a
  particular aspect solves his problem and then point him to a
  more detailed explanation.
- Accessibility: distribution in a form that allows the least computer initiated to stumble along with few impediments. If it
  takes a nerd to get at the necessary knowledge, it might as well
  lie buried in a Mayan tomb.
- Layers: arrangement so the user can dive deeply into the information or navigate comfortably near the surface.
- Connection to the source: encouragement for users to contact
  the folks who contributed particular bits of wisdom to the
  product.
- Training support: instruction available from the practitioners
  who developed the product. This can range from formal,

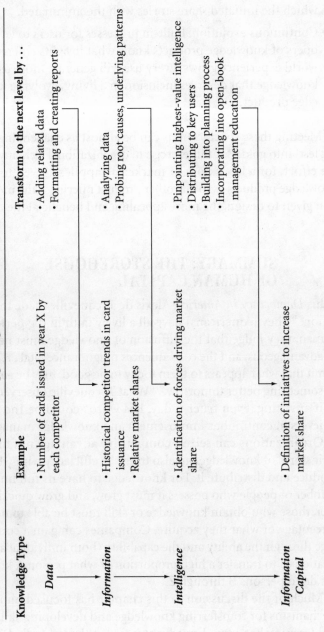

Figure 7.1. Upgrading Data to Information Capital.

Knowledge Type	Example	Transform to the next level by . . .
Data	• Number of cards issued in year X by each competitor	• Adding related data • Formatting and creating reports
Information	• Historical competitor trends in card issuance • Relative market shares	• Analyzing data • Probing root causes, underlying patterns
Intelligence	• Identification of forces driving market share	• Pinpointing highest-value intelligence • Distributing to key users • Building into planning process • Incorporating into open-book management education
Information Capital	• Definition of initiatives to increase market share	

company-sponsored training (best delivered to teams and practice communities at their local sites) to informal sessions in which the initiated share stories with the uninitiated.

• Continuous evolution: built-in processes for users to let developers of knowledge products know what insights emerge as real-world experience grows. Every use will generate more useful knowledge that deserves inclusion in a living, evolving knowledge product.

Meeting these specifications can be almost as challenging as turning lead into gold. But this exercise in organizational alchemy is worth the effort, for a key axiom of marketing applies as well to internal knowledge products as to any other product offering—the more attention given to design, the more appealing and beneficial the result.

SUMMARY: THE STOREHOUSE OF HUMAN CAPITAL

In his *Democracy in America,* Alexis de Tocqueville made this observation: "They [Americans] have all a lively faith in the perfectibility of man, they judge that the diffusion of knowledge must necessarily be advantageous, and the consequences of ignorance fatal . . . and they admit that what appears to them today to be good, may be superseded by something better tomorrow."[44] What Tocqueville observed in 1835 is, if anything, even truer today. His words could be the credo of believers in continuous improvement and knowledge management.

Organizations can seize a competitive advantage not only from their stores of knowledge but also from the efficiency with which they produce and distribute it. For knowledge to have its full impact, the number of people who possess it must grow, and grow quickly. Moreover, those who obtain knowledge or skill must be able to use a high percentage of what they acquire. Companies can gain a competitive edge through the ability and the capability (both individual and organizational) to transfer a high proportion of what person A knows and can do to persons B through Z.

Much of the discussion in this chapter has focused on informal mechanisms for transferring knowledge and developing skills. Informal learning has some key advantages, not the least of which is the speed with which learning occurs. Teams and communities of practice create tacit knowledge merely by collecting people in one place and giving them a reason to talk about something of common interest. As the IRL's Wenger puts it, "There is no distinction between learning and social participation, and that is what makes learning possible, enduring, and meaningful."[45] Given its social nature, learning is far too spontaneous to be shrink-wrapped and confined to a three-ring binder. It intertwines much too tightly with work practice for restriction to a classroom.

And yet classroom learning has a place in most human capital–building strategies. A catalyst for communities of practice, a facilitator of knowledge sharing, a clearinghouse for best practices—these are the roles to which training departments should aspire. Those that can reinvent themselves along these lines can find a place as contributors to the storehouse of human capital. They do so by helping companies make tacit knowledge explicit and by getting explicit knowledge into the hands—and minds—of more people.

After completing their work at Motorola and other organizations with advanced learning strategies, EDC researchers concluded that organizational culture profoundly affects informal learning. Although we haven't used the label *culture,* we could apply that term to the investment-eliciting factors from Chapters Five and Six. We can see how some of those investment-supporting elements could act as prerequisites not only for human capital investment but also for encouraging learning. Remember these four elements:

1. *Competence seeking,* which both supports investment and grows as a result of knowledge and skill development

2. *Autonomy,* another factor that underlies the investment of human capital and contributes to the effectiveness of informal learning activities

3. *Reinforcement* of individual and group effort, a stimulus for the human capital investment required to seek out and transform individual and local knowledge

4. *Alignment* between knowledge-building efforts and business strategy, a contextual factor addressed in Chapter Five and a prerequisite for maximizing the value of knowledge products

Each factor has two effects: contributing to human capital growth and encouraging its investment. Each therefore represents an opportunity for organizations to achieve a human capital double dip—two benefits for the price of one.

Any company that wants to influence the future must find ways not only to support the social development of individual learning but also to hold on to those individuals. When you get right down to it, organizations do not learn, any more than they own the human capital of their workers. The "learning organization" is a worthy metaphor for the collective ability of a group to expand continuously its capacity to create its future.[46] The coming together and cooperation of learning individuals create such an organization, however. Human capital is, in the words of *Fortune* writer Thomas Stewart, "like a joint checking account on which both you and your employer can draw."[47] Therefore, the question for would-be managers of human capital holders and investors is not this: "How do we control our investment in human capital building so people learn only what they can use in our company?" Instead, it is this: "Given that we have helped build employees' human capital, how do we keep them within our organization and investing in the organization's interests?"

We take up that question in Chapter Eight.

CHAPTER EIGHT

Holding On to Human Capital Investors

I f you had to pick a fairy tale to represent the modern workplace experience, which would you choose? *The Emperor's New Clothes*, perhaps, to reflect the self-delusion and hubris of some CEOs? Maybe *Jack and the Beanstalk*, to underscore that one can prosper through hard work and cunning? My choice would be *The Ugly Duckling*. In this tale, a homely hatchling is rejected by his mother and his adopted duckling brethren. Rejection later becomes acceptance (indeed, praise and envy) for the mature version of the same qualities that had offended his barnyard buddies. This process of rejection followed by acceptance must seem familiar to workers who felt unloved in the late 1980s and early 1990s. Scarcely half a decade later, they suddenly found themselves in demand, swans in a labor market that became, from the employer perspective, strictly for the birds.

But don't kid yourself; we haven't seen the last buyer's market for human capital. The persistence of labor market oscillation makes one pause to wonder: As employment conditions vary, do worker attitudes toward job stability change? Evidence I have seen suggests that workers' feelings about sticking with their employers seem to stay remarkably constant from one market to the next. For example, 58 percent of the participants in a 1988–1991 National Opinion Research Center analysis said that they were not at all likely to leave their companies during the next twelve months.[1] In 1991, you'll recall, job elimination hit a peak, with 56 percent of companies surveyed by the American Management Association saying they had cut jobs.[2] Unemployment in Silicon Valley, that cradle of knowledge work, peaked the following year at 6.9 percent.[3] When Towers Perrin did its *Workplace Index* analysis in 1995, a tighter labor market (Silicon Valley unemployment had dropped to 5.0 percent), 61 percent of the respondents gave the same answer; they said that they were unlikely to seek new employment during the next year. We asked the question again in 1996 (Silicon Valley unemployment—less than 4.0 percent) and again got consistent results, with 62 percent saying they would not likely try to change jobs.[4] The Families and Work Institute asked respondents to its 1997 workforce survey whether they planned to make a genuine effort to change employers in the next year; 62 percent said "not at all likely." That percentage remained unchanged from the Institute's 1977 survey.[5]

This pattern emerges across the economy at large. In 1997, *Wired* magazine did a broad-ranging survey covering Americans' attitudes on everything from jobs to politics to social issues.[6] They divided their respondents into four classes, differentiated by levels of technological familiarity and proficiency. At one end of the spectrum they put the Superconnected, people who make heavy use of e-mail, cell phones, laptops, beepers, and home computers. At the other end are the Unconnected, who use none of these technologies. The Connected and Semiconnected occupy the space in the middle. *Wired* asked people in all four groups: Assuming that responsibilities and money were roughly the same, would you prefer to have one job for twenty years or five different jobs for four years each? Between two-thirds and three-quarters of the respondents in the Superconnected, Connected, and Semiconnected groups said they would rather stay put. The percentage preferring one job jumped to 82 percent for the Unconnected.

Companies thus find themselves caught between a secular pattern of people wanting to stick with an organization and a cyclical trend of defections in tight labor markets. When markets are tight, the natural response is for organizations to offer enticements to stay put, to get workers to say "not interested" when the headhunter calls. People struggle with the decision to stay or go, balancing tangible and intangible, transactional and relational elements of return on workplace investment. The struggle, though difficult, is far from irrational, however. Sam Gould of the University of Texas at Arlington has developed a model that depicts how people analyze the decision to quit. His equation generates what he calls the *net value of leaving*. The Gould model, adapted somewhat, works like this:[7]

> *Step 1.* You grow irritated by inadequate ROI_w from your present job in your current company or intrigued by the possibility that a job somewhere else offers more of something you want. In either case, you begin to doubt the relative value of your present situation. Call this ValCurrentPosition.
>
> *Step 2.* A headhunter calls to tell you about an opening for a senior vice president of something interesting at Cool Company. You're impressed with Cool Co., and you think a job there will provide a higher ROI_w. Call this higher return ValNewPosition.
>
> *Step 3.* You are not sure you can land this position, however, or that it really will be better, so incorporate a probability factor. This is ProbReallyBetter.
>
> *Step 4.* You interrupt your daydream about the value of Cool Co. options and consider the cost of leaving your present organization. Cost includes things like pensions lost and bonuses forgone (you are, after all, having a dynamite year). If you have any compunction about breaking moral obligations to your company or your team or worries about looking like a job-hopping flake, you add them in here. Let's use the term CostQuitting to refer to the total of these factors.

Putting these pieces together, you get:

$$\text{Net value of leaving} = [\text{ProbReallyBetter} \times (\text{ValNewPosition} - \text{ValCurrent Position})] - \text{CostQuitting}$$

You'll consider packing up your old kit bag if you can confidently predict that the ROI_w from a new job in a new company will beat what you have now by more than the cost of quitting. We know from earlier discussions, however, that human capital investment depends not only on ROI_w but also on the interplay of organizational environment and job attachment factors. This interplay, in turn, influences our old friends, commitment and engagement. As we'll see in a few pages, commitment and engagement have a direct effect on whether a worker stays with an organization or leaves for greener pastures.

Whereas Chapters Four through Seven dealt with acquiring, drawing forth, and building human capital investment capacity, this chapter is about preservation. We begin with a discussion of the analysis an organization should undertake to diagnose the worker retention challenges it faces. From there, we consider ways companies and workers together can increase the value of individual jobs and broader organizational relationships.

ANALYZING TURNOVER CAUSES

Companies facing turnover problems commonly lament their ill fortune, curse the competition that stoops to buying people with stock options, and resolve to put in retention bonuses. What they should do first is identify turnover patterns and interpret their meaning. This analysis provides a rational basis for the retention initiatives discussed in a few pages.

Figure Out Who Is at Risk

The analysis of turnover aims to identify workers who meet two criteria: they have human capital that the organization values highly and show characteristics that make them likely to depart. Companies need to search for patterns along two dimensions: when and why.

Different jobs in different companies naturally have distinct fracture points, the juncture at which people show the greatest likelihood of leaving the company. Such factors as the timing of formal advancement steps, experience required for professional certification (like the CPA), and typical lengths of project commitments all influence turnover timing. Researchers from Ohio State University and the University of Texas at Arlington looked at turnover trends covering multiple years of individual job experience. Using data from the Department of Labor's National Longitudinal Survey of Youth, they first substantiated a general relationship between job satisfaction and turnover. Their calculations showed that a one standard deviation increase in job satisfaction corresponds to a 16 percent reduction in the probability an individual will quit his job.[8]

The researchers also discovered, however, that the relationship between job satisfaction and the risk of turnover does not remain constant. Their analysis showed that the positive effect of job satisfaction on tenure lasts about four years. That is, for the first four years, workers with high job satisfaction are less likely to quit than those with low job satisfaction.[9] After four years, the effect of satisfaction appears to wear off. At that point, satisfied workers are about as likely as unsatisfied ones to get the itch to move on. Other factors, like organizational commitment, might still bind them, but the inherent satisfaction from the job has largely worn off.

For any individual company, assessment of tenure patterns will reveal whether the itch occurs at four years or some other point. Of course, the when and why of turnover are bound to intertwine. Therefore, the turnover analysis should test for patterns not only by tenure but also by these kinds of factors:

- Type of position (for example, manager, exempt, nonexempt)
- Professional classification (engineer, scientist, paraprofessional)
- Function (sales, marketing, information technology)
- Geographic location
- Facility type (factory, field office, headquarters)
- Demographics (gender, race and ethnicity, marital status)
- Education type and level
- Skill or experience type
- Performance level
- Compensation level and type (above market, below market, eligible for bonuses and stock)

The goal of a high-level turnover analysis is to uncover problems in specific populations. You know you are losing engineers but which ones? Those with special skills, or with five years' experience, or with particular kinds of responsibilities? To management, they may be strong contributors whose compensation (financial and other) hasn't fully caught up with their value to the company. To the employees themselves, they are exploited minions who can cash in their human capital for big returns (psychic and other) somewhere else.

At Cypress Semiconductor, a top-level analysis revealed that the highest proportional turnover occurs in the first and fifth years of worker tenure.[10] The Year One bulge in turnover, Cypress found, was especially heavy for nonexempt employees and direct labor workers in fabrication facilities.

This kind of analysis tells managers where trouble spots lie, but the analytical challenge does not end here. The organization needs to delve more deeply into the turnover patterns. Cypress did that, with interesting results.

Analyze Root Causes

The next stage of turnover analysis goes to the root causes of trends that emerge in the first-stage assessment. Secondary sources like managers, mentors, and peers can provide useful information about why people with particular characteristics or in specific situations might (or actually did) decide to move on. Information obtained through direct contact with employees in the at-risk groups yields the richest insights about causes of turnover and possible responses. Surveys, focus groups, and interviews of the members of at-risk populations can provide important clues about how current members view their jobs. These sources can also reveal concerns about their organizational attachments and their return on workplace investment.

Cypress took the next step in its turnover analysis by surveying employees who had been at the company for six years or more, that is, those who had survived the five-year danger point. The human resource department divided the survey population into three groups, differentiated by performance level. They used recent salary increases and number of promotions as performance indicators. It also turned out that these performance proxies correlated well with number of opportunities to leave the organization. Among respondents in the highest raise category, 42 percent had been turned around between one and three times in their six years with the company. In other words, they had decided to quit at least once but someone had talked them into staying. About 25 percent of respondents in the lowest raise category had been turned around.[11]

Table 8.1. Factors That Bind People and Companies.

Q: Why have you stayed with Cypress Semiconductor,
in spite of opportunities to leave?

| Performance Category[b] | Three Most Important Factors and Average Ratings[a] | | | | | |
| | #1 | | #2 | | #3 | |
	Factor	Rating	Factor	Rating	Factor	Rating
Top	Interesting work	8.0	Good wages	6.5	Growth opportunities	6.3
Middle	Interesting work	6.8	Good wages	6.2	Recognition	5.9
Bottom	Good wages	7.0	Stock options	6.6	Interesting work	6.3

[a]On a scale from 1 to 10, where 10 = "very important to my decision to stay" and 1 = "not at all important."

[b]Determined by salary increase percentage and number of promotions while at Cypress.

Source: Internal company documents.

Cypress asked the survey group to rate ten factors according their importance in binding people to the company. Table 8.1 shows the results for the top three factors.

The survey findings gave the company important clues about where to focus its retention-improvement efforts. For the top and middle-level performers, interesting work clearly has the greatest influence in getting people over the five-year hump. Financial elements are not trivial, but they play a distinctly subordinate role for all but the bottom group. Do the top performers shine because they focus on the job instead of the money? Do people who exhibit lower performance feel frustrated by job demands and therefore turn their attention to compensation? Perhaps those who focus chiefly on money take their eye off the ball and lose performance momentum. Or maybe the oppressive bonds of their programmatic commitment work to lessen their motivation.

Whatever the direction of causation, analysis like this begins to suggest where the organization needs to focus its attention. The data should provoke the company to ask a series of ever-more-focused questions. Consider this flowchart:

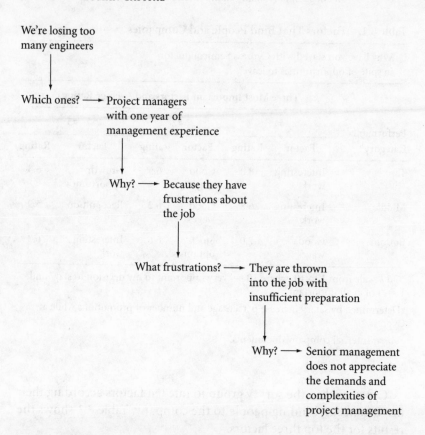

We're losing too
many engineers

Which ones? ⟶ Project managers
with one year of
management experience

Why? ⟶ Because they have
frustrations about
the job

What frustrations? ⟶ They are thrown
into the job with
insufficient preparation

Why? ⟶ Senior management
does not appreciate
the demands and
complexities of
project management

In this example, following the root-cause process would lead an organization to try solutions addressing job content and preparation for
responsibilities. Without delving for root causes, a company might
instead decide (as many have) that retention bonuses are the answer.
Appealing as that response might be, it would not go to the heart of
the problem.

This kind of analysis gives a foundation on which to build a
retention-improvement strategy. To complete the picture, however, a
company needs another bit of information.

Analyze ROI$_w$ Elements Against
Competitive Offerings

In Chapter Four, we noted the importance of having a competitive
perspective on all elements of ROI$_w$ offered at the time of hire. That
knowledge is equally important when companies face the challenge

of retaining their best human capital owners. It is a competitive world, after all; if you have good people, someone out there wants to take them away from you. Remember that dissatisfaction alone does not drive turnover. People need an alluring alternative (ValNewPosition) to break the bonds of commitment. Assessing where your organization's return-on-investment offering stands in relation to competitive offerings is a key part of the analytical foundation needed to fight and win the retention wars.

You can get the competitive information you need from a variety of sources:

- Data published in industry trade journals or provided by professional organizations to which HR staff and others belong
- Surveys available from consulting firms
- Information provided by people you hire away from your competitors, provided they stay within the bounds of confidentiality agreements
- Similar kinds of information from people who get job offers from competitors but decide to stay with your company
- Executive recruiters who focus on your industry
- Consulting firms that specialize in collecting and analyzing competitive information, often as part of their strategic planning services

Do not stop with data on the financial element of ROI_w. It takes cleverness, tenacity, and energy to get information on the other ROI_w elements, but this is critical knowledge to have, for all the reasons we know so well.

The most obvious benefit from knowing an organization's competitive position is the opportunitiy to address big ROI_w gaps. Recognizing gaps is the first step to closing them and reducing comparative disadvantages in holding on to key people. Similarly, if a company can point out the superior elements of its deal (ValCurrentPosition) to an at-risk employee, it may be possible to reduce the value of leaving to below zero.

There is another advantage, more subtle, to having an accurate competitive perspective. It has to do with the uncertainty factor (ProbReallyBetter) included in the value-of-leaving equation. This factor reflects risk, a concept we will explore further in a few pages. A worker thinking about quitting knows for sure what she has now but has only a sense of what the future (however rosy it may seem) might bring. Uncertainty runs especially high concerning the relational elements of ROI_w. An organization that can make a competitive juxtaposition places its certain offering against an unknown future, a future that must be discounted for its uncertainty. Call this the bird-in-the-hand strategy; it can work because of archetypal human aversion to risk. Underlying risk aversion is loss aversion—the tendency for people to be more sensitive to reductions in their well-being than to increases.[12] Economists have even gone so far as to put a number on relative risk aversion; they estimate that people are twice as unhappy about losing some amount as they are happy about winning the same amount.[13] The prospect of changing jobs usually carries risk; the possibility of a loss in ROI_w reduces the probability factor and therefore the potential value of leaving.

People are also averse to change. According to Denise Rousseau, "The cognitive processes involved are both lazy and conservative. People do not work hard on changing contracts or any other established mindset. People work hard on fitting experiences into them."[14] An organization that can prove it offers a competitive (even if not distinctly superior) ROI_w package may benefit from the change aversion of someone who might otherwise pack up and go.

Another principle of risk response says that people have a bias in favor of the familiar. This means that they tend to judge an event likely if they can easily remember or imagine it.[15] If a worker has prospered in your organization, the possibility of continuing prosperity may seem comfortably likely. Your company can bolster familiarity bias in two ways: by presenting credible comparative information on your deal and by creating an individual human capital investment plan that bodes well for future ROI_w. Of course, convincing someone to stay under these circumstances may constitute a new deal between organization and individual. Mutually beneficial implementation of this deal requires individual and organization alike to be mindful of the deal-execution criteria of Chapters Four through Six. Both parties should put special emphasis on the trust that underlies acceptance. Hence this warning—never offer a please-don't-quit deal you cannot live up to. It will not work long term, and the effects of broken promises will reach far beyond one individual.

INCREASING VALUE AND STRENGTHENING TIES

Chapter Two introduced the dual ideas of engagement in the job and commitment to the organization. In the human capital model, they preceded investment and grew with return on investment. They also play a role in our understanding of retention. Researchers Gary Blau and Kimberly Boal have explored the effect on retention of both factors. They defined organizational commitment in terms similar to those used in Chapter Two—the degree to which an individual identifies with the goals of an organization and wishes to maintain membership. They defined engagement (in their terms, *involvement*) as the extent to which a worker feels psychologically linked with her job.[16] Workers who have both high organizational (especially attitudinal) commitment and high job engagement display characteristics that show up on every organization's wish list:

- They value the intrinsic elements of their work.
- They value the social relationships they form at work and the financial rewards they receive.
- They outperform people with lower levels of commitment and engagement.
- They tend to want to preserve their organizational ties.

Manage the Value of the Relationship

As Exhibit 8.1 indicates, high levels of commitment and engagement reinforce each other. In its latest research, the Families and Work Institute found that "employees with better-quality jobs are substantially more likely than other employees to plan on staying with their current employers."[17] In other words, the features of a great job—which the Families and Work Institute defined as autonomy, learning opportunities, meaningfulness of the job, job security, and personal opportunities for advancement—tend to increase not only job engagement but also organizational commitment.

We'll take advantage of this convergence to advance the discussion of retention. We'll focus on ROI_w as the driver of commitment and engagement, the essence of ValCurrentPosition, and therefore the

Exhibit 8.1.   Results from Building Both Commitment and Engagement.

	Low Job Engagement	High Job Engagement
High Organizational Commitment	Value social relationships Moderate performance High propensity to stay	Value work itself, future with company, pay, social relationships Best performance Highest propensity to stay
Low Organizational Commitment	Value pay Poorest performance Moderate propensity to stay	Value work itself, working conditions, pay Moderate performance Moderate propensity to stay

Y-axis: Organizational Commitment (Low to High); X-axis: Job Engagement (Low to High)

Job Engagement

Source: Adapted from G. J. Blau and K. B. Boal, "Conceptualizing How Job Involvement and Organizational Commitment Affect Turnover and Absenteeism," *Academy of Management Review,* 1987, 12(2), and adapted from J. C. Casal, "Shoot for the 'Stars,'" *Journal of Health Care Marketing,* 1996, 16(2).

centerpiece of prolonged attachment to an organization. To simplify the discussion, we'll combine the effects of all return-on-investment elements into a single function: "Willingness to invest human capital." It subsumes both organizational ("I'm committed to staying here and making my investment in ways this organization values") and job-level ("My work is so interesting that I want to keep making a major effort") bonds. Figure 8.1 depicts the exchange of human capital for the combined bundle of ROI_w elements. The figure looks like a good old-fashioned utility curve; it shows how preference for different amounts of ROI_w affects variable willingness to invest human capital. We will return to this consolidated utility curve in Chapter Nine. We will see how to build the curve from its components and analyze the

Figure 8.1.   Equilibrium Curve of Human Capital Exchange.

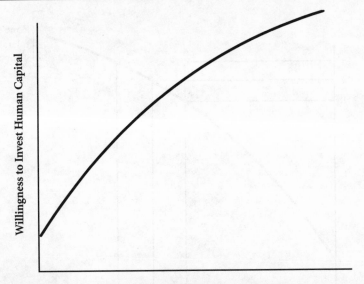

Return on Investment in Work (ROI$_w$)

costs and effects of delivering individual return-on-investment elements.

Let's think of the curve as representing a deal-focused exchange between a rational individual and an equally rational organization. The points that make up the curve denote equilibrium—exchanges of investment and return both worker and company consider fair. The shape of the curve varies by individual, reflecting unique personal propensities. The shape may also change over an individual's career. Fluctuating market demand for a particular skill or other human capital component may increase or decrease the worker's bargaining power and shift the balance of the exchange.

The objective for the organization is to prolong human capital investment by achieving and maintaining equilibrium. To do so, managers must understand all they can about the relative component weights and shapes of workers' exchange curves. Figure 8.2 shows the exchange equilibrium curve with some additional reference points. Think of point A as the equilibrium achieved by a specific job within a particular company—the product development position at Perpetual Petals, for example. At point A, the product developer invests I1 of human capital, and receives a total return of R1 on that investment.

Figure 8.2.   Points on and off the Equilibrium Exchange Curve.

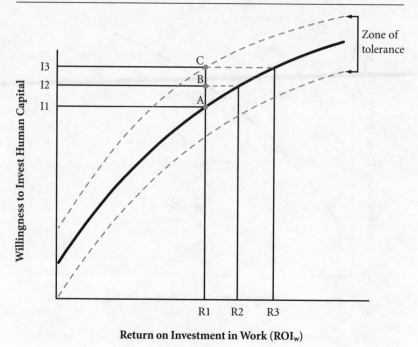

Return on Investment in Work (ROI$_w$)

Now suppose that our product developer's job lies not at point A but at B, just above the solid line curve but below the dashed line. At point B, the exchange is noticeably, if only slightly, out of kilter. As defined by Gould, the area containing point B, banded by the dashed lines above and below the solid curve, represents the zone of tolerance.[18] Within this zone, worker and company either do not perceive disequilibrium (more investment than return justifies, or vice versa) or they consider it tolerable. At point B, the product developer is willing to invest more human capital (signified by I2 on the human capital investment axis) than the point A position rewards. She still receives R1 return on investment rather than the R2 that would maintain equilibrium. She may have agreed, for example, to take on a special project (joining a team analyzing a potential acquisition, let us say) while still carrying her full product development load. If team membership turns out to be a waste of time (perhaps because of a restrictive team mandate or a clumsy structure), she will receive little personal value from participating. Because the additional human capital investment is small

(I2 − I1), our heroine takes the position and (temporarily at least) accepts the disequilibrium in the organization's favor.

Now consider point C, which lies outside the upper bound of the zone of tolerance. Here, the organization wants her to invest I3 human capital (near her maximum potential) while still receiving R1 return on her investment. Management may have persuaded her to sit on the company's public relations committee, a time-consuming job yielding no additional ROI_w save the occasional long meeting with stale doughnuts. The exchange represented by point C will not last long. The company has exploited the individual and can expect her to readjust the return-on-investment relationship.

The easiest response for the individual is to ignore the disequilibrium and continue investing human capital as before. Tolerance of a wage freeze is a common example. A person may also try to restore the lost return on investment by approaching the organization and asking for an ROI_w increase. For instance, a worker may request training to enable her to move out of a postdownsizing job that has become routine. When this is not feasible, the worker may escalate the response by withdrawing some amount of human capital investment and thereby moving back onto the equilibrium curve. Absenteeism is a common form of investment reduction. This approach appeals to workers who believe themselves powerless to change their employer's behavior.[19] If these actions prove unsatisfactory, a worker may take more radical steps. One alternative is to withdraw human capital investment completely but temporarily. Workers take this route when they go on strike. The most dramatic remedy available to the worker is, of course, to quit the organization altogether, permanently withdrawing investment. We can think of turnover, therefore, as a disequilibrium situation in which either individual or organization—or both—lack the ability or the will to define a job-specific exchange that gets them back on the equilibrium curve.

The discussion of the equilibrium curve has focused on the relationship between an individual worker and an organization. However, organizations frequently act in ways that throw whole groups of workers into disequilibrium. Redirection of strategy, mergers or acquisitions, widespread introductions of new technology—any one can disrupt the investment-ROI_w balance. A bit later in the chapter we will assess the risk management implications of large-scale change. For now, we consider how organizations can get themselves and their workers back onto the equilibrium curve.

The case of Wawa Food Markets, a company with some five hundred premium convenience stores in the mid-Atlantic region, shows how a company can take action to analyze and fix a disequilibrium problem.[20] Wawa (whose name means "wild goose" in a Native American language) is a privately held company with 1997 sales of about $1 billion. The organization employs about eleven thousand part-time store associates, of whom two-thirds are female and two-thirds fall into the Generation X category. Wawa has an aggressive growth strategy, expecting to double its revenue by 2001. This might be a modest ambition for a Silicon Valley start-up, but it's impressive for a food retailer. To achieve that goal, the organization will need twenty thousand high-performing associates in its stores—and not just any associates either, but employees capable of providing the legendary customer service that has made Wawa famous.

High turnover in stores inhibits the organization's ability to get and keep the people it will need to expand its business. With most of its attention focused on growth, management had not systematically adapted its reward systems to meet the human capital needs of the business strategy. The result has been turnover at 100 percent per year—not out of line for the retail industry but not good enough for Wawa. The organization simply is not willing to hire two associates for each position every year.

Wawa's analysis of its turnover experience showed that employee departures had little to do with money. Only 11 percent of the respondents to a survey of departing employees said insufficient pay was a problem. Instead, turnover correlated more directly with the work environment created by store managers. For employees who left the company within the first three years, concerns about management quality and behavior carried about half the weight in their decision to quit; no other single factor was nearly as important. Among those who left after three or more years with the company, concerns about management performance and work environment made up 90 percent of the rationale for quitting.

In restructuring the deal, the organization concentrated on the areas that Generation X employees said were most important: providing interesting and varied work, creating avenues for employees to control their work processes, sharing company success, and generating career advancement opportunities based on learning and skill acquisition. Most of these factors involve employee engagement in the job, and most fall under the local manager's control. A continuing initiative called "Store Manager of the Future" will improve managers' ability to deliver key ROI_w elements. The program began when the organization zeroed in on a group of about twenty exemplary store managers whose stores had achieved excellent financial results. They found that people-management skills correlated with financial success. Managers whose stores prospered tended to give informal recognition by celebrating success, to give feedback on employee performance, to support team spirit, and to take time to orient new employees. Wawa plans to use a formal training program to spread these behaviors to another one hundred managers and from there to the rest of the store network. Of course, the organization also improved its compensation and benefits packages. Wawa brought starting pay to market medians and began allowing managers flexibility to meet local market conditions. The benefits program also received two enhancements: a medical cost reimbursement account and school tuition coverage.

Any organization that wants to double revenue in four years has to have goals and numbers to manage by. Therefore, Wawa management set specific objectives for turnover reduction. The organization expects that changes in the financial aspects of its deal will produce a 10 percent drop in turnover almost immediately. Improvements in store culture and learning environment, management believes, will generate an additional 30 percent reduction by 2001.

There is no magic elixir that cures a turnover problem. An equilibrium relationship is the culmination of the full range of human capital management elements. The joint energies of individual and organization to find the right equilibrium point should reflect this broad perspective. Exhibit 8.2 summarizes the main elements of the human capital management system pieced together in Chapters Three through Seven. It incorporates ROI_w and all the other factors that determine whether worker and supervisor can find the equilibrium point that best suits both the person and the organization.

Much of the responsibility for executing the factors listed in Exhibit 8.2 falls to the first-line manager. In effect, the supervisor delivers the deal for the organization. Although the supervisor's influence works chiefly at the job level, he also functions as the agent of the organization. In that capacity, he calculates the individual's worth to the company and helps to dole out commensurate returns on investment. Supervisor behavior thus goes a long way toward determining whether individual workers develop sufficient commitment and engagement to stick with the organization.

**Exhibit 8.2.   Human Capital Management Context—
A Checklist for Assessing Equilibrium.**

Strategic Linkage
- Is it clear which organization capabilities the individual's human capital supports?
- Do organization structure, process, and technology support and complement the individual's human capital investment?

Making the Deal
- Was the deal fully communicated and agreed to during the hiring process? Did the worker and the organization agree on duration, consideration, and flexibility?
- Was the process valid from both individual and organizational perspectives?
- Did the deal suit the worker and the organization from the start?

Framework for Investment—Organization Level
- Does a clear link exist between the organization's strategic requirements and the human capital investment expected from the individual? Did the person participate in crafting the link? Do people know how the business works and how they contribute?
- Do the individual and the organization have a consistent understanding of the current deal? Does the worker know what investment and performance the organization expects? Does the organization know how the individual values various elements of return on investment in all four ROI_w areas?
- Does the individual trust the organization to accept and stick with the deal? Does the organization trust the individual to invest human capital as required by her end of the bargain?

Framework for Investment—Job Level
- Is competence building engineered into the individual's job?
- Does the worker have autonomy to define and execute her role within reasonable bounds? Do competence and autonomy support one another to bring about high performance in a diverse, challenging job?
- Does the organization deliver return on workplace investment in a way that reinforces human capital investment in the job? Do people have a reasonable choice in constructing ROI_w portfolios? Are rewards allocated justly?

Human Capital Building
- Do formal learning opportunities build the human capital most beneficial to the organization? Do they benefit the individual by boosting desirable ROI_w?
- Do informal learning approaches benefit both the organization and the person?
- Does the individual have opportunities to help develop and transform explicit knowledge derived from tacit knowledge?

Turnover Analysis and Risk Management
- Has the organization analyzed turnover patterns? Does the organization know who is at risk and why?
- Does the organization have accurate information on the ROI_w provided by industry and labor market competitors?
- Does the organization use information and its distribution to preserve human capital investment during risky times?

In each of four key roles, the supervisor has the opportunity to influence the kinds and amounts of ROI_w that flow to the individual. To fulfill the roles of contract maker, ROI_w provider, investment adviser, and information communicator, the supervisor must be prepared to:

- Contribute to the definition of strategic direction and the determination of human capital required to carry out business strategy
- Take the lead in making sure employees start with (and maintain) a solid understanding of the main elements of the psychological deal (duration, consideration, and flexibility) and of how the organization intends to live up to its end of the compact
- Help workers craft and clarify the link between their contribution of human capital and the success of the business
- Ensure that the organization upholds its part of the deal by seeing to it that procedures for reward allocation and outcomes of reward distribution meet high standards of justice
- Keep promises and involve workers in key business decisions to build the bonds of trust between individual and company
- Act as a teacher, a builder of teams, and a supporter of interpersonal connections among workers, thereby creating a workplace rich in formal and informal opportunities to build competence
- Fashion an appreciation-rich workplace through both formal and informal recognition of excellent performance
- Understand individual needs and help people create human capital development plans that build the ability to act with effective autonomy
- Give people the information they need to manage their risky investment of human capital

Of course, supervisors who do all this well are rare and valuable investors, worthy themselves of heroic retention efforts. Their most important achievement, perhaps, is that they increase the value of nonfinancial return-on-investment elements. By so doing, they make employees tougher targets for headhunters whose siren song is chiefly a chorus of financial enticements. Smart companies hone their hiring systems, invest in development programs, and craft an appealing deal so they can create and preserve the pool of first-line managerial ability.

Here is another way to think about turnover—companies should worry less about making workers *feel* better and more about enabling them to *do* better. Remember that performance produces job satisfaction, not vice versa. The thoughts of a Generation X manager are enlightening on this point. Brent Frei is a software entrepreneur and CEO of ONYX Software Corp. In a *San Francisco Examiner* newspaper article, he talked about his ideas for stopping the "high-stakes hopscotch" of workers jumping from company to company. These are some of his comments:[21]

> "Give your employees the power to judge what it takes to get the job done."
>
> "Companies should hire self-managing people and entrust them to do the right thing."
>
> "Hire people with high values and outstanding abilities, give them plenty of accountability and authority, let them share the financial rewards, and make sure work is fun."
>
> "Give people the freedom to interact with each other and the best ideas will flow freely."
>
> "Team managers and leaders should be accountable for ensuring outstanding communication and flow of information, and for providing support, coaching and career development opportunities."
>
> "Make sure your employees are unencumbered."
>
> "A company must offer a product or service to its customers that is of the highest quality, something that employees can truly be proud of."

Frei's points address a few key themes: hire well, give people autonomy, give them a high return on their investment in work, count on groups to create knowledge and spread it around. "A company that puts these principles into practice can stop worrying about motivating and retaining employees and begin harnessing the positive attitude, fighting spirit, respect and commitment it needs from each employee to succeed," he says. Good performance makes the job fun and produces the business results that stoke the value of stock options.

BOUNDED RATIONALITY

In discussing the arrangements between individual and organization, we postulated that a worker can act rationally in managing his way to an equilibrium position. In real life, however, there are bounds on the ability of human capital investors to act with the rationality classically attributed to their financial counterparts.

Consider portfolio diversification. Depending on the amount of money available for investment, a financial investor can choose as many different securities as he wants. By diversifying, he eliminates what economists call unique or unsystematic risk, the potential ROI fluctuations that afflict individual companies.[22] In contrast, workers automatically overinvest in the companies that employ them. They have no choice—most derive the majority of their financial income and a sizable portion of their other ROI_w from a single source. The seven million Americans who toil at more than one job do so more to survive economically than to reduce the chance of financial harm if they lose one of their jobs.[23]

Second, think about the different degrees of control exercised by financial and human capital investors. Equity and bond holders can, for the most part, decide when to buy or sell their holdings. In the main, they choose the form of their investments and returns (debt or equity, dividends, appreciation, or interest payments) at the time of purchase. Moreover, they have complete control over whether the relationship continues or ends. Investors can shed their investments, but stock and bond issuers do not, under most circumstances, dump their investors. In contrast, employers share with workers roughly equal control over termination of the employment relationship. Organizations participate actively in human capital transactions; they are not merely passive recipients of investors' contributions. Consequently, workers find themselves striving for an equilibrium point in concert with an active, interested partner rather than simply aiming for maximum returns. A company can modify a compensation arrangement, redefine a role, or cut a training budget. Imagine how difficult it would be for a company to attract financial investors if it could summarily dismiss them or pay quarterly dividends in antique doorknobs instead of money. Those are realities that worker-investors face in a world where the organization holds most of the ROI_w cards.

Third, human capital investors enjoy much less investment liquidity than do their financial-investor counterparts. As Nobel economist Gary Becker has noted, "Human capital is a very illiquid asset—it cannot be sold and is rather poor collateral on loans."[24] Although a worker can sell his services for money, the human capital required to do the job remains in his mind, muscles, and heart. Other than taking a job or selling blood plasma, there is no way to transform it into cash.

Finally, financial and human capital investors face different kinds and degrees of risk and have different risk management responses available to them. Financial investors have difficulty enough assessing and managing risk, and it becomes even more elusive in the workplace. Adam Smith noted that most of us have an ill-formed sense of the risks we undertake: "The chance of gain is by every man more or less over-valued, and the chance of loss is by most men under-valued, and by scarce any man, who is in tolerable health and spirits, valued more than it is worth. . . . The contempt of risk and the presumptuous hope of success, are in no period of life more active than at the age at which young people chuse their professions."[25]

Preserve Investment During Times of Uncertainty

The last section of Exhibit 8.2 refers to risk management, a notion introduced in the value-of-leaving equation. In that equation, the probability factor reflects risk. Risk comes from uncertainty about the return on investment from a new job. However, risk can attach to the existing job too.

The *Oxford English Dictionary* says *risk* means "to *expose* to the *chance* of injury or *loss*." *Exposure* means the degree to which one is subject to the effects of a change within the organization. If someone else's department is downsizing but yours is safe, your exposure is nil—for now. *Chance* refers to the probability of suffering a loss. It ranges between the book ends of certain loss and certain gain; certainty eliminates chance, whereas uncertainty heightens it. The significance of loss hinges on the impact of the possible effects; significance depends on the size of the effect (measured in dollars, utiles of satisfaction, or other units) and importance (the value attached to the ROI_w aspects affected). For instance, a big change in the assignment of parking spaces might have a large magnitude (no more spot right next to the building). It will have little significance, however, if parking spaces do not matter to you (given that you just bought your lifetime bus pass).

Putting all the terms together, we can define workplace risk as the possibility that the return on a worker's investment in the job will decrease significantly because of changes in a worker's situation. Risk falls in the middle of a biblical chain: change begets risk, risk begets uncertainty, uncertainty begets . . . a pause. But this is no pause to refresh, no benign breather. It is a full-stop brake-slammer to take a compass reading, check the wind, get the lay of the land, and let things shake out. It is an interruption in the investment of human capital, shorter-lived than a full-fledged departure, but an interruption nonetheless. The only way to prevent it, or at least to reduce its duration, is to manage risk.

Information is the sine qua non of risk management. Referring back to our definition of risk's three components (exposure, chance, and significance of loss), the kinds of information for which workers hunger appear in Exhibit 8.3. To answer these questions companies must manage the content of the information they provide about change, accelerate its initial availability, maximize its frequency, and choose carefully the media through which they convey it.

What follows is not a primer on change management or a comprehensive communication strategy. It is, rather, a few thoughts on how organizations can use information to reduce the effects of uncertainty on human capital investment.

PROVIDE CRITICAL CONTENT Among the changes that create risk and leave workers uncertain about the future, mergers must come out near the top of the list. To find out how information content might alter the way people act during a merger, researchers David Schweiger and Angelo DeNisi set up an experiment.[26] Their laboratory consisted of two similar light manufacturing plants belonging to a pair of Fortune 500 companies that had announced a merger. Employees in the control plant received no formal information about the merger except an announcement letter from the CEO. In the experimental plant, management began a comprehensive program of merger-related communication with employees. The experimental information was comprehensive indeed. It included answers to questions concerning layoffs, transfers, promotions and demotions, and changes in pay, jobs,

Exhibit 8.3.   Companies Should Answer Risk-Management Questions.

Risk Components		
Exposure	Chance	Significance
Who is affected (location, division, plant, organization level)?	What certainties can be identified?	Why is change occurring?
Who is specifically not affected?	What uncertainties remain?	What changes are expected?
How will gains and losses be allocated?	What general probabilities can be attached to uncertainties?	How dramatic will the changes be?
When will the change begin?	How will the uncertainties be resolved: more analysis, future decisions, external acts?	What about the organization is not changing?
When will it end?		What purely positive effects can be expected?
Will change occur at once or in phases?	When will the uncertainties be resolved?	What purely negative effects can be expected?
What can we do to affect the outcome?		Is the change like anything we have experienced or observed before? How is it similar or different?
How has the company prepared to respond to this change?		
How can we learn more about what is going on, now and as change unfolds?		

and benefits that would take place in their work units. The employees in the experimental plant also received weekly briefings from the plant manager and the vice president of human resources. Throughout the process, the plant manager met personally with individual employees whenever management made a decision directly affecting them. To test the effect of enhanced information, the researchers surveyed employees in both plants at four different times: once before the major announcement, once after the announcement, and twice after the information campaign began.

If all this sounds familiar, think back to the critical hiring information described in Chapter Four. Management in the experimental plant took a lesson from companies that give realistic job previews to hirees. They used a similar structure for the worker-specific information provided to employees.[27] As the graphs in Figure 8.3 show, the information program was associated with reduced employee uncertainty and better job performance in the experimental plant.

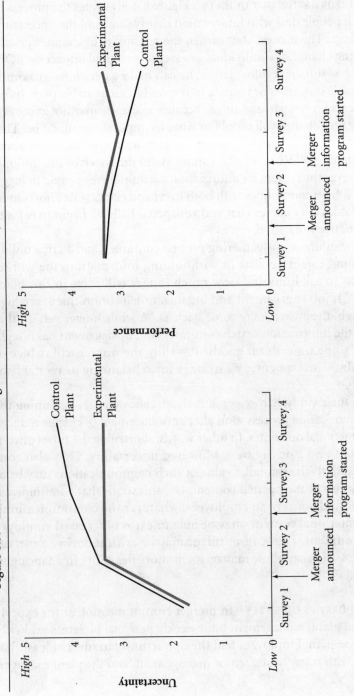

Figure 8.3. Effects of Realistic Merger Information on Uncertainty and Job Performance.

Source: D. M. Schweiger and A. S. DeNisi, "Communication with Employees Following a Merger: A Longitudinal Field Experiment," *Academy of Management Journal*, 1991, 34(1), pp. 123, 127. Used by permission.

GET INFORMATION OUT QUICKLY   Figure 8.4 illustrates the process by which people deal with information deprivation and the uncertainty it brings. The process starts when the possibility of change appears. Sensing change, the individual assesses its potential impact on ROI_w. If he has sufficient information, he can make a decision—maximize favorable outcomes or prepare to respond to unfavorable ones. Information may be sparse or absent because managers may not know precisely how change will unfold or what its implications might be. They may worry about alerting competitors to what is going on, or about frightening off workers who cannot stand the shock of disruption.[28] Whatever the reason, an information vacuum leaves people to juggle their job responsibilities with both overt and clandestine efforts to fill the void. Water cooler chat and whispered hall talk begin to eat into productive work time.

The information-gathering process continues, and a crisis builds. If management persists in withholding information, the worker begins to ask himself: "How much longer will I live in this black hole?" If job engagement and organizational commitment are high enough, the answer may come back as, "A while longer yet." In that case, the information search continues, and management has bought itself some time. But if goodwill is thin, the worker will reduce or withdraw investment, as a strategy for rebalancing or reestablishing ROI_w.

In their study, Schweiger and DeNisi showed that beginning the communication process soon after announcement of change reduced dysfunctional outcomes. In other words, shortening the time between points 1 and 2 on Figure 8.4 lowered uncertainty. They also concluded that "the symbolic value of such communications may be as important as their actual content. Organizations that communicate caring and concern to employees, whatever the communication's informational content, may be able to expect increased employee commitment. That commitment may be critical during a merger process and may allow management more flexibility in adapting to changes."[29]

BROADCAST FREQUENTLY   In merger communication at the experimental plant, management built weekly personal bulletins explicitly into the plan. Employees had the opportunity to meet at least that often with supervisors, senior management, and the plant manager.

Figure 8.4. Response to Change Depends on Speedy Resolution of Uncertainty.

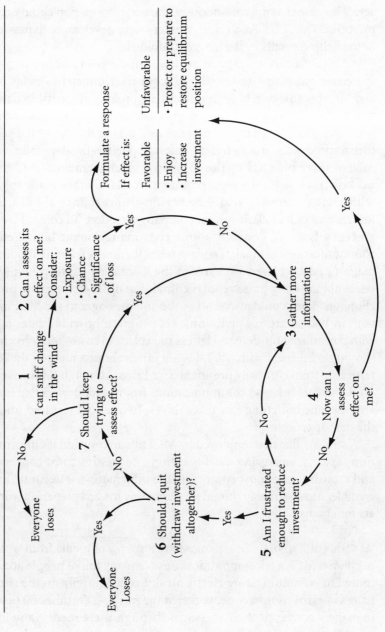

Equally important, the organization provided a telephone hot line. Through the hot line, workers had access to a human resource manager who passed along continuously updated information about organizational changes.[30] As a result, workers were never more than a few hours behind events as the merger unfolded.

At MCI Communications in 1997, uncertainty accompanied aggressive courtship from would-be acquirers. Ultimately, WorldCom and MCI became one, but not until after a prolonged courtship dance that featured flirtation between MCI and several other suitors. As MCI executives pored over their sales results near the end of the year, they noticed a disturbing trend—sales dropped in the days following each of three bids to buy the company.[31] Management feared that workers (especially sales reps) had stopped attacking the marketplace with their customary zeal. The reason—uncertainty about their futures and lack of clarity about company direction. To combat complacency born of concern about risk, management launched a communications campaign code-named Rainmaker. Frequent information updates played a key role in the Rainmaker strategy. Employees could get daily pulse reports containing up-to-the-minute press clippings. They could also send outbound messages to the MCI bigwigs in Washington. The Rainmaker program provided sales reps with customized on-demand letters to explain to customers why they should do business with MCI despite jitters about a merger; the letters came from company president Tim Price. Although Rainmaker's implementers believed communications from headquarters had been ample—one bulletin every three days—frequency increased under the new approach.

A strategy like that employed by MCI fills an individual's information capacity, answering most questions, addressing most concerns, and crowding out most rumors. If the information is accurate and credible, such a strategy should go a long way toward preparing workers for change.

MANAGE YOUR MEDIA   Companies have an array of media from which to choose. MCI, a telecommunications company full of people accustomed to communicating electronically, relied heavily on the company's internal computer networks. At the merging Fortune 500 plant, managers conveyed their messages through three media: a twice-monthly merger newsletter, a telephone hot line, and personal meetings between managers and workers, both in groups and individually.

Although personal contact may seem the least glamorous way to transfer information, it is in many ways the best. Writing in the *Harvard Business Review,* authors T. J. and Sandar Larkin give blunt advice to executives about communicating change: "The next time you communicate major change to your frontline employees, do it differently. Communicate only facts; stop communicating values. Communicate face-to-face; do not rely on videos, publications, or large meetings. And target frontline supervisors; do not let executives introduce the change to frontline employees." Supervisor communications meetings may not seem revolutionary, say the Larkins, but they are: "In a company that institutes such briefings, a frontline employee who wants to know what's happening has only one way to get that information: by asking the supervisor. And that information probably will be communicated one-on-one and will be in the supervisor's own words. No big meeting, no grand announcement, no executive road shows, no speeches relayed by satellite. All the resources previously spent communicating indiscriminately are aimed at communicating with supervisors, who are given information, influence, and thereby increased power and status. As a result, they are more likely to help implement change."[32]

Does this mean that senior management has no role in communicating with employees? Not at all; it just means that organizations should not expect that an eloquent, high-profile speech by the silver-tongued CEO will give employees what they need to cope with change and manage risk. Again, the Larkins make their point bluntly: "No matter what the change—merger, restructuring, downsizing, reengineering, the introduction of new technology, or a customer service campaign—the first words frontline employees hear about a change should come from the person to whom they are closest: their supervisor. . . . Spend 80 percent of your communication time, money, and effort on supervisors. . . . Supervisors—not senior managers—are the opinion leaders in your organization."[33] Because of their centrality in the social network of the work unit, the information they provide is both immediate and relevant. It comes in a familiar context that heightens its impact and believability.

GIVE PEOPLE CONTROL We know from our discussions of trust in Chapter Five that involvement in, and control over, evolving circumstances can help ensure an equitable outcome. The same holds for managing the risk associated with organizational disruption. The more people control their own fate, helping to design the architecture of change, the more power they have over the high-value elements of work. Realizing this, enlightened organizations solicit worker participation in change. One organization even set aside money saved from a downsizing effort to reward survivors who made efficiency-improving suggestions.[34] Kodak, which underwent its share of layoffs in the 1980s, found that the postlayoff environment provided fertile ground for employee participation in redesigning work.[35] Control over work redesign, in turn, increased intrinsic satisfaction.

RAISING THE COST OF QUITTING

The last term in the turnover equation refers to the cost of quitting the organization. Most managers think of this as a literal financial cost, because management dedication to the easiest lever (that is, monetary rewards) continues unabated. Respondents to a 1997 Society for Human Resource Management survey on retention rated a list of strategies according to effectiveness in retaining employees.[36] Survey takers gave four of the top five spots to financial rewards of one sort or another: salary levels and increases, health care benefits, and retirement savings plans. Only one nonfinancial strategy, open communications, sneaked into the top five, holding down the number three spot. Robert Half, the temporary services and recruiting firm, reports that "competitive benefits" constitute the number one strategy companies use to prevent recruitment of their people.[37] The theory, consistent with our definition of programmatic commitment, seems to be that the best way to bind people is to make it monetarily costly for them to quit. But we already know the weaknesses of programmatic commitment, especially its feeble relationship with worker motivation.

There is a more robust way to bind people to the organization, however. Perhaps the strongest, most energizing bond an organization can develop goes to its role as the locus of interpersonal networks that make jobs and connections more fulfilling and enriching. Remember Brent Frei's words about the importance of the workplace network. Remember also our discussion of the power represented by growth and learning opportunities. We know that teams and practice communities form a trelliswork of personal contacts that sustain us emotionally and enrich us intellectually. What better way to engender loyalty-based commitment? What better place to find this complex of interconnections than at work?

Values guru Brian Hall says that, paradoxically, group intimacy and support help us cope with the fundamental reality that each of us alone has responsibility for everything we do.[38] Hall studied the evolution of values in two large organizations from the 1950s to the present, documenting a fundamental shift from a task-based to a relationship-based orientation.[39] People, it seems, want to share attitudes, beliefs, and knowledge as well as space and time, to form bonds with each other and with the organization. When *Wired* magazine asked what is most important in getting ahead, the results for the technologically sophisticated group confirmed the old saw—who you know counts for more than what you know.[40] People who work in an organization that provides a rich environment for forming personal networks will be loath to walk away. A web of contacts is a sticky web indeed. Breaking away exacts a high psychic price.

When researchers at the Corporate Leadership Council (CLC, a Washington, D.C., think tank that analyzes human resource issues) looked for turnover-reduction success stories, they found an aerospace defense contractor that used a network-building strategy to reduce defections of new managers.[41] As CLC lead consultant Devashree Gupta tells the story, this $1 billion manufacturer discovered that technical experts had difficulty making the transition into project management roles. The company threw them into a tough job with little preparation or attention from their bosses. They felt abandoned and unappreciated. Consequently, nearly 40 percent of newly promoted project managers left the company within a year of taking the position. The organization suffered in two ways: it lost a steady stream of high-potential leaders and had to foot the bill for direct turnover costs to boot.

The company responded by creating a process to help technical experts become competent managers. They start with individual contributors who show management potential and interest. Most managers-in-waiting spend between three and five years with the company to prove the depth of their technical knowledge. Members of this group become apprentice project managers for six to twelve months, learning the ropes from an experienced manager and forming peer-level bonds. Apprentices then graduate to a comanager position for another six to twelve months. During this stint, they help manage product development and similar cross-functional projects, assisted by a coach. When ready, they move on to become full-fledged project managers, capable of handling projects on their own and taking on their own apprentices. The company also assigns a senior executive sponsor who monitors the apprentice throughout the project. An executive sponsor holds monthly one-on-one checkpoint meetings, helps with presentations to senior management, and conducts a post-project debriefing. At the end of the preparation period, the new project manager has strengthened her personal network both horizontally (with peers) and vertically (with superiors). Says Gupta, the program has produced impressive results: "Not only has the company improved the performance of its project managers, but they've also reduced turnover of key performers. Since starting the program, turnover has dropped to 2 percent." The turnover reduction comes not from higher salaries or three-year vesting periods for stock options, but rather from an elevated sense of competence, high fulfillment from the job, and a strong network of contacts binding individual to organization.

SUMMARY: MAINTAINING INVESTMENT

This chapter began with a paradox—if people prefer to stick with a single employer over the long term, why does turnover periodically become a big problem? Maybe people want to stay in one place but cannot fight off the temptation to move when attractive opportunities come along. Maybe, in the wake of downsizing, they do not trust companies to live up to an equilibrium deal. And maybe companies use all the wrong strategies to retain the people they need, focusing on money when intangibles are more important.

An equilibrium deal, fairly balancing the interests of both individual and organization, lies at the heart of any successful retention strategy. Equilibrium reinforces engagement in the job as well as the distinct but related contribution of organizational commitment. It takes both commitment and engagement to bind people to the organization and maintain their interest in investing discretionary effort. Blau and Boal express the dual effect succinctly—the job itself enables an individual to meet intrinsic growth needs, whereas the organization can help an individual meet social and other extrinsic reward needs.[42] High levels of attitudinal commitment and job engagement tend to reinforce each other, producing dramatic human capital investment effects.

Many organizations, however, adopt a short-term, throw-money-at-it strategy to address a worker retention problem. The idea is right—make the cost of quitting high enough to dissuade defection—

but the tactic is wrong. An organization that provides the network where learning occurs, competency grows, and intrinsic satisfaction thrives creates the enduring emotional and social links that hold people more surely than money. In a healthy economy, almost any company can pay a transactional premium to get someone it wants. Far fewer can create a work environment so rich in relational factors that people cannot afford to leave, for reasons that have nothing to do with money. Which do you think has the advantage in holding on to the human capital required for competitive success?

Chapter Eight also underscored the role of the supervisor. Besides a multifaceted role in delivering the deal, the supervisor also functions as information source and repository of organizational values. In that role, the supervisor ensures that the individual has enough information to reduce uncertainty and make wise choices about human capital investment. Students of individual self-determination like to quote Thomas Jefferson on this point: "I know no safe depository of the ultimate powers of the society but the people themselves; and if we think them not enlightened enough to exercise their control with a wholesome discretion, the remedy is not to take it from them, but to inform their discretion."[43] Enlightenment and informed discretion are never more important than during times of change, when risk creates the uncertainty that makes people suspend their human capital investment. Of the many potential sources of information for risk management, the supervisor is paramount.

These first eight chapters have set forth the components of a human capital management system. In Chapter Nine, all the elements come together to suggest how an organization that takes a holistic view can make the most of the investments-and-returns framework.

CHAPTER NINE

Optimizing and Measuring Human Capital Investment

Managers love numbers. In their respect for numerical insights, they share kinship with William Thomson, Lord Kelvin, the nineteenth-century British physicist. Kelvin formulated the second law of thermodynamics and conceptualized absolute zero, the temperature characterized by the complete absence of heat. More relevant for us, Kelvin was a devotee of measurement: "When you can measure what you are speaking about, and express it in numbers, you know something about it; but when you cannot measure it, when you cannot express it in numbers, your knowledge is of a meager and unsatisfactory kind."[1]

It turns out that Kelvin, apart from (or perhaps because of) his skill in quantitative physics, was a notably arrogant fellow. He applied his theories of thermodynamics to estimate the age of the earth, attempting to reform, in a single stroke, a field of science outside his own.[2] On the one hand, his age estimates of between twenty million and a hundred million years represented a vast improvement over the biblical chronologies of his time. Old Testament adherents in the late nineteenth century admitted an age of no more than a few thousand years. On the other, Kelvin based his figures on an incorrect assumption about the source of the earth's heat. The subsequent discovery that radioactive decay produces the heat in the earth's core led to a determination that the earth is about 4.5 billion years old. Kelvin's highest estimate undershot that figure by a Montana mile.

We in the human capital business can learn from Kelvin's embarrassment. We should share his dedication to quantification. We should also bear in mind, however, that it never pays to assume that everything important is readily apparent or amenable to easy measurement.

This chapter approaches the challenge of measurement from two directions. The first section builds on the equilibrium investment and return notion established in Chapter Eight. The discussion elaborates on ways to estimate the shape of the equilibrium curve and define suitable exchanges. Defining these points will become an optimization challenge. From there, the chapter will suggest how a system of interlocking measures can reflect the effectiveness with which individuals and organizations together manage human capital and its investment. We will revisit our friends at Perpetual Petals one last time to see how managers might apply the measurement approaches. Through it all, we will maintain a sense of perspective about the quest for quantification, keeping in mind that even a great scientist can miss the mark by an order of magnitude or two. Kelvin's experience should give us the anti-hubris perspective needed to approach measuring the intangible.

OPTIMIZING

The discussion of reinforcement in Chapter Six alluded to a dual responsibility of managers—delivering an attractive ROI_w package while husbanding the organizational resources required to provide that package. Chapter Eight introduced the idea of achieving equilibrium between an individual's propensity to invest human capital and the return on investment funded by the company. Put these two ideas together, and you get optimization. To understand and determine the optimal exchange, we will borrow concepts and tools from basic economic theory, consumer market research, and operations research. The ideas are straightforward (and there is computer software that experts can use to make application easier). Here are the basic steps.

Step 1. Start by defining what your organization means by each return-on-investment element: intrinsic fulfillment, growth opportunities, recognition, and financial rewards. I don't mean develop broad definitions; rather, define specifically the components that go into each element for work groups in your company. Intrinsic fulfillment, for example, may mean choosing frequently from a variety of projects, having discretion over one's work schedule, or participating in important strategic decisions. At Southwest Airlines, for instance, a fulfilling environment includes working in a place oozing with energy, humor, and team spirit.[3] The most important growth opportunities in an organization may include membership on teams doing advanced product development or participation in executive graduate programs. Workers in high-tech organizations place especially high value on such factors. Recognition may encompass public awards for specific kinds of performance and companywide acknowledgment of certain special accomplishments (exotic trips for big sales successes, perhaps). Sales forces in pharmaceutical companies might be oriented this way. Define the elements that seem to have the greatest value in your organization; involve employees in the definition process, and make sure the list is comprehensive.

Step 2. Determine a utility curve for each of the four return-on-investment elements. We introduced the term in Chapter Six when we said that utility represents a value metric reflecting individual preferences for tangible, intangible, relational, and transactional rewards. In Chapter Eight, we combined utilities for all ROI_w elements into a single curve; we refined the definition to mean individual motivation to invest human capital, as affected by return on that investment. For the employee group in question, break the consolidated curve into separate curves that show how much value (measured in units called utiles) individuals gain from various amounts of each ROI_w element. Four versions of such curves appear in Figure 9.1; the four shapes represent examples only, though the patterns are classic. The financial rewards curve displays the traditional diminishing returns phenomenon. The convex curve representing intrinsic fulfillment shows the rapid upward slope that means utility grows quickly with each bit of added fulfillment, after a slow start. A sigmoid shape like that shown for the sample recognition curve signifies that the first and last increments of recognition produce significant value; middling amounts, however, create little additional utility. The linearity of the growth opportunities utility curve depicts a constant relationship of incremental opportunity and utility.

You could probably derive the shape of each curve through careful questioning of the workers in the group. Marketing research science,

Figure 9.1. Four Examples of Utility Curves.

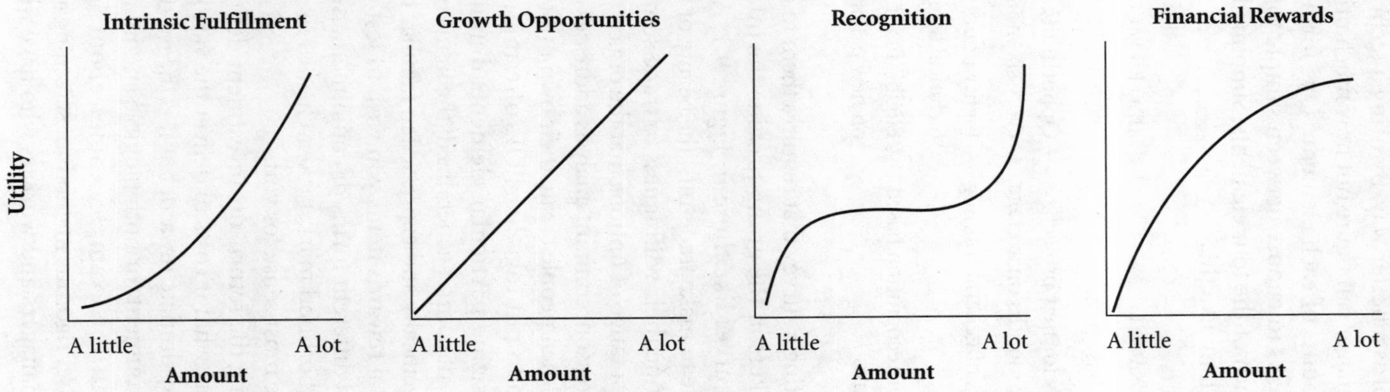

however, affords a better way. By using a technique called conjoint analysis, a manager can figure out how much utility workers get from different amounts of each element.[4] One form of conjoint analysis calls for subjects to choose between sample total rewards packages comprising each of the four elements. Simplified somewhat, a sample choice might look like this:

REWARD PACKAGE 1	REWARD PACKAGE 2
$100,000 in base pay	$80,000 in base pay
Opportunity for new project every twelve months on average	Opportunity for new project every six months on average
Thirty hours of general training annually	Eighty hours of training on technical topics annually
Eligibility for recognition based on new patents	Eligibility for recognition based on new patents

By completing a survey that requires them to choose between such bundles, workers in the group provide the information needed to draw utility curves like those in Figure 9.1. A conjoint approach requires people to make trade-offs; the beauty of it is that workers, not managers, define their willingness to trade some ROI_w elements for others, within a range of options that the organization pledges to provide. For this reason, conjoint analysis addresses the concern raised in Chapter Six. When people create their own utility curves and companies use them to put together ROI_w offerings, the risk of over- or underemphasizing particular elements diminishes. The example shown here is, of course, generalized; the items in each package must be defined specifically and expressed in familiar terms. Depending on how many total rewards items you wish to test, you can select from among several different forms of conjoint analysis. Check with your friendly neighborhood market research guru to choose the approach that makes the most sense for you.

Step 3. Using the return-on-investment definitions developed in step 1, calculate what it costs to deliver the various elements. Money may not be the ultimate reward, but it is the mother's milk that nourishes the environment for both tangible and intangible ROI_w. Intrinsic fulfillment, for example, comes about in part because an organization uses rigorous methods of screening and selection to make sure it hires managers and workers who have what it takes to create fulfilling work in an energizing environment. At Southwest Airlines, the organization uses a series of group exercises to identify which potential hirees have the stuff it takes to fit into the company's fun-loving but customer-focused culture.[5] In one such exercise, called the Fallout Shelter, job applicants act as a committee responsible for rebuilding civilization after a nuclear war. They have a list of fifteen people from different occupations, including a nurse, teacher, athlete, biochemist, and pop singer. The group has ten minutes to reach a unanimous decision about which seven can remain in the fallout shelter. As the exercise unfolds, some candidates remain passive, some take part, and some lead; a team of Southwest recruiters observes the group and decides whom to invite back for interviews. It takes time and money to build and use such a hiring system, and these represent costs you can quantify. Creating intrinsically fulfilling jobs might require other identifiable organizational investments as well; for example:

- Investment in the development of recruiting and selection approaches to find and hire supervisors who can deliver the deal

- Expenditures for training of those critical supervisors and mentors

- Funding for teams and communities of practice

- Acquisition of job-enhancing technology

- Provision of time for workers to do community service work or teach at the local college

- Support for occasional meetings of managers to share successful practices

- Provision of time for supervisors to learn and begin practicing open-book management techniques

Identifying and tracking such costs may not be easy, but it is worth the effort, as you will see.

Figure 9.2 shows the four utility curves with dollar figures included along the horizontal axis. For each element, a sample current situation shows the utility generated by company expenditures in each reward area. In the example, for the $20,000 this organization spends per capita to heighten intrinsic fulfillment, each individual gets an average of 40 utiles. Expenditures of $25,000 and $15,000 per person

Figure 9.2. Utility Curves with ROI_W Delivery Costs Added.

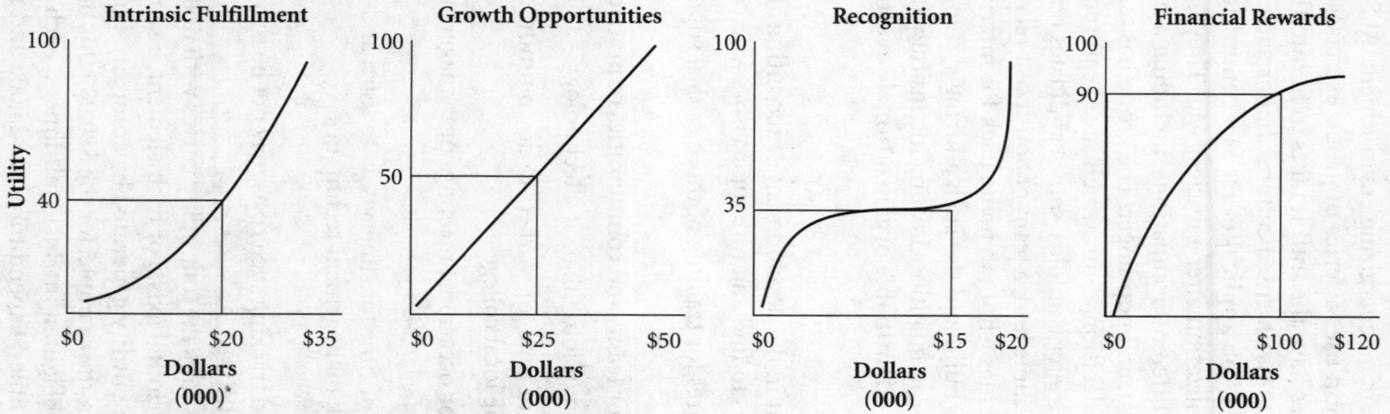

in growth opportunities and recognition yield 50 and 35 utiles, respectively. It spends $100,000 in annual financial rewards per individual, yielding an average of 90 utiles of value on the financial rewards curve. Add it all up, and you get a per-person average of 215 utiles and a cost to the organization of $160,000. Although each curve extends to zero dollars on the left-hand side, in real life each would have practical lower constraints. No organization, for example, would propose an ROI_w package with no expenditure for compensation.

Step 4. Now recombine the points on each of the four utility curves to produce a single summary curve like the ones shown in Chapter Eight. An economist would call this the *efficient frontier,* a term used also in portfolio optimization analysis. The efficient frontier represents all of the points for which company investment and employee utility are in balance, that is, the places where the optimum trade-offs occur. Table 9.1 presents five example ROI_w packages, A through E. For each, the company expenditure by element appears, as does the utility that results from that expenditure. The utility and expenditure numbers come from the curves in Figure 9.2. In package A, for example, $120,000 in financial rewards yields 93 utiles. Spending $35,000 for intrinsic fulfillment produces 100 utiles, and so on for a total expenditure of $225,000 per person and 393 total utiles. Packages B through E were similarly derived.

Plotting the points represented by A through E would begin to form the efficiency curve shown in Figure 9.3. Notice that three points—those corresponding to total reward packages A, B, and C— lie on the efficient frontier. Packages D and E, in contrast, fall inside the frontier, showing that they are not optimum points. At point D, for example, an expenditure of $160,000 yields a suboptimal result. Inefficient allocation among the four reward categories produces a utility of only 215 utiles (check Table 9.1 to see where the total comes from). The efficient allocation of the same $160,000 per person could generate 331 utiles, as denoted by point B on the curve. Similarly, the $122,000 spent to provide package E yields 189 utiles; read off the curve at $122,000, however, and you see that an efficient use of the same funds could produce about 230 utiles.

Knowing the shape and position of the efficient curve allows the organization to pursue either of two human capital strategies:

1. Develop the highest-utility ROI_w package given a specific financial constraint on expenditure; for example, an organization

Table 9.1. Five ROI_w Packages: Expenditures and Utilities.

ROI_w Package	Per Capita Company Expenditure ($000)	Utility in Utiles				
		Intrinsic Fulfillment	Growth Opportunities	Recognition	Financial Rewards	Total Utility
Package A						
Intrinsic fulfillment	35	100				100
Growth opportunities	50		100			100
Recognition	20			100		100
Financial rewards	120				93	93
Total expenditure	225					393
Package B						
Intrinsic fulfillment	30	85				85
Growth opportunities	30		60			60
Recognition	20			100		100
Financial rewards	80				86	86
Total expenditure	160					331
Package C						
Intrinsic fulfillment	0	0				0
Growth opportunities	0		0			0
Recognition	0			0		0
Financial rewards	80				86	86
Total expenditure	80					86
Package D						
Intrinsic fulfillment	20	40				40
Growth opportunities	25		50			50
Recognition	15			35		35
Financial rewards	100				90	90
Total expenditure	160					215
Package E						
Intrinsic fulfillment	20	40				40
Growth opportunities	15		30			30
Recognition	15			35		35
Financial rewards	72				84	84
Total expenditure	122					189

Figure 9.3. Efficient Frontier of Rewards and Utility.

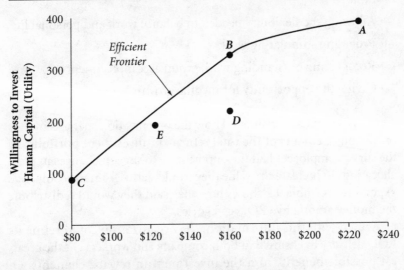

with only $80,000 to spend per person would produce the greatest utility by putting all the money into compensation.

2. Figure out what it will cost to generate the high utilities (that is, propensity to invest human capital on the company's behalf) on the right side of the curve. A company wanting to produce the investment propensity implied by 380 utiles should be prepared to invest about $200,000 per person in ROI$_w$.

Plotting a few dozen points like the five shown on Figure 9.3 would allow a manager to approximate the shape of the efficient frontier. Another way to approximate employee valuations is to do a simple preference survey. At a southern California cellular telephone company, management combined a written survey with focus groups to explore the optimum allocation of company expenditures on workplace investment returns.[6] Employees rated eighteen items, indicating how important each was to overall worker satisfaction with the company. In order, here were the top seven factors:

• Providing career opportunities for people who do good work

• Providing benefit programs that meet worker needs

- Making available top-quality tools and technology to get the job done
- Allowing the flexibility needed to balance work and personal life
- Providing stimulating work
- Recognizing outstanding work group accomplishments
- Giving the opportunity for income growth

Management also estimated how the organization spent its money on various elements of the total return-on-investment portfolio. In the survey, employees had the opportunity to suggest changes in these allocations to increase the value they would derive from the company's expenditures. Table 9.2 shows how they said they would redistribute the money among five ROI_w categories.

Armed with this information, the organization could refine its ROI_w delivery to ensure that both company and workers got the greatest possible benefit from the investment in reward elements. Of course, this approach yields only a rough sense of the best portfolio; it also works on the assumption of a fixed pie of dollars to invest in ROI_w. Going further to plot the efficient frontier of expenditures on ROI_w and utility can tell a company more about optimum utility and investment relationships.

Rigorous optimization analysis is conventional in such fields as financial portfolio management and operations research. Software exists to help with such problems. My model-building friends tell me the programs can handle far more than the few variables discussed here. (Readers can ask a colleague in finance or operations to provide computer support.)

Table 9.2.   Preferred Redistribution of Company Expenditures.

Reward Component	Current Percentage	Preferred Percentage	Percentage Difference
Cash compensation	80	74	−8
Health and welfare benefits	10	12	+20
Retirement programs	5	7	+40
Learning and development programs	4	5	+25
Lifestyle enhancements	1	2	+100

This example has focused on learning the trade-off preferences of a work group. As we know, however, individual reward preferences may deviate from group norms. The organization should therefore strive to offer as much choice as it legally and administratively can, allowing individuals to customize their choices, especially in the three nonfinancial ROI_w categories. In other words, use the utility and optimization approaches to ensure that the menu available to employees contains attractive options. I encourage companies to take a Tootsie Roll Pop approach to defining ROI_w portfolios. Define a central group of reward elements that are, in the main, the same for everyone (the chocolate center, if you will). Then supplement the standard offerings with a wide array of options in areas affecting intrinsic job fulfillment, growth opportunities, and informal aspects of recognition (the variously flavored candy shell).

Remember too that attractive ROI_w is a necessary but not sufficient requirement for human capital investment. The six factors from Chapters Five and Six help draw out investment potential and make it effective.

MEASURING

By determining utility curves and an efficient investment frontier, managers can refine their understanding of human capital as a contributor to strategic success. But contribution, the denominator of the productivity fraction, tells only half the story. Managers need measures of results—indicators of how the investment of human capital has helped to propel the organization toward competitive advantage. To reflect the results of the human capital management system, we need an array of measures. These measures must link and together show how effectively individual and organization have managed human capital acquisition, building, and investment. First, however, let us stipulate some principles to measure by.

Measurement Criteria and Definitions

As they develop systems for measuring human capital, managers would do well to heed these four criteria. In keeping with the first criterion, they boil down to a simple few:

1. Embrace simplicity. The best measures are the easiest to derive. Conversely, measures that rely on too many assumptions or

interdependent calculations may produce Kelvin-like inaccuracy. About 600 B.C., the Chinese philosopher Lao-tzu urged his followers to manifest plainness and embrace simplicity. His advice applies as well to measurement as it does to life.

2. Count only what counts. Albert Einstein, no slouch at the numbers game, has been quoted as saying that not everything that counts can be counted, and not everything that can be counted counts. Regardless of whether the words are his, the wisdom is Einsteinian. Keep track of what really matters to customers, workers, and shareholders, making sure that the measures reflect your strategic position on cost, quality, and innovation. The rest, apart from what the Internal Revenue Service requires, is probably optional.

3. Make measures understandable. While I am quoting scientists, here is a thought from Stephen Hawking. He is talking about the whole universe, but his idea fits our little corner too: "If we do discover a complete [unified] theory [of the universe], it should in time be understandable in broad principle by everyone, not just a few scientists."[7] Measures should be clear enough that anyone with a basic understanding of the business can figure out how the business is doing.

4. Build in a compass. A good measure of "what" should point to the underlying "why." The point of measuring, after all, is to suggest goals and reveal the actions required to reach them (and thereby make measures improve). Having fewer steps between measuring and acting means a more useful measurement system.

Exhibit 9.1 shows the kinds of measures that meet these criteria. The left-hand column lists the system components developed in Chapters Three through Eight. They flow from top to bottom, starting with the connection between human capital and strategic capabilities and ending with retention. The middle column offers eleven key indicators of human capital management effectiveness. These items emphasize results that make a difference to strategic success and shareholder value. The right-hand column gives examples of contributory measures—indicators that suggest how well individual actions and programs support the results measures. Most of these

Exhibit 9.1.   Suggested Human Capital Measures.

Elements of Human Capital System	Results Measures	Contributory Measures
Linkage of human capital with strategy	Improvement in key strategic capabilities Use of human capital to strengthen capabilities	Growth of human capital elements supporting key capabilities
Hiring human capital investors	Contribution of hiring to strengthening capabilities	Size of applicant pipeline, especially for pivotal jobs Percentage of top candidates hired Hiring cycle time Hiring cost
Context for performance	Unit productivity per employee Revenue per employee Profit per employee Market capitalization per employee	Employee attitudes toward each element of ROI_w Employee attitudes toward each of the three organization environment elements (strategic alignment, deal understanding, deal acceptance) Employee attitudes toward each of the three job execution elements (competence, autonomy, reinforcement) Levels of employee commitment and engagement
Building human capital	Contribution of learning to strengthening of key capabilities Tobin's q People value-added	Success of teams in meeting goals Number and strength of practice communities Total training investment Training ROI Spread of training hours and dollars by position
Retention of investors	Retention of committed and engaged people in pivotal jobs	Competitive comparison of ROI_w elements Turnover in pivotal jobs Position of ROI_w packages relative to efficient frontier

should seem familiar. They are the success metrics that well-run organizations use consistently to monitor their performance across a range of initiatives focused on people, quality, and customers.

By no means does the list in Exhibit 9.1 contain all of the useful measures of human resource management. Rather, in keeping with the second criterion for measurement, it sets out a few of the prominent alternatives that convey the most insight about human capital management. Most of the measures in the middle column of Exhibit 9.1 are intuitive, but a few deserve more comment. We will come back to the strengthening of strategically important capabilities; we'll also return to the contribution of hiring and learning to capability improvement and retention of dedicated people in critical jobs.

The measure called Tobin's q is a recommended general metric of intangible capital (including but not limited to human capital). It comes from capital investment theory and the thinking of Nobel laureate James Tobin. Tobin theorized that a company's investment rate depends on the market's valuation of returns on a marginal investment project compared with the project's cost of capital. He denoted this ratio as q.[8] Whereas Tobin concerned himself with the implications of q for capital investment, it also suggests how much mileage an organization gets out of its intangible assets. We determine this by interpreting Tobin's q as the ratio of a company's market capitalization (stock price times shares outstanding) to the replacement cost of tangible assets. If the ratio exceeds 1, it means that something other than tangible assets has produced value recognized by the securities market. That something must be the firm's intangible assets. Besides human capital, intangible assets include things like documented product and process ideas (transformed tacit knowledge, in Chapter Seven terms), patents, trademarks, customer relationships, and supplier connections.[9] All of this may be intangible, but it has concrete value. Researchers have discovered, for example, that differing amounts of intangible capital contribute to variations in Tobin's q among semiconductor companies.[10]

Another useful value metric, one that suggests the effectiveness of human capital investment, is people value-added (PVA). The PVA ratio measures the economic value created by an organization for each dollar invested in employee costs. The numerator is your favorite measure of economic value-added—say, the premium of market value over book value. The denominator consists of the capitalized value of employee costs—wages, salaries, and benefits, discounted at an appropriate interest rate. Devotees of PVA point out that the ratio is strategic, meaning that it focuses on economic value, which is close to the hearts of shareholders. In effect, PVA shows how well a firm uses all of its resources. It thus relies on the assumption that financial value comes from the organization's ability to employ intellectual capital to direct the use of other capital. As PVA expert Robert Schneier has noted, "This is a sensible assumption, since the assets of the company have no innate ability to create profits—the organization's human resource applies the knowledge, skill, and efforts needed to convert those resources into cashflow."[11] In other words, human capital catalyzes tangible capital.

MEASURE FOR MEASURE

Companies that dedicate themselves to counting tough-to-count intangibles as well as financially denominated assets apparently distinguish themselves by superior performance. A survey conducted by Wm. Schiemann & Associates, an East Coast consulting firm, turned up evidence that what they called "measurement-managed" companies outperform other organizations.[12] Measurement-managed companies meet two criteria: senior management reports agreement on measurable criteria for strategic success, and managers review semiannual performance data in at least three of six categories. The six categories are financial performance, operating efficiency, customer satisfaction, employee performance, innovation and change, and community/environmental issues. Companies that track performance in these areas excel in three ways: identification as an industry leader over the prior three years (74 percent of measurement-managed companies versus 44 percent of others), financial performance in the top third of the industry (83 percent versus 52 percent), and self-reported success at major cultural or operational change (97 percent compared with 55 percent).

Willingness to measure does not make it easy, however. The survey found evidence of a sizable gap between the value that managers place on certain kinds of information and their inclination to bet on its accuracy. Fully 85 percent of the responding executives said that they value customer service data, but only 29 percent said they would bet their jobs on the quality of those data.[13] Information on employee performance exhibited a similar gap; 67 percent said they value it, but only 16 percent (a 51 percentage point gap) said it passes quality muster. Concerns about information quality are hardly surprising, given that only 17 percent of the respondents said that employee performance measures are clearly defined. This is the opinion of the Conference Board Research Director who commented on human resource measures: "Most efforts to measure HR's performance . . . are either too general and of limited value, such as headcount or payroll costs, or so complex that managers are unable or unwilling to use them."[14] Perhaps that is why senior executives have not historically paid much attention to conventional HR measures. The Conference Board reports, for example, that corporate executives, financial analysts, and portfolio managers all give short shrift to measures like employee turnover.[15]

That seems to be changing, however, as managers and analysts come to realize that workers' feelings about their jobs and companies make a big difference in company performance. The consultants at Wm. Schiemann & Associates concluded that a focus on employee measurement is the single biggest factor differentiating successful firms from less successful ones.[16] And CalPERS (the huge California Public Employees Retirement system) has pressured companies in its portfolio to reduce layoffs and account for management practices that show insensitivity to worker needs.[17] On the mutual fund front, Massachusetts Financial Services (MFS) markets a fund called Union Standard Equity, which targets "labor-sensitive" companies for its investment portfolio.[18] MFS has its investments screened by the independent Labor Advisor Board and by American Capital Strategies (ACS); companies that make the cut get onto the ACS Labor Sensitivity Index. According to the prospectus, ACS criteria include "whether the company is or has been involved in strikes or lock-outs and whether the company has demonstrated patterns of noncompliance with applicable labor or health and safety laws." Qualitative factors considered include "patterns of outsourcing and associated plant closings."

Many organizations use employee attitude and organizational climate surveys to try to track worker happiness. But remember that job satisfaction (a commonly measured attitude factor) does not produce, but instead results from, job performance. Measurement systems need to reflect this; a simple index of worker bliss will not tell management whether the storehouse of human capital is increasing or decreasing, or whether human capital investment benefits worker and organization.

An Application Example

Let us go back to the strategy planning meeting on which we eavesdropped in Chapter Four. Recall that the sales and marketing manager had just reviewed the strategy plan with the unit head of Perpetual Petals, producer of ersatz flowers. We saw how the manager might take one strategic organization capability—speedy development and launching of new products—and define human capital elements required to strengthen it. To measure the development and application of human capital, however, takes more. After a triple espresso (this human capital measurement stuff isn't for wimps), the sales and marketing manager sets to work.

IDENTIFY CAPABILITY GAPS Figure 9.4 shows four major elements in the human capital system devised for product development at Perpetual Petals. (Actually, it comes from Towers Perrin's work in a variety of industries, so it should have broad application.) The upper left-hand graphic (denoted as A) shows a simplified plot of the organization capabilities required for Perpetual Petals to be successful. Thus we have the organization's first measurement question: How well positioned is each capability? The horizontal axis measures the strategic importance of each capability. Importance ranges from "needed to play" (necessary for an organization just to get into the competitive game) to "needed to win" (potential opportunities to achieve a competitive advantage). The vertical axis indicates how well the organization performs in comparison with competitors. To plot its competitive position in product development, management could use such data as number of new products introduced compared with the number of competitor introductions; new-product revenue versus competitors' new-product success; or comparative new-product appeal in consumer tests. To identify the horizontal coordinate, the organization would consider such factors as the positions of its current offerings on the industry's product maturity curve, the importance of new-product revenue in the Perpetual Petals strategy, or the length of time since the last successful product introduction.

In this example, new-product development falls in the lower right-hand corner. This means that creating and introducing new offerings is a competitively important but comparatively weak capability for Perpetual Petals. The sales and marketing manager must find ways to improve performance so that product development moves into the

Figure 9.4. A Human Capital Measurement System.

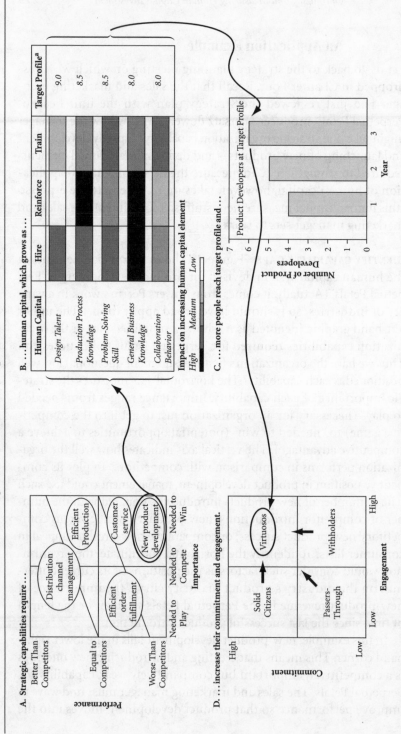

[a]On a scale from 1 to 10, where 1 means the job requires "very little" of a human capital element and 10 means the job requires "quite a lot" of an element.

Source: Graphic D derives from Exhibit 8.1, which is adapted in part from J. C. Casal, "Shoot for the 'Stars,'" *Journal of Health Care Marketing,* 1996, 16(2).

alignment zone depicted by the diagonal lines in graphic A. For capabilities in this zone, the strength of competitive performance roughly matches strategic importance. The company has achieved alignment for efficient flower production and order fulfillment; Perpetual Petals's performance is consistent with the strategic significance of these capabilities. The unit may have overinvested in distribution channel management; competitive performance exceeds the level required by this capability's strategic importance. The head of sales and marketing knows that pulling one or more implementation levers will address the product development problem. We will focus here on how the manager can monitor the effectiveness of the organization's use of the human capital lever.

TRACK THE GROWTH OF CRITICAL HUMAN CAPITAL   We know from the discussion in Chapter Four that a silk flower designer needs a combination of human capital elements. Success at acquiring, building, and managing these will determine how well and how quickly the organization closes the new-product performance gap. The head of sales and marketing should plot a course by gathering the information shown in graphic B. The left-hand column contains an abbreviated list of human capital elements for a product developer. In the middle columns is the organization's assessment of the feasibility of potential strategies for increasing the key elements. The far right-hand column carries the key measurement information. That is where the product development manager figures out the mix of human capital elements required by a successful product designer. The target profile that results represents an aggregate against which the organization can hire and develop. Consider the three most important human capital elements in this example: hiring protocols will focus on talent acquisition, problem solving will call for a mixed hire-and-reinforce strategy, and the organization will face a make-or-buy decision on production process knowledge.

The target human capital profile also serves as the model against which to compare both newly hired and incumbent product developers. By deciding how many product development staffers meet or exceed the profile, the organization can answer the second measurement question: How are we doing in increasing the necessary human capital through our hiring and building efforts? Of course, finding out how well the population of product developers matches up against the profile requires an individual assessment of each worker. This can take place when manager and worker go through the IPO process outlined in Chapter Five. More product developers meeting the target profile signifies more success at working the human capital implementation lever. Graphic C in Figure 9.4 shows a simple way to illustrate the organization's progress. The goal, of course, is for the whole product development group to reach the target profile for each position. The top number on the vertical axis reflects the goal; it should correspond to 100 percent of the population in the function.

MONITOR THE DEDICATION OF WORKERS IN PIVOTAL JOBS   We will call the positions that contribute most directly to an organization's competitive success, positions like the product developers at Perpetual Petals, *pivotal jobs;* these jobs encompass substantial amounts of capability-boosting human capital. Store managers, COBOL programmers, account executives—they have different names in different organizations. However, let's not forget that we live in the age of the nonjob job. The need for flexibility, the assignment of work to teams, and the growth of individual autonomy have knocked down the fences separating one job from another. These days, many organizations have a mix of job types. Some rigidly defined jobs will remain; these have a clear connection to strategy and a stable set of human capital requirements. A few, the most important to strategic success, are pivotal. Simultaneously, many amorphous jobs have emerged—situations in which key people make a range of contributions. The modern project manager, for instance, moves from gig to gig, doing important work but having a vaguely definable (and constantly changing) job. Brokers who move between communities of practice make contributions that defy easy categorization into a job type. For these positions (*roles* is a better word), the individual's human capital makes him or her pivotal; there is no cast-in-stone job definition to serve as an intermediary filter.

At Perpetual Petals, product developers who reach the targeted human capital profile fall into the pivotal job group. But simply having their human capital in the organization is not enough. The organization must also provide a high return on human capital investment, plus an environment that supports its effective investment. The desired result is implied by the third measurement question: How are we doing at keeping our pivotal workers committed to the organization and engaged in their jobs? Management should monitor the individual elements supporting commitment and engagement, as suggested by the contributory measures in Exhibit 9.1. It also makes sense to keep track of key results ratios like productivity, profit, and market cap per employee, and value metrics like Tobin's q and PVA; these indicate the results produced by effective human capital investment.

To go beyond what those measures tell, Perpetual Petals should construct a chart that looks like graphic D in Figure 9.4. Graphic D derives its logic from Exhibit 8.1. To construct the graphic, management would count the number of at-profile product developers (from graphic C) and, using attitude survey results, place each in a quadrant of graphic D. The quadrant labels tell the story. The lower-right box has the highly engaged but dubiously committed Withholders; they have the necessary human capital but lack the commitment to keep them from taking their assets to another company. In the upper-left box are the Solid Citizens, who stay because of ties to the organization; frankly, however, they have grown bored with their jobs. People in the lower-left box show neither commitment nor engagement; better act fast to move passers-through up and to the right.

In fact, the organization should strive to move everyone toward the upper-right box—the ZIP code where Virtuosos live—and minimize turnover to keep them there. Virtuosos meet the targeted human capital profile and display both commitment and engagement. Most important, their human capital endowment and dedication to job and organization make them the organization's best hope to push the product development capability into strategic alignment.

The measurement system depicted in Figure 9.4 meets the four measurement criteria. The measures are simple, strategically focused, and easy to understand. They encourage the establishment of goals: everyone reaching the targeted profile, all capabilities in the alignment zone, low turnover among Virtuosos. They also suggest actions for achieving goals: improve hiring and development to create more Virtuosos and do what it takes to hang on to them.

SUMMARY: THE HUMAN CAPITAL YARDSTICK

The measurement discussion makes a suitable capstone for all the pages that precede it. Here in Chapter Nine we have considered measurement from two perspectives: as a tool for defining optimum combinations of utility and return-on-investment expenditure and as a means to monitor progress in managing human capital strategically.

Taking the measurement approaches described here to full application requires undeniable tenacity and dedication. The effort is worth it for several reasons besides the value of measures themselves. Deriving utility curves requires managers to think long and hard about the returns on investment people want, and to ask the people themselves to define their own trade-offs. Both requirements reinforce sound management practice in the era of the free-agent human capital investor. Moreover, it is hard to imagine going through the process without engaging people in profound discussions about work and its meaning; such discussions are invaluable by-products of the measurement effort.

To do its job, the measurement system must yield insights about vital human capital owners. Indeed, hiring, developing, and holding onto Virtuosos may be the single most important strategic challenge facing knowledge-intensive companies. When times are prosperous and labor markets are constricted, this kind of human capital analysis and measurement can help an organization build its population of Virtuosos. When times get tough and cost cutting becomes inevitable, the system can help managers identify who is critical for survival and can help them monitor success at preserving commitment and engagement from this pivotal population. Moreover, understanding the cost of delivering appealing return-on-investment bundles helps an organization manage the financial implications of commitment and engagement. Companies that can do this have an advantage in any economic environment.

But contemplate the story that has unfolded in these pages, and you can see another shoe and another foot. Instead of worrying about calculating the worth of human assets, companies should concern themselves with defining what human capital owners get out of their association with a business. In other words, they should focus less on the value of the individual to the organization, and more on the value of the organization to the individual. This is the true value that deserves attention from managers who hope to create lasting success.

The measurement system set forth in this chapter reveals a lot about an organization's success at acquiring, eliciting, building, and preserving human capital. Having the will to measure also speaks volumes about the organization itself; it tells the world that here is a company with foresight enough to invest time and resources in understanding its appeal as a workplace. Companies that care enough to measure the value of the organization to the employee will attract people looking for the best place to put their human capital. These organizations position themselves to increase other forms of value—tangible, intangible, and financial. Such companies will prosper, at the expense of competitors and headhunters.

⟿ Notes

Preface

1. K. Q. Seelye, "House Turns Back Measures to Limit Terms in Congress," *New York Times*, Mar. 30, 1995, p. A20.
2. J. Ortega y Gasset, *The Dehumanization of Art* (n.p., 1948).

Chapter One

1. U. Sinclair, *The Jungle* (New York: Penguin Books, 1985), p. 346. (Originally published 1906)
2. Ibid., p. 376.
3. A. Smith, *Wealth of Nations* (New York: P. F. Collier & Son, 1937), p. 103. (Originally published 1776)
4. According to sociologists Larry Moore and Brenda Beck, "Charismatic leaders are persons who are especially skilled in the manipulation of such meanings, doing so through their symbolic use of speech and other key behaviors. . . . The quality or character of the imagery a leader uses in relating various contextual influences and tensions constitutes the essence of personal style." L. F. Moore and B.E.F. Beck, "Leadership Among Bank Managers: A Structural Comparison of Behavioral Responses and Metaphorical Imagery," in J. G. Hunt, D. Hosking, C. A. Schriesheim, and R. Stewart (eds.), *Leaders and Managers: International Perspectives on Managerial Behavior and Leadership* (New York: Pergamon Press, 1984), p. 241.

Iain Mangham, a professor of management development at the University of Bath, believes that some metaphors are downright indispensable for understanding what goes on in business: "Imagine purging all organization and management texts of reference to goals that we aim for and struggle to reach, of directions, of missions, of cross-roads and junctions, of obstacles and blockages that we have to get round. . . . The thoughts that organizations are games, are political, are plays, similarly appear to be indispensable parts of our ways of seeing and being in the world." I. Mangham, "Some

Consequences of Taking Gareth Morgan Seriously," in D. Grant and C. Oswick (eds.), *Metaphor and Organizations* (Thousand Oaks, Calif.: Sage, 1996), p. 29.

5. J. Pfeffer, *Competitive Advantage Through People: Unleashing the Power of the Work Force* (Boston: Harvard Business School Press, 1994), p. 109.

6. American Management Association, *1994 AMA Survey on Downsizing: Summary of Key Findings* (New York: American Management Association, 1994), p. 1.

7. J. Gordon, "Training Budgets: Recession Takes a Bite," *Training*, Oct. 1991, p. 41.

8. American Management Association, *Corporate Job Creation, Job Elimination, and Downsizing: Summary of Key Findings* (New York: American Management Association, 1997), p. 1.

9. "Training Budgets," *Training*, Oct. 1997, p. 41.

10. Towers Perrin, *The People Strategy Benchmark Awareness and Attitude Study* (New York: Towers Perrin, 1995), pp. 2, 3.

11. E. G. Flamholtz, *Human Resource Accounting* (San Francisco: Jossey-Bass, 1985), p. 35.

12. M. Twain, "The Art of Authorship," in W. Blair (ed.), *Selected Shorter Writings of Mark Twain* (Boston: Houghton Mifflin, 1962), p. 226.

13. The first (and so far, only) time I have seen workers referred to as investors in the business press is in T. A. Stewart's article, "A New Way to Think About Employees," *Fortune*, Apr. 13, 1998, pp. 169, 170.

14. Smith, *Wealth of Nations*, p. 103.

15. J. S. Lublin and J. B. White, "Throwing Off Angst, Workers Are Feeling in Control of Careers," *Wall Street Journal*, Sept. 11, 1997, p. A1.

16. L. M. Lynch and S. E. Black, *Beyond the Incidence of Training: Evidence from a National Employers Survey*, Working Paper No. 5231 (Cambridge, Mass.: National Bureau of Economic Research, 1995), p. 22.

17. U.S. Bureau of the Census, *Statistical Abstract of the United States, 1995* (Washington, D.C.: U.S. Government Printing Office, 1995), p. 426.

18. C. Handy, *The Age of Unreason* (Boston: Harvard Business School Press, 1989), p. 153.

19. U.S. Bureau of the Census, *Statistical Abstract of the United States, 1996* (Washington, D.C.: U.S. Government Printing Office, 1996), pp. 159, 192, 193.

20. U.S. Bureau of the Census, *Statistical Abstract of the United States, 1996*, p. 428.

21. Bureau of Labor Statistics, Local Area Unemployment Statistics, [http://stats.bls.gov/lauhome], Mar. 31, 1998.

22. Quoted in D. M. Gordon, *Fat and Mean: The Corporate Squeeze of Working Americans and the Myth of Managerial "Downsizing"* (New York: Free Press, 1996), p. 223.

23. M. Hopkins and J. L. Seglin, "Americans @ Work," *Inc.*, Special Edition on the State of Small Business, 1997, 19(7), p. 85.

24. S. Caulkin, "Skills, Not Loyalty, Now Are Key If You Want Job Security," *San Francisco Examiner*, Sept. 7, 1997, p. J-3.

25. *Statistical Handbook of Working America* (Detroit: Gale Research, 1995), p. 180.

Chapter Two

1. Biblical references come from Genesis 2:9, 3:23.

2. S. Terkel, *Working: People Talk About What They Do All Day and How They Feel About What They Do* (New York: Pantheon Books, 1974), Introduction.

3. W. H. Whyte, Jr., *The Organization Man* (New York: Simon & Schuster, 1956), p. 15.

4. E. G. Flamholtz and J. M. Lacey, *Personnel Management, Human Capital Theory, and Human Resource Accounting.* Industrial Relations Monograph Series, No. 27 (Los Angeles: Institute of Industrial Relations, University of California, Los Angeles, 1981), p. 19.

5. G. S. Becker, *Human Capital: A Theoretical and Empirical Analysis with Special Reference to Education* (Chicago: University of Chicago Press, 1993).

6. R. Crawford, *In the Era of Human Capital* (New York: HarperBusiness, 1991), p. 5.

7. C. Ammer and D. S. Ammer, *Dictionary of Business and Economics* (New York: Free Press, 1977), p. 424.

8. W. C. Borman, D. Dorsey, and L. Ackerman, "Time-Spent Responses as Time Allocation Strategies: Relations with Sales Performance in a Stockbroker Sample," *Personnel Psychology*, 1992, no. 45, pp. 770, 771.

9. Ibid., pp. 774, 775.

10. The discussion of commitment comes from several sources. See R. Eisenberger, R. Huntington, S. Hutchison, and D. Sowa, "Perceived Organizational Support," *Journal of Applied Psychology*, 1986, 71(3), pp. 500–507; J. E. Mathieu and D. M. Zajac, "A Review and Meta-Analysis of the Antecedents, Correlates, and Consequences of Organizational Commitment," *Psychological Bulletin*, 1990, 108(2), pp. 171–194; A. E. Reichers, "Conflict and Organizational Commitments," *Journal of Applied Psychology*, 1986, 71(3), pp. 508–514.

11. J. P. Meyer and N. J. Allen, *Commitment in the Workplace: Theory, Research, and Application* (Thousand Oaks, Calif.: Sage, 1997), p. 11.

12. L. M. Shore and S. J. Wayne, "Commitment and Employee Behavior: Comparison of Affective Commitment and Continuance Commitment with Perceived Organizational Support," *Journal of Applied Psychology,* 1993, 78(5), p. 774.

13. Meyer and Allen, *Commitment in the Workplace,* p. 24.

14. H. S. Becker, "Notes on the Concept of Commitment," *American Journal of Sociology,* 1960, 66(1), p. 36.

15. Meyer and Allen, *Commitment in the Workplace,* p. 25.

16. Ibid., p. 93; Shore and Wayne, "Commitment and Employee Behavior," p. 775.

17. J. P. Meyer and N. J. Allen, "Testing the 'Side-Bet Theory' of Organizational Commitment: Some Methodological Considerations," *Journal of Applied Psychology,* 1984, 69(3), p. 373.

18. D. Yankelovich and J. Immerwahr, *Putting the Work Ethic to Work: A Public Agenda Report on Restoring America's Competitive Vitality* (New York: Public Agenda, 1983), p. 17.

19. G. J. Blau and K. B. Boal, "Conceptualizing How Job Involvement and Organizational Commitment Affect Turnover and Absenteeism," *Academy of Management Review,* 1987, 12(2), p. 289.

20. R. Garner, "Gimme Some Respect! Annual Job Satisfaction Survey," *Computerworld,* May 26, 1997, p. 89.

21. C. T. Hall, "Wanted: Biotech Help," *San Francisco Chronicle,* Apr. 20, 1998, p. B1.

22. Genentech, *1997 Annual Report,* p. 1.

23. Interview with J. Heyboer, senior vice president of human resources, Genentech, Mar. 27, 1998.

24. Blau and Boal, "Conceptualizing," p. 289.

25. Meyer and Allen, *Commitment,* p. 28.

26. T. A. DeCotiis and T. P. Summers, "A Path Analysis of a Model of the Antecedents and Consequences of Organizational Commitment," *Human Relations,* 1987, 40(7), p. 466.

27. Ibid., p. 467.

28. Eisenberger, Huntington, Hutchison, and Sowa, "Perceived Organizational Support," p. 501.

29. Meyer and Allen, *Commitment,* p. 52.

30. E. E. Lawler III, and L. W. Porter, "The Effect of Performance on Job Satisfaction," *Industrial Relations,* 1967, no. 7, pp. 27, 28.

31. Yankelovich and Immerwahr, *Putting the Work Ethic to Work,* p. 29.

32. See two sources: Blessing/White, *You Can Demand Their Time But Not Their Commitment: A Study of Discretionary Effort in the Workplace* (Princeton,

N.J.: Blessing/White, 1994), pp. 6–8; "Employees Aren't Encouraged to Give Extra Effort, Study Concludes," *Management Review Executive Forum, Management Review,* July 1996, pp. 2, 3.

33. E. Galinksy, J. T. Bond, and D. E. Friedman, *The Changing Workforce: Highlights of the National Study* (New York: Families and Work Institute, 1993), p. 14.

34. The discussion of transactional and relational elements comes from M. Barringer and G. Milkovich, *Changing Employment Contracts: The Relative Effects of Proposed Changes in Compensation, Benefits and Job Security on Employment Outcomes,* Working Paper 95–14 (Ithaca, N.Y.: Center for Advanced Human Resource Studies, Cornell University, 1995), pp. 8, 21.

35. R. Gordon, "Muni Driver Takes the High Road," *San Francisco Examiner,* Dec. 28, 1997, pp. D-1, D-4.

36. J. Milton, *Paradise Lost,* line 262.

37. A. Lucchetti, "An Auto Worker Earns More Than $100,000 but at a Personal Cost," *Wall Street Journal,* Aug. 1, 1996, p. A1.

38. M. Selz, "Entrepreneurs May Be More Widespread Than Thought," *Wall Street Journal,* Dec. 13, 1996, p. B11B.

39. S. N. Mehta, "More Women Quit Lucrative Jobs to Start Their Own Businesses," *Wall Street Journal,* Nov. 11, 1996, p. A1.

40. Ibid.

41. R. Berner, "The Rolls-Royce of Leather Jackets Is Hard to Come By," *Wall Street Journal,* Nov. 22, 1996, pp. A1, A10.

Chapter Three

1. H. Mintzberg, *The Rise and Fall of Strategic Planning* (New York: Free Press, 1994), pp. 23, 24.

2. Ibid., p. 26.

3. T. A. Stewart, "Trying to Grasp the Intangible," *Fortune,* Oct. 2, 1995, p. 157.

4. Conference Board, *New Corporate Performance Measures: A Research Report* (New York: Conference Board, 1995), p. 15.

5. S. Henry, "Culture Club: Signing Up the High-Tech Workforce," *Tech-Capital,* Mar.–Apr. 1998, p. 43.

6. M. E. Porter, *Competitive Strategy: Techniques for Analyzing Industries and Competitors* (New York: Free Press, 1980), p. 3.

7. The discussion of product and market themes and organization capabilities comes from an internal Towers Perrin document, *An Analytic Framework for Strategy Clarification,* June 1996. The document was produced in

conjunction with Paul Tiffany, professor of business policy and strategy at the Wharton School of the University of Pennsylvania and the Haas School of Business at the University of California, Berkeley.

8. The telemedia analysis comes from an internal Towers Perrin project conducted in 1996 and 1997.

9. J. Helyar and J. S. Lublin, "Do You Need an Expert on Widgets to Head a Widget Company?" *Wall Street Journal,* Jan. 21, 1998, p. A1.

10. R. Ornstein, *The Roots of the Self: Unraveling the Mystery of Who We Are* (San Francisco: HarperSanFrancisco, 1993), p. 26.

11. Towers Perrin, *IT Hot Skills Database: Workplace and Reward Practices* (New York: Towers Perrin, 1998), p. 23.

12. Ibid., p. 24.

13. Ibid., p. 25.

14. K. Alvares, vice president of human resources at Sun Microsystems, speaking before the Senate Judiciary Committee hearing on the temporary visa program for high-tech workers, Feb. 25, 1998.

15. R. Garner, "Gimme Some Respect! Annual Job Satisfaction Survey," *Computerworld,* May 26, 1997, p. 91.

Chapter Four

1. H. Melville, *Bartleby the Scrivener,* in *The Shorter Novels of Herman Melville* (New York: Grosset & Dunlap), 1928, p. 117. (Originally published 1856)

2. J. E. Hunter, F. L. Schmidt, and M. K. Judiesch, "Individual Differences in Output Variability as a Function of Job Complexity," *Journal of Applied Psychology,* 1990, 75(1), p. 36.

3. Olsten Corporation, *Staffing Strategies: The Olsten Forum on Human Resource Issues and Trends* (Melville, N.Y.: Olsten Corporation, 1996), p. 1.

4. O. L. Gallaga, "High-Tech Firms Rely More on New Breed of Temp Worker," *Wall Street Journal,* July 31, 1996, p. B8.

5. Internal company documents.

6. D. M. Rousseau, "Changing the Deal While Keeping the People," *Academy of Management Executive,* 1996, 10(1), p. 50.

7. Ibid., p. 51.

8. J. C. Mowen, *Judgment Calls: Making Good Decisions in Difficult Situations* (New York: Simon & Schuster, 1993), p. 248.

9. P. Herriot, quoted in J. W. Smither and others, "Applicant Reactions to Selection Procedures," *Personnel Psychology,* 1993, 46, p. 52.

10. T. H. Macan, M. J. Avedon, M. Paese, and D. E. Smith, "The Effects of Applicants' Reactions to Cognitive Ability Tests and an Assessment Center," *Personnel Psychology,* 1994, 47, pp. 717, 718.

11. H. Schuler, "Social Validity of Selection Situations: A Concept and Some Empirical Results," in H. Schuler, J. L. Farr, and M. Smith (eds.), *Personnel Selection and Assessment: Individual and Organizational Perspectives* (Hillsdale, N.J.: Erlbaum, 1993), p. 12.

12. Smither and others, "Applicant Reactions," p. 54.

13. Schuler, "Social Validity," pp. 15–19; Smither and others, "Applicant Reactions," p. 71.

14. Schuler, "Social Validity," p. 18.

15. N. Munk and S. Oliver, "Think Fast!" *Forbes,* Mar. 24, 1997, p. 147.

16. Schuler, "Social Validity," p. 15.

17. T. J. Rodgers, "No Excuses Management," *Harvard Business Review,* July–Aug. 1990, p. 84.

18. Ibid., p. 85.

19. Internal company documents.

20. J. Cole, "Flying High at Southwest," *HR Focus,* May 1998, p. 8.

21. Numbers in these ranges appeared in several publications in 1998 and were confirmed by Libby Sartain, vice president—people, Southwest Airlines.

22. "Up Close Q&A," *Career Pilot,* Aug. 1996, p. 10.

23. Schuler, "Social Validity," p. 15.

24. C. L. Adkins, C. J. Russell, and J. D. Werbel, "Judgments of Fit in the Selection Process: The Role of Work Value Congruence," *Personnel Psychology,* 1994, 47, p. 609.

25. Ibid., pp. 611, 612.

26. D. M. Rousseau and M. M. Greller, "Human Resource Practices: Administrative Contract Makers," *Human Resource Management,* 1994, 33(3), p. 389.

27. L. W. Porter and E. E. Lawler III, "What Job Attitudes Tell About Motivation," *Harvard Business Review,* Jan.–Feb. 1968, p. 124.

Chapter Five

1. R. W. Emerson, *Compensation* (New York: P. F. Collier & Son Corporation, 1937), pp. 96, 97. (Originally published 1841)

2. S. Bowles, D. M. Gordon, and T. E. Weisskopf, quoted in D. Yankelovich and J. Immerwahr, *Putting the Work Ethic to Work: A Public Agenda Report on*

Restoring America's Competitive Vitality (New York: Public Agenda, 1983), p. 39.

3. Kepner-Tregoe®, *Minds at Work: How Much Brainpower Are We Really Using?* (Princeton, N.J.: Kepner-Tregoe®, 1997), p. 5.

4. Data in this chapter come from Towers Perrin, *The 1997 Towers Perrin Workplace Index* (New York: Towers Perrin, 1997).

5. J. Case, "The Open-Book Revolt," *Inc.*, June 1995, p. 29.

6. J. Case, *The Open-Book Experience* (Reading, Mass.: Addison-Wesley, 1998), p. 202.

7. J. C. Shaffer, "Creating a Business of Business People," *Strategic Communication Management*, Apr.–May 1997, pp. 3, 4.

8. G. Witherall, "Workers Are Bonded to the Business," *Los Angeles Times*, Nov. 29, 1996, pp. D1, D4.

9. Sculley, quoted in D. Whyte, *The Heart Aroused* (New York: Currency Doubleday, 1994), p. 78.

10. D. M. Rousseau and M. M. Greller, "Human Resource Practices: Administrative Contract Makers," *Human Resource Management*, 1994, 33(3), pp. 388, 389.

11. F. R. Bleakly, "A Bastion of Paternalism Fights Against Change," *Wall Street Journal*, Jan. 16, 1997, pp. B1, B2.

12. *Fireman's Fund Partnership Portfolio* (internal document), p. 1.

13. F. Fukuyama, *Trust: The Social Virtues and the Creation of Prosperity* (New York: Free Press, 1995), p. 25.

14. Ibid., p. 25.

15. Ibid., pp. 27, 28.

16. P. Slovic, "Perceived Risk, Trust, and Democracy," *Risk Analysis*, 1993, 13(6), pp. 677, 678.

17. A. Smith, *Wealth of Nations* (New York: P. F. Collier & Son, 1937), p. 10. (Originally published 1776)

18. M. Hopkins and J. L. Seglin, "Americans @ Work," *Inc.*, Special Edition on the State of Small Business, 1997, 19(7), pp. 77, 78.

19. Slovic, "Perceived Risk," p. 677.

20. D. E. Morrison, "Psychological Contracts and Change," *Human Resource Management*, 1994, 33(3), p. 357.

Chapter Six

1. M. Twain, *The Adventures of Tom Sawyer* (New York: Bantam Books, 1981), pp. 10–16. (Originally published 1876)

2. J. Piaget, quoted in R. W. White, "Motivation Reconsidered: The Concept of Competence," *Psychological Review,* 1959, 66(5), p. 316.

3. White, "Motivation Reconsidered," pp. 321, 322, 323.

4. *Fireman's Fund Partnership Portfolio* (internal document), p. 5.

5. Interview with A. Rich, senior vice president of human resources, Williams-Sonoma, May 18, 1998.

6. Aon Consulting, *The 1997 Survey of Human Resource Trends Report* (Detroit: Aon Consulting, 1997), pp. 34, 35.

7. Center for Workforce Development, Education Development Center, Inc., *The Teaching Firm: Where Productive Work and Learning Converge* (Newton, Mass.: Center for Workforce Development, Education Development Center, Jan. 1998), pp. 126, 127.

8. Ibid., p. 127.

9. L. Berton, "Many Firms Cut Staff in Accounts Payable and Pay a Steep Price," *Wall Street Journal,* Sept. 5, 1996, p. A1.

10. J. Falvey, "The Art of Selling," *Wall Street Journal,* July 15, 1996, p. A10.

11. D. Yankelovich and J. Immerwahr, *Putting the Work Ethic to Work: A Public Agenda Report on Restoring America's Competitive Vitality* (New York: Public Agenda, 1983), p. 12. Yankelovich and Immerwahr in turn quote W. J. Heisler and John W. Houch, *A Matter of Dignity* (Universitiy of Notre Dame Press, 1977), p. 66.

12. T. Aeppel, "Not All Workers Find Idea of Empowerment as Neat as It Sounds," *Wall Street Journal,* Sept. 8, 1997, p. A1.

13. E. L. Deci with R. Flaste, *Why We Do What We Do: Understanding Self-Motivation* (New York: Penguin Books, 1995), pp. 134, 135.

14. A. S. Tannenbaum, paraphrased in L. E. Parker and R. H. Price, "Empowered Managers and Empowered Workers: The Effects of Managerial Support and Managerial Perceived Control on Workers' Sense of Control over Decision Making," *Human Relations,* 1994, 47(8), p. 914.

15. "Rethinking Work," *Business Week,* Oct. 17, 1994, p. 77.

16. E. Galinsky, J. T. Bond, and D. E. Friedman, *The Changing Workforce: Highlights of the National Study* (New York: Families and Work Institute, 1993), p. 20.

17. T. Schellhardt, "Want to Be a Manager? Many People Say No, Calling Job Miserable," *Wall Street Journal,* Apr. 4, 1997, p. A1.

18. J. C. Collins and J. I. Porras, *Built to Last: Successful Habits of Visionary Companies* (New York: HarperCollins, 1994), pp. 209, 210.

19. T. J. McCoy, paraphrased in B. Ettorre, "The Empowerment Gap: Hype Versus Reality," *Management Review,* July–Aug., 1997, p. 13.

20. Deci with Flaste, *Why We Do What We Do,* p. 71.

21. "Rethinking Rewards," *Harvard Business Review*, Nov.–Dec. 1993, p. 42.

22. T. Amabile, as quoted in "Creativity's Rewards," an interview with Michelle Trudeau on National Public Radio, Mar. 28, 1997.

23. M. Lewis, "The Bonus Holdup," *New York Times Magazine*, Sept. 10, 1995, p. 28.

24. P. D. Sweeney and D. B. McFarlin, "Workers' Evaluations of the 'Ends' and the 'Means': An Examination of Four Models of Distributive and Procedural Justice," *Organizational Behavior and Human Decision Processes*, 1993, no. 55, pp. 23, 24.

25. K. A. Brown and V. L. Huber, "Lowering Floors and Raising Ceilings: A Longitudinal Assessment of the Effects of an Earnings-at-Risk Plan on Pay Satisfaction," *Personnel Psychology*, 1992, 45, p. 282.

26. P. Nulty, "Incentive Pay Can Be Crippling," *Fortune*, Nov. 13, 1995, p. 235.

27. G. S. Leventhal, paraphrased in J. P. Meyer and N. J. Allen, *Commitment in the Workplace: Theory, Research, and Application* (Thousand Oaks, Calif.: Sage, 1997), p. 111.

28. Brown and Huber, "Lowering Floors," p. 299.

29. R. L. Heneman, D. B. Greenberger, and S. Strasser, "The Relationship Between Pay-for-Performance Perceptions and Pay Satisfaction," *Personnel Psychology*, 1988, 41, p. 746.

30. Lewis, "Bonus Holdup," pp. 28, 29.

31. L. K. Gundry and D. M. Rousseau, "Critical Incidents in Communicating Culture to Newcomers: The Meaning Is the Message," *Human Relations*, 1994, 47(9), pp. 1065, 1066.

32. Ibid., p. 1079.

33. D. Brinburg and P. Castell, "A Resource Exchange Theory Approach to Interpersonal Interactions: A Test of Foa's Theory," *Journal of Personality and Social Psychology*, 1982, 43(2), p. 261.

34. H. Lancaster, "Life Without Titles: What Makes Bosses Bosses, Peons Peons," *Wall Street Journal*, May 16, 1995, p. B1.

Chapter Seven

1. *The Other Shoe: Education's Contribution to the Productivity of Establishments*, Catalog No. RE02 (Philadelphia: National Center on the Educational Quality of the Workforce, 1995), p. 2.

2. *First Findings from the EQW National Employer Survey*, Catalog No. RE01 (Philadelphia: National Center on the Educational Quality of the Workforce, 1995), pp. 9, 10.

3. "Industry Report: 1998," *Training,* Oct. 1998, p. 49.

4. "Industry Report: 1996," *Training,* Oct. 1996, p. 43; "Industry Report: 1997," *Training,* Oct. 1997, p. 41.

5. L. M. Lynch and S. E. Black, *Employer-Provided Training in the Manufacturing Sector: First Results from the United States,* Catalog No. WP34 (Philadelphia: National Center on the Educational Quality of the Workforce, 1996), pp. 3, 4.

6. *Job Skills Training in the California Workforce* (San Francisco: Field Institute and Future of Work and Health, 1996), graph 12.

7. "Industry Report: 1998," pp. 56, 60.

8. R. Marshall and M. Tucker, *Thinking for a Living: Education and the Wealth of Nations* (New York: Basic Books, 1992), p. 69.

9. Center for Workforce Development, Education Development Center, Inc., *The Teaching Firm: Where Productive Work and Learning Converge* (Newton, Mass.: Center for Workforce Development, Education Development Center, Jan. 1998), p. 9.

10. A. R. Damasio, *Descartes' Error: Emotion, Reason, and the Human Brain* (New York: Grosset & Dunlap, 1994), p. 249.

11. "Industry Report: 1998," p. 58.

12. Damasio, *Descartes' Error,* pp. 173, 174.

13. I. Nonaka, "A Dynamic Theory of Organizational Knowledge Creation," *Organization Science,* 1994, 5(1), p. 22.

14. E. J. Langer, *The Power of Mindful Learning* (Reading, Mass.: Addison-Wesley, 1997), p. 130.

15. Nonaka, "Dynamic Theory of Organizational Knowledge Creation," p. 18.

16. Ibid., p. 16.

17. *From Training to Learning: Preparing for Success in a Digital World* (Menlo Park, Calif.: Institute for Research on Learning, 1997), pp. 20, 21.

18. S. Stucky, quoted in P. A. Galagan, "The Search for the Poetry of Work," *Training and Development,* Oct. 1993, p. 36.

19. Center for Workforce Development, *Teaching Firm,* p. 53.

20. Ibid., p. 133.

21. Ibid., p. 222.

22. Ibid., p. 222.

23. Ibid., pp. 223–225.

24. Ibid., p. 225.

25. C. Darrouzet and others, *Rethinking "Distance" in Distance Learning,* Report No. IRL 19.101 (Menlo Park, Calif.: Institute for Research on Learning, May 1995), p. 5.

26. S. Stucky, quoted in ibid., p. 6.

27. Interview with S. Stucky, associate director, Institute for Research on Learning, July 15, 1997.

28. Darrouzet and others, *Rethinking "Distance,"* p. 18.

29. "Boss' View of Telecommuting," *USA Today,* Nov. 28, 1995, p. B1.

30. H. Wild, L. Bishop, and C. L. Sullivan, *Building Environments for Learning and Innovation* (Menlo Park, Calif.: Institute for Research on Learning, Aug. 1996), p. 22.

31. K. A. Jehn and P. P. Shah, *Interpersonal Relationships and Task Performance: An Examination of Mediating Processes in Friendship and Acquaintance Groups,* Working Paper WP 96–24 (Philadelphia: Reginald H. Jones Center, Wharton School, University of Pennsylvania, 1996), pp. 3, 34.

32. Ibid., p. 34.

33. A. Taranta, "The Double Life of Islands," *Pacific Discovery,* Summer 1995, p. 35.

34. J. Donne, *Devotions upon Emergent Occasions, Meditation XVI,* 1624.

35. Stucky, interview.

36. Ibid.

37. M. Aring, quoted in D. Stamps, "Learning Ecologies," *Training,* Jan. 1998, p. 34.

38. E. Wenger, quoted in ibid., p. 38.

39. Interview with L. Bishop, research scientist, Institute for Research on Learning, Aug. 15, 1997.

40. E. G. Flamholtz and J. M. Lacey, *Personnel Management, Human Capital Theory, and Human Resource Accounting,* Industrial Relations Monograph Series, No. 27 (Los Angeles: Institute of Industrial Relations, University of California, Los Angeles, 1981), pp. 41, 42.

41. T. A. Stewart, "Beat the Budget and Astound Your CFO," *Fortune,* Oct. 28, 1996, p. 187.

42. Ibid.

43. T. H. Davenport and L. Prusak, *Working Knowledge: How Organizations Manage What They Know* (Boston: Harvard Business School Press, 1998). Summarized in Audio-Tech Business Book Summaries. T. H. Davenport is not related to me.

44. A. de Tocqueville, *Democracy in America,* pt. 1, chap. 3, 1835.

45. E. Wenger, "Communities of Practice: The Social Fabric of a Learning Organization," *Healthcare Forum Journal,* July–Aug. 1996, p. 22.

46. P. M. Senge, *The Fifth Discipline: The Art and Practice of the Learning Organization* (New York: Currency Doubleday, 1990), p. 14.

47. T. A. Stewart, *Intellectual Capital: The New Wealth of Organizations* (New York: Currency Doubleday, 1997), p. 216. Stewart refers to what he calls "intellectual capital," which incorporates human capital. I have interpreted his phrase liberally.

Chapter Eight

1. National Opinion Research Center, University of Chicago, *General Social Surveys, 1972–1996: Cumulative Codebook* (Storrs, Conn.: Roper Center for Public Opinion Research, University of Connecticut, Nov. 1996), p. 401.
2. American Management Association, *Corporate Job Creation, Job Elimination, and Downsizing: Summary of Key Findings* (New York: American Management Association, 1997), p. 1.
3. Bureau of Labor Statistics, Local Area Unemployment Statistics, [http://stats.bls.gov/lauhome], Mar. 31, 1998.
4. Towers Perrin, *The 1997 Towers Perrin Workplace Index* (New York: Towers Perrin, 1997).
5. J. T. Bond, E. Galinsky, and J. E. Swanberg, *The 1997 National Study of the Changing Workforce* (New York: Families and Work Institute, 1998), p. 115.
6. J. Katz, "The Digital Citizen," *Wired,* Dec. 1997, p. 82.
7. S. Gould, "An Equity-Exchange Model of Organizational Involvement," *Academy of Management Review,* 1979, 4(1), p. 56.
8. D. N. Dickter, M. Roznowski, and D. A. Harrison, "Temporal Tempering: An Event History Analysis of the Process of Voluntary Turnover," *Journal of Applied Psychology,* 1996, 81(6), p. 710.
9. Ibid., p. 711.
10. Internal company documents.
11. Ibid.
12. S. Benartzi and R. H. Thaler, "Myopic Loss Aversion and the Equity Premium Puzzle," *Quarterly Journal of Economics,* Feb. 1995, p. 73.
13. Ibid., p. 79.
14. D. M. Rousseau, "Changing the Deal While Keeping the People," *Academy of Management Executive,* 1996, 10(1), pp. 51, 52.
15. P. Slovic, B. Fischhoff, and S. Lichtenstein, "Facts and Fears: Understanding Perceived Risk," in R. C. Schwing and W. A. Albers Jr. (eds.), *Societal Risk Assessment: How Safe Is Safe Enough?* (New York: Plenum Press, 1980), p. 183.
16. G. J. Blau and K. B. Boal, "Using Job Involvement and Organizational Commitment Interactively to Predict Turnover," *Journal of Management,* 1989, 15(1), p. 116.
17. Bond, Galinsky, and Swanberg, *1997 National Study of the Changing Workforce,* p. 129.
18. Gould, "Equity-Exchange Model," p. 57.
19. S. L. Robinson, M. S. Kraatz, and D. M. Rousseau, "Changing Obligations and the Psychological Contract: A Longitudinal Study," *Academy of Management Journal,* 1994, 37(1), p. 149.

20. Internal company documents.

21. B. Frei, "Halting Workplace Hopscotch," *San Francisco Examiner*, Mar. 22, 1998, pp. B-5, B-6.

22. R. Brealey and S. Myers, *Principles of Corporate Finance* (New York: McGraw-Hill, 1981), p. 121.

23. L. Alderman, "Here Comes the Four-Income Family," *Money*, Feb. 1995, p. 150.

24. G. Becker, *Human Capital: A Theoretical and Empirical Analysis with Special Reference to Education* (Chicago: University of Chicago Press, 1993), p. 91.

25. A. Smith, *Wealth of Nations* (New York: P. F. Collier & Son, 1937), pp. 109, 111. (Originally published 1776)

26. D. M. Schweiger and A. S. DeNisi, "Communication with Employees Following a Merger: A Longitudinal Field Experiment," *Academy of Management Journal*, 1991, 34(1), pp. 110–135.

27. Ibid., p. 113.

28. Ibid., pp. 111, 112.

29. Ibid., p. 130.

30. Ibid., p. 118.

31. J. Helyar, "MCI Brass Sets Out to Rally Dispirited Troops," *Wall Street Journal*, Nov. 3, 1997, p. B1.

32. T. J. Larkin and S. Larkin, "Reaching and Changing Frontline Employees," *Harvard Business Review*, May–June 1996, pp. 95, 102, 103.

33. Ibid., pp. 101, 102.

34. J. Brockner, "Managing the Effects of Layoffs on Survivors," *California Management Review*, 1992, 34(2), p. 24.

35. Ibid., p. 25.

36. Society for Human Resource Management, *1997 Retention Practices Mini-Survey*, June 1997, p. 8.

37. Robert Half International, *How to Keep Your Best People* (n.p.: Robert Half International, 1997), p. 7.

38. B. P. Hall, *Values Shift: A Guide to Personal & Organizational Transformation* (Rockport, Mass.: Twin Lights Publishers, 1995), p. 89.

39. T. A. Stewart, "Gray Flannel Suit? Moi?" *Fortune*, Mar. 16, 1998, p. 82.

40. Katz, "Digital Citizen," p. 82.

41. Corporate Leadership Council, *Forced Outside: Leadership Talent Sourcing and Retention* (Washington, D.C.: Advisory Board Company, 1998), p. 220; interview with Devashree Gupta, lead consultant, June 22, 1998.

42. G. J. Blau and K. B. Boal, "Conceptualizing How Job Involvement and Organizational Commitment Affect Turnover and Absenteeism," *Academy of Management Review*, 1987, 12(12), p. 289.

43. T. Jefferson, letter to W. C. Jarvis, Sept. 28, 1820.

Chapter Nine

1. W. Thomson, Lord Kelvin, *Popular Lectures and Addresses*, 1891–1894.

2. S. J. Gould, *The Flamingo's Smile: Reflections in Natural History* (New York: Norton, 1985), pp. 126, 127.

3. P. Carbonara, "Hire for Attitude, Train for Skill," *Fast Company*, Aug.–Sept. 1996, p. 74.

4. I am indebted to Bryan Orme, a conjoint analysis expert from Sawtooth Software, for his help with the explanation of conjoint. Sawtooth is located in Sequim, WA.

5. Carbonara, "Hire for Attitude," p. 74.

6. Internal company documents.

7. S. W. Hawking, *A Brief History of Time: From the Big Bang to Black Holes* (New York: Bantam Books, 1988), p. 175.

8. NCI Research, *Evaluating Intangible Assets in Capital Investment Decision-making*, report prepared for U.S. Department of Commerce, Economic Development Administration (Evanston, Ill.: NCI Research, June 1995), p. 11.

9. L. Edvinsson and M. S. Malone, *Intellectual Capital: Realizing Your Company's True Value by Finding Its Hidden Brainpower* (New York: HarperBusiness, 1997), p. 11.

10. P. Megna and M. Klock, "The Impact of Intangible Assets on Tobin's q in the Semiconductor Industry," *AEA Papers and Proceedings*, May 1993, p. 268.

11. R. Schneier, "People Value Added: The New Performance Measure," *Strategy and Leadership*, Mar.–Apr. 1997, p. 16.

12. J. H. Lingle and W. A. Schiemann, "From Balanced Scorecard to Strategic Gauges: Is Measurement Worth It?" *Management Review*, Mar. 1996, p. 60.

13. Ibid., pp. 57, 58.

14. L. S. Csoka, "Measuring HR's Performance," *HR Executive Review: Measuring the Value of HR* (New York: Conference Board, 1995), 3(3), p. 3.

15. Conference Board, *New Corporate Performance Measures: A Research Report*, Report No. 1118–95-RR (New York: Conference Board, 1995), p. 53.

16. Lingle and Schiemann, "From Balanced Scorecard," pp. 58, 59.

17. B. Ettorre, "The HR Factor," *Management Review*, Dec. 1994, p. 26.

18. MFS Union Standard Equity Fund, Prospectus, Aug. 1, 1997, pp. 4, 5.

―∿― Index

A

Ability, in human capital, 19–20
Acceptance: index of, 117–119; in workplace environment, 96, 111–119
Accommodation, and contract flexibility, 78
Ackerman, L., 229
Adam, 17
Adkins, C. L., 233
Aeppel, T., 235
Alderman, L., 240
Alignment. *See* Strategy alignment
Allen, N. J., 230, 236
Alvares, K., 232
Amabile, T., 133, 236
America Online, 50
American Capital Strategies, 218
American Dietetic Association, reinforcement at, 140–141
American Management Association, 5, 9n, 170, 228, 239
Ammer, C., 229
Ammer, D. S., 229
Aon Consulting, 125, 235
Apple, understanding at, 104–105
Aring, M., 158, 238
Asset: criteria for, 6; market value of, 46; workers as, 4–7
AT&T, 50
Attitudinal commitment, 24, 30
Attitudes, toward job stability, 169–170
Automation, costs of, 127–128
Autonomy: and competence, 131–132; and investment, 128–134; and learning, 148–149, 151; and

rewards, 132–134; and work processes, 130–132
Avedon, M. J., 233

B

Barringer, M., 231
Beck, B.E.F., 227
Becker, G. S., 19, 190, 229, 240
Becker, H. S., 25, 230
Behaviors: by company, 88; in human capital, 20; increasing, 68
Bell System: and contracts, 79; in telemedia industry, 50
Benartzi, S., 239
Berner, R., 231
Berton, L., 235
Bethlehem Steel Co., work processes at, 21
Bishop, L., 159, 238
Black, S. E., 145, 228, 237
Blau, G. J., 180n, 230, 239
Bleakly, F. R., 234
Blessing/White, 230–231
Boal, K. B., 180n, 230, 239
Boeing, and informal learning, 151
Bond, J. T., 231, 235, 239
Bonded Motors, and strategy alignment, 103
Borman, W. C., 229
Boundary spanners, for communities of practice, 156
Bounded rationality, and retention, 189–190
Bowles, S., 233
Brealey, R., 240

Brinburg, D., 236
Brockner, J., 240
Brookings Institution, 46
Brown, K. A., 236
Budgets, for training, 159–160
Buffet, W., 136–137
Bureau of Labor Statistics, 11, 12n, 228, 239

C

California, job training in, 145
California Public Employees Retirement, 218
Capabilities: measuring gaps in, 219–221; organizational, and strategy, 48–49, 51–53
Carbonara, P., 241
Casal, J. C., 180n, 220n
Case, J., 101, 234
Castell, P., 236
Caulkin, S., 229
Center for Workforce Development, 146n, 235, 237. *See also* Education Development Center
Change: and contract flexibility, 77–81; managing, 80–81
Clews, H., 18
Cole, J., 233
Collins, J. C., 130–131, 235
Commitment: and acceptance, 118–119; and contract duration, 73; and engagement, 26–28, 179–198; and friendship, 154; monitoring, 222–223; to organization, 24–26; and performance, 28–30; and return on investment, 29–34; and strategy alignment, 104–105; and understanding, 110–111
Communities of practice, for learning, 152–156
Competence: and autonomy, 131–132; building, 143–168; and investment, 122–128; as organizational value, 127–128; and strategy alignment, 124–126; teaching and learning for, 126

Competition: and information, 102; strategy for, 44–62
Conference Board, 218, 231, 241
Confucius, 4
Conjoint analysis, and utility curves, 206
Consultants, trainers as, 158–159
Contract: duration of, 73–75; flexibility of, 77–81; full-disclosure, 83–89; and information, 103; and participation, 115; and selection, 72–81; and trust, 111–119; and understanding, 104–111; and value exchanged, 75–77
Control: and autonomy, 129; of human capital, 7–8; and retention, 189–190; and rewards, 41–42; and risk management, 197–198; in selection process, 82–83
Cooperation, and friendship, 154
Corporate Leadership Council, 199, 240
Costs: of automation, 127–128; of quitting, 198–200; of reinforcement, 140; of return-on-investment elements, 206–209; and selection, 71; and trust, 112–113
Crawford, R., 19, 229
Creativity, and rewards, 133
Critical incidents, and reinforcement, 137–138
Csoka, L. S., 241
Customers, and information, 102–103
Customization, for reinforcement, 138–142
Cypress Semiconductor: selection at, 74–75, 84–87; turnover at, 174–175

D

Damasio, A. R., 148, 237
Darrouzet, C., 237, 238
Data, and knowledge, 163, 165
Davenport, T. H., 162–163, 238
DeBella, R., 40
Deci, E. L., 129, 131, 132n, 235
DeCotiis, T. A., 29, 230
DeNisi, A. S., 191, 192n, 193n, 194, 240

Descartes, R., 147
Details, in strategy, 57
Dickter, D. N., 239
Disney, 50
Donne, J., 155, 238
Donnelley & Sons, R. R., and strategy alignment, 97, 101, 103
Dorsey, D., 229
Downsizing trends, 5
Dumbing-down theory, 36

E

Eastman Chemical Co., understanding at, 106
Easton Corp., empowerment at, 129
Eck, A., 11*n*
Edison, T. A., 57
Education Development Center (EDC): and competence, 126, 127, 235; and training, 145, 146*n*, 150–152, 158, 167, 237
Edvinsson, L., 241
Efficient frontier, and optimization, 209–213
Effort, in human capital, 20–21
Einstein, A., 214
Eisenberger, R., 229
Emerson, R. W., 94, 233
Employment cost index, 10–11
Employment relationships: alternative, 68, 70–71; value of, 179–190. *See* Retention of investors; Selection
Empowerment: and autonomy, 128–129; and trust, 114–115
Engagement, and commitment, 26–28, 179–198
Entrepreneurship, and rewards, 41–42
Environment. *See* Workplace environment
Equilibrium: checklist for assessing, 186; curve for, 181–183
Equity, individual, 136–138
Ethical issues, and trust, 112
Ethnographers, trainers as, 159
Ettorre, B., 235, 241
Eve, 17

Evolution, and contract flexibility, 78–79
Exchange: optimization of, 203–213; of value, 75–77
Execution, of strategy, 57
Expectancy, and return on investment, 29–30

F

Face validity, in selection, 82
Fairness, procedural, 135–136
Falvey, J., 128, 235
Families and Work Institute, 36, 130, 170, 179
Feedback, in selection process, 83
Field Institute, 145
Fireman's Fund Insurance Company: and competence, 123; understanding at, 106–107, 109
Fischhoff, B., 239
Flamholtz, E. G., 6, 159–160, 228, 229, 238
Flaste, R., 132*n*, 235
Flexibility: of contract, 77–81; in reinforcement, 139–140; and rewards, 42; of workers, 12–13
Ford, and informal learning, 151
Frei, B., 188, 198, 240
Friedman, D. E., 231, 235
Friendship, and learning, 154–155
Frontier, efficient, and optimization, 209–213
Fukuyama, F., 112, 113*n*, 234

G

Galagan, P. A., 149*n*, 237
Galinsky, E., 231, 235, 239
Gallaga, O. L., 232
Garner, R., 230, 232
Gateway 2000, and strategy alignment, 97
Genentech, commitment at, 27–28, 230
General Electric, and competitive strategy, 46
General Motors, and strategy, 48
Goal statements, for understanding, 107

Golden West Financial Corp., and trust, 117

Gordon, D. M., 229, 233

Gordon, J., 228

Gordon, R., 231

Gould, S., 171, 182, 239

Gould, S. J., 241

Greenberger, D. B., 236

Greller, M. M., 233, 234

Growth opportunity, and return on investment, 33–34, 39

Gundry, L. K., 137, 236

Gupta, D., 199–200, 240

H

Hadary, S., 41

Hall, B. P., 199, 240

Hall, C. T., 230

Handy, C., 10, 228

Hansen, D., 42

Harrison, D. A., 239

Hawking, S. W., 214, 241

Helyar, J., 232, 240

Heneman, R. L., 236

Henry, S., 231

Heraclitus, 77

Herriot, P., 232

Hewlett-Packard: autonomy at, 130–131; community of practice at, 153; contracts at, 79

Heyboer, J., 27–28, 230

Hiring. *See* Selection

Hopkins, M., 114*n*, 229, 234

Huber, V. L., 236

Human capital: action for, 63–225; brain surgery example of, 23–24; building, 143–168; challenges of, 202–225; and competitive strategy, 44–62; components of, 18–24; concepts of, 18–19; context for, 1–62; equation for, 22–24; equilibrium curve for, 181–183; hiring, 65–93; as implementation lever, 49, 55; and intangibles, 42–43; investments and returns for, 17–43, 121–142; measures for, 215–216; models for, 54–60; optimizing, 203–213;

overview on, 13–15; ownership and control of, 7–8; and perception gap, 34–42; principles for, 125–126; requirements for, 66–67; retention of, 169–201; return on investment for, 8; sources of, 67–72; themes of, 14–15; tracking growth of, 221–222; workplace environment for, 94–120

Hunter, J. E., 232

Huntington, R., 229

Hutchison, S., 229

I

Immerwahr, J., 26, 95, 230, 233, 235

Implementation levers, and strategy, 49–50, 53–55

Incentives, for knowledge, 162–163

Information: capital, and knowledge, 164–166; content of, 191–194; frequent, 194–196; and knowledge, 163, 165; and media management, 196–197; in risk management, 191–197; sharing, and friendship, 155; for strategy alignment, 101–103; timely, 194–195

Information technology: accelerating change in, 61–62; and competitive strategy, 59–60, 62; impact of, 16; as implementation lever, 49, 55; and job engagement, 27

Institute for Research on Learning (IRL), 150, 152, 153, 154, 159, 167, 238

Intangible capital, measuring, 216

Intelligence, and knowledge, 163–164, 165

Interviews, for selection, 87–88, 90–92

Investment: approaches for, 121–142; and autonomy, 128–134; challenges of, 202–225; and competence, 122–128; conditions for, 24–34; discretionary, 31–34; measuring, 213–223; optimizing, 203–213; preserving, 190–198; and reinforcement, 134–142; summary on, 142

Investment plan options (IPO), 107–109

Investors: aspects of workers as, 3–16; as assets, 4–7; categories of, 9–10; characteristics of, 8–13; education of, 10–12; flexibility of, 12–13; metaphor of, 7–8; retaining, 169–201; summary on, 15–16

J

Japan, knowledge creation in, 148–149
Jarvis, W. C., 240
Jefferson, T., 201, 240
Jehn, K. A., 238
Job engagement, and commitment, 26–28, 179–198
Job fulfillment, and return on investment, 33–34, 39
Job satisfaction: factors in, 211–212; and performance, 188–189; and rewards, 31; and turnover, 173
Job titles, and reinforcement, 140–141
Judiesch, M. K., 232
Justice, and reinforcement, 134–142

K

Katz, J., 239, 240
Kelleher, H., 89
Kelvin, Lord, 202–203, 214, 241
Kennedy, J. F., 81
Kepner-Tregoe®, 95, 234
Klock, M., 241
Knowledge: and ability, 19; explicit, 149, 156–166; increasing, 68; marketplace for, 160–163; product design for, 163–166; tacit, 149–156; transforming, 162; uncovering, 162
Knowledge workers trend, 9
Kodak, work redesign at, 198
Kraatz, M. S., 239
Kraft, C., 81

L

Labor Advisor Board, 218
Lacey, J. M., 159–160, 229, 238
Lancaster, H., 236
Langer, E. J., 237
Langlitz Leathers, and rewards, 42

Lantech, reinforcement at, 135
Lao-tzu, 214
Larkin, S., 197, 240
Larkin, T. J., 197, 240
Lasorda, T., 24
Lawler, E. E., III, 31, 93, 230, 233
Learning: categories of, 151; communities of practice for, 152–156; for competence, 126; formal, 146–147, 157–160, 167; and friendship, 154–155; informal, 145–146, 150–152, 157–160; neuroprocessing system for, 147–149; synergies in, 157–160
Learning organization, 168
Leaving: cost of, 198–200; net value of, 171–172
Leventhal, G. S., 236
Levers, implementation, and strategy, 49–50, 53–55
Lewis, M., 236
Lichtenstein, S., 239
Lingle, J. H., 241
Loyalty-based commitment, 25–26, 30
Lublin, J. S., 228, 232
Lucchetti, A., 231
Lynch, L. M., 145, 228, 237

M

Macan, T. H., 233
Malone, M. S., 241
Managers: in apprenticeships, 199–200; capabilities of, 57–60; and communities of practice, 155–156; as engineers, 35; and reinforcement, 141; roles of, 130; and strategy, 56–57; and strategy alignment, 100–101
Management, open-book, 101–103
Mangham, I., 227–228
Marshall, R., 237
Massachusetts Financial Services, 218
Mathieu, J. E., 229
McCoy, T. J., 131
McFarlin, D. B., 236
MCI Communications: information at, 196; in telemedia industry, 50
Measurement: criteria and definitions in, 213–214; example of, 219–223;

Measurement *(continued)*
insights from, 224–225; and investment, 213–223; and performance, 217–218; summary on, 223–225
Megna, P., 241
Mehta, S. N., 231
Melville, H., 65, 232
Mercedes Benz, and strategy, 47
Metaphors, power of, 4, 227
Meyer, J. P., 230, 236
Microsoft, 50
Milkovich, G., 231
Milton, J., 40–41, 231
Minnesota, University of, research at, 154
Mintzberg, H., 44–45, 61, 231
Monitoring: of commitment, 222–223; and friendship, 155
Moore, L. F., 227
Morrison, D. E., 116, 234
Morrow, L., 12
Motivation, and competence, 123, 131. *See also* Commitment
Motorola, informal learning at, 151–152, 158, 167
Mowen, J. C., 232
Munk, N., 233
Myers, S., 240

N

National Aeronautics and Space Administration, and selection process, 81
National Bureau of Economic Research, 8
National Center on Educational Quality of the Workforce, 143, 236
National Employer Survey, 143
National Foundation for Women Business Owners, 41
National Longitudinal Survey of Youth, 172–173
National Opinion Research Center, 170, 239
NCI Research, 241
Networks, and retention, 199

Neuroprocessing system, and learning, 147–149
Niebrugge, V., 35n
Nixon, R. M., 17–18
Nonaka, I., 148–149, 237
Nulty, P., 236

O

Ohio State University, research at, 172–173
Oliver, S., 233
Olsten Corporation, 70, 232
ONYX Software Corp., and retention, 188
Optimization: and efficient frontier, 209–213; of exchange, 203–213
Organization: capabilities of, and strategy, 48–49, 51–53; commitment to, 24–26; and competence, 127–128; and knowledge, 161–162, 166, 168; structure of, as implementation lever, 49, 55
Orme, B., 241
Ornstein, R., 232
Ortega y Gasset, J., 227

P

Paese, M., 233
Parker, L. E., 235
Participation, trust built with, 113–116
Pennsylvania, University of, research at, 154
People value-added (PVA), measuring, 216–217
Perception gap, and human capital, 34–42
Performance: and commitment, 28–30; and job satisfaction, 188–189; and measurement, 217–218; and time, 22
Pfeffer, J., 228
Piaget, J., 122, 235n
Planning, for strategy, 47
Porras, J. I., 130–131, 235
Porsche, and strategy, 48
Porter, L. W., 31, 93, 230, 233

Porter, M. E., 47, 231
Predictive validity, in selection, 82
Price, R. H., 235
Price, T., 196
Productivity, and training, 143–144
Programmatic commitment, 24–25, 30
Prusak, L., 162–163, 238
Psychological contract, concept of, 72.
   See also Contract
Public Agenda, 26, 31–32

Q

Quitting: cost of, 198–200; net value of,
   171–172

R

Rank Xerox, and knowledge, 162
Rationality, bounded, and retention,
   189–190
Reciprocity, and return on investment,
   29–31
Recognition, and return on investment,
   33–34, 38–39
Recruitment: and interviews, 91;
   process for, 82. *See also* Selection
Reichers, A. E., 229
Reinforcement: customization for,
   138–142; and individual equity,
   136–138; and investment, 134–142;
   and procedural fairness, 135–136;
   and titles, 140–141
Replacement, and contract flexibility, 79
Retention of investors: approaches for,
   169–201; and bounded rationality,
   189–190; commitment and engagement in, 179–198; and cost of quitting, 198–200; factors in, 175,
   184–185; patterns of, 169–171, 173;
   and risk management, 190–198;
   summary on, 200–201; trends in,
   12–13; and turnover causes,
   172–179
Return on investment: and commitment, 29–34; defining, 107–108; elements in, 33–34; and expected
   return, 108; for human capital, 8;

model of, 36–37; optimization for,
   203–213; transactional and rela-
   tional types of, 38–40
Rewards: and autonomy, 132–134;
   elements in, 206; and return on
   investment, 30–31, 33–34, 38–39;
   varying, 40–42
Rich, A., 124–125, 235
Risk, concepts of, 190–191
Risk aversion, and turnover, 178
Risk management, and retention,
   190–198
Robert Half International, 198, 240
Robinson, S. L., 239
Rodgers, T. J., 84, 233
Rousseau, D. M., 79, 137, 178, 232, 233,
   234, 236, 239
Roznowski, M., 239
Russell, C. J., 233

S

Salomon Brothers, and reinforcement,
   136–137
San Francisco, Muni drivers in, 40
Sandler, H., 117
Sandler, M., 117
Sartain, L., 89–90, 233
Schellhardt, T., 235
Schiemann, W. A., 241
Schmidt, F. L., 232
Schneier, R., 217, 241
Schuler, H., 82, 233
Schultz, T. W., 19
Schweiger, D. M., 191, 192n, 193n, 194,
   240
Sculley, J., 104–105, 234
Seelye, K. Q., 227
Seglin, J. L., 114n, 229, 234
Selection: aspects of, 65–93; interviews
   for, 87–88, 90–92; process for,
   81–89; strategies for, 66–72; sum-
   mary on, 90–93; validity of process
   for, 82–83
Selz, M., 231
Senge, P. M., 238
Shaffer, J. C., 234

Shah, P. P., 238

Shareholder pressure theory, 36

Shore, L. M., 230

Side bets, and programmatic commitment, 25

Siemens, and informal learning, 151

Sinclair, U., 3–4, 227

Skill: and ability, 19–20; increasing, 68

Slovic, P., 116, 234, 239

Smith, A., 4, 7, 8, 114, 190, 227, 228, 234, 240

Smith, D. E., 233

Smither, J. W., 232, 233

Social learning theory, 153–154

Social norms and structure, and trust, 111–112

Social validity, in selection, 82–83

Society for Human Resource Management, 198, 240

Somatic-marker hypothesis, 148

Southwest Airlines: optimization at, 204, 207; selection at, 89–90, 233

Sowa, D., 229

Springsteen, B., 42

Stallone, S., 42

Stamps, D., 238

Standard & Poor's, 137

Stanford University, videotaped lectures from, 153

Stevenson, W., 129

Stewart, T. A., 168, 228, 231, 238, 240

Stinnette, J., 106

Strasser, S., 236

Strategy: aspects of, 44–62; components of, 45–50; concepts of, 44, 46–48; example of, 50–54; formulation of, 61–62; and implementation levers, 49–50, 53–55; models for, 54–60; and organization capabilities, 48–49, 51–53; requirements for, 51–52; for selection, 66–72; summary on, 60–62; typology of, 44–45

Strategy alignment: and competence, 124–126; index of, 103–104; information for, 101–103; and learning, 151; and understanding, 109–110; in workplace environment, 96, 97–101

Stucky, S., 150, 153, 237, 238

Sullivan, C. L., 238

Summers, T. P., 29, 230

Sun Microsystems, and competitive strategy, 61, 232

Supervisors, and retention, 187–188, 197, 201

Swanberg, J. E., 239

Sweeney, P. D., 236

T

Talent: and ability, 20; increasing, 68

Tannenbaum, A. S., 235

Taranta, A., 238

Taylor, F. W., 21, 128–129, 130

TCI, 50

Technology. *See* Information technology

Telecommuting, and friendship, 154–155

Telemedia industry, strategy in, 50–54, 57–60

Terkel, S., 17, 229

Texas at Arlington, University of, research at, 172–173

Thaler, R. H., 239

Thomson, W., 202–203, 214, 241

Tiffany, P., 232

Time, in human capital, 21–22

Tobin, J., 216

Tocqueville, A. de, 166, 238

Towers Perrin: and competitive strategy, 50, 51, 52n, 53n, 58n, 59, 231–232; and retention, 170, 239; and worker as investor, 5, 238; and workplace environment, 95, 104n, 105n, 110n, 111n, 118n, 234

Training: approaches for, 143–168; bias for, 144–149; budgets for, 159–160; for competence, 126; expenditures for, 144, 145; and explicit knowledge, 156–166; summary on, 166–168; and tacit knowledge, 149–156; of trainers, 159; and worker as asset, 5, 8; of workers, 10–12

Trudeau, M., 236

Trust: and contract, 111–119; and costs, 112–113; nurturing, 116–117; and participation, 113–116

Tucker, M., 237

Turnover: analyzing, 172–179; and competitive offerings, 176–178; as disequilibrium, 183–185; patterns of, 172–174; root causes of, 174–176

Twain, M., 7, 121, 228, 234

U

Understanding: general, 106–107; index of, 110–111; specific, 107–110; in workplace environment, 96, 104–111

U.S. Bureau of the Census, 228

U.S. Department of Labor, 145, 172–173

Utility curves, for return-on-investment elements, 204–206, 207–208

V

Validity, of selection process, 82–83

Value: coincidence of, 113–115; competence as, 127–128; exchange of, 75–77; and networks, 199

Visa International, and strategy alignment, 97

Volkswagen, and strategy, 47

W

Wawa Food Markets, and turnover, 184–185

Wayne, S. J., 230

Weisskopf, T. E., 233

Welch, J., 46

Wenger, E., 152, 158, 167, 238

Werbel, J. D., 233

White, J. B., 228

White, R. W., 122–123, 131, 235

Whyte, D., 234

Whyte, W. H., Jr., 18, 229

Wild, H., 238

Wm. Schiemann & Associates, and measurement, 217–218

Williams-Sonoma, and competence, 124–125, 235

Witherall, G., 234

Women, as entrepreneurs, 41–42

Work ethic, 17–18, 20

Work processes: and autonomy, 130–132; as implementation lever, 49, 55

Workers. *See* Investors

Workplace environment: acceptance in, 96, 111–119; aspects of, 94–120; background on, 94–97; elements in, 95–97; for informal learning, 150–152; strategy alignment in, 96, 97–101; summary on, 119–120; understanding in, 96, 104–111

Workplace Index, 103–105, 110, 117–118

World Savings, 117

WorldCom, 196

Y

Yankelovich, D., 26, 95, 230, 233, 235

Z

Zajac, D. M., 229